T0332474

# CACHE AND INTERCONNECT ARCHITECTURES IN MULTIPROCESSORS

# CACHE AND INTERCONNECT ARCHITECTURES IN MULTIPROCESSORS

edited by

**Michel Dubois**
University of Southern California

and

**Shreekant S. Thakkar**
Sequent Computer Systems

**KLUWER ACADEMIC PUBLISHERS**
**Boston/Dordrecht/London**

Distributors for North America:
Kluwer Academic Publishers
101 Philip Drive
Assinippi Park
Norwell, Massachusetts 02061 USA

Distributors for all other countries:
Kluwer Academic Publishers Group
Distribution Centre
Post Office Box 322
3300 AH Dordrecht, THE NETHERLANDS

Library of Congress Cataloging-in-Publication Data

Cache and interconnect architectures in multiprocessors / [edited] by
   Michel Dubois and Shreekant S. Thakkar.
      p.   cm.
   Papers presented at a workshop titled Cache and Interconnect
Architectures in Multiprocessors, held in Eilat, Israel, May 25-26,
1989.
   Includes index.
   ISBN 0-7923-9074-1
   1. Computer network protocols—Congresses.   2. Multiprocessors—
Congresses.   3. Computer network architectures—Congresses.
I. Dubois, Michel, 1953-      .   II. Thakkar, S. S.   III. Title:
Interconnect architectures in multiprocessors.
TK5105.5.C33   1990
004.5—dc20                                          90-37022
                                                       CIP

# Contents

# Preface

## Cache And Interconnect Architectures In Multiprocessors

Eilat, Israel

May 25-26 1989

**Michel Dubois**

*University of Southern California*

**Shreekant S. Thakkar**

*Sequent Computer Systems*

The aim of the workshop was to bring together researchers working on cache coherence protocols for shared-memory multiprocessors with various interconnect architectures. Shared-memory multiprocessors have become viable systems for many applications. Bus-based shared-memory systems (Eg. Sequent's Symmetry, Encore's Multimax) are currently limited to 32 processors. The first goal of the workshop was to learn about the performance of applications on current cache-based systems. The second goal was to learn about new network architectures and protocols for future scalable systems. These protocols and interconnects would allow shared-memory architectures to scale beyond current imitations.

The workshop had 20 speakers who talked about their current research. The discussions were lively and cordial enough to keep the participants away from the wonderful sand and sun for two days. The participants got to know each other well and were able to share their thoughts in an informal manner. The workshop was organized into several sessions. The summary of each session is described below. This book presents revisions of some of the papers presented at the workshop.

Session 1: Cache and TLB Consistency Protocols

Michael Carlton talked on "Efficient Cache Coherency for Multiple Bus Multiprocessor Architectures." He described the work in progress at Berkeley on a scalable shared-memory architecture for Parallel Prolog. This proposed architecture is a multiple bus multiprocessor, an extension of current bus-based shared-memory multiprocessors. It is similar to, but more general, than the Wisconsin Multicube. The coherency protocol uses both snooping and directory schemes. Their architecture takes advantage of the locality of processor references on a single bus and supports broad-cast messages over a bus using a snooping cache coherency protocol. A directory style cache coherence scheme is used to ensure correctness among buses. Mike sparked a lively discussion when he reviewed some of the design decisions involved in the development of the protocol.

Gurindar Sohi was the next speaker and he talked on "Cache Coherence Mechanisms for Multiprocessors with Arbitrary Interconnects." The basic mechanism is a distributed cache directory that is maintained as a doubly-linked list across the system. The proposed coherence mechanism requires much less memory than an equivalent main memory directory based scheme. The scheme obviates the need for multi-level inclusion in hierarchical multiprocessors; it works well in cluster-based systems where the individual clusters are bus-based multiprocessors.

Pat Teller was the final speaker in the session. Pat's talk was refreshingly different from the majority of the talks since she addressed the problem of "Consistency-Ensuring TLB Management and Its Scalability," a rarely discussed topic. She described several consistency-ensuring methods of managing TLBs in a shared-memory multiprocessor system. These methods differ not only in strategy but also in their generality, performance, and scalability. The performance of such a management scheme can be quantified by examining its effect on TLB miss rates, page fault rates, memory traffic, and execution time. She discussed the pros and cons of each of the described TLB management schemes and outlined a methodology for comparing them.

Session 2: System Architectures

Erik Hagersten gave an interesting talk on "The Data Diffusion Machine" which is another architecture to support Parallel Prolog. This is a hierarchically-organized architecture where the memory is physically distributed and globally addressed. A block of memory may reside in any processor memory and there maybe multiple copies of the same block, just as in a cache-based multiprocessor. The processors and their memory are at the leaves of a tree-like hierarchy and the branches form the clusters of processors. The clusters interface through directory caches. Erik described the coherency protocol for this system.

Rae McLellan described the implementation of the ISM multiprocessor, supporting up to sixteen CRISP processors on a single backplane. Among the features of this system are multi-level caches accessed with virtual addresses. A new term, "snarfing", was coined to refer to a bus-watching mechanism which reduces contention to synchronization primitives.

Vason Srini talked about the "Xbar Multi Processor (XMP) Architecture." Vason outlined the design of a massively parallel, cache coherent shared memory system. It is based on bus-based shared-memory multiprocessors interconnected by a low latency crossbar switch. His talked focused on the implementation of the crossbar switch.

Session 3: Bus/Network Architectures

Trevor Mudge was supposed to talk on "Cache Behavior in a Logical Shared-Bus Multiprocessor." However, he had to postpone his journey to Israel at the last moment. We missed him.

Alan Jones talked on "Multiprocessor for high-density Interconnects." Alan described simulation studies to evaluate the performance of multiple bus and wide bus multiprocessors architectures. The coherence protocol used in the study was based on the Berkeley model. The conclusion of the study was that the multiple narrow buses perform better than wider buses.

Paul Sweazy gave a description of the "Directory-based Cache Coherence on SCI." This is the work of the IEEE Scalable Coherent Interconnect standards committee. The SCI project was started to overcome the scalability limits of bus-based shared-memory multiprocessors. The interconnect standard allows a system to connect an arbitrary number of nodes. The interconnect standard is topology independent. Paul described a linked-list based directory coherence protocol that is independent of the interconnect. This is similar to the scheme described earlier in the day by Gurindar Sohi.

To cap off the day, Dimitris Lioupis made a short impromptu presentation on the "Chess Multiprocessor", an architecture in which groups of processors share caches. Dimitris's presentation was mostly on the packaging of his machine. On his slide, the alternation of processors and caches looked like a checkerboard.

Session 4: Performance

Philip Bitar gave a "A Critique of Trace-Driven Simulations for Shared-Memory Multiprocessors." Philip's contention was that it is difficult for trace-driven simulations to produce a valid representation of interacting processes in a multiprocessor system. Trace-driven simulations, like high-level modeling, must be verified by low-level simulation, or by actual execution. His talk sparked a lively discussion of trace-driven simulation techniques used in several current studies. Some of the researchers of these studies were in the audience and defended their approach.

Shreekant Thakkar described the "Performance of Cache Coherence Protocols." He talked on the performance of the Sequent's Symmetry write-through and copyback protocols for several different (parallel, database and multi-user) applications. The performance study related bus utilization and cache coherence traffic with the application performance. These statistics were collected on a 30 processor Symmetry multiprocessor using embedded hardware monitoring technique. The statistics revealed that the copyback protocol allowed the system to be scaled to large number of processors for many applications. The talk also described the performance of the current hardware synchronization mechanism and compared it with several software synchronization mechanisms.

Michel Dubois described his "Experience using analytical program models to predict cache overhead in parallel algorithms." An analytical model for the sharing behavior of parallel programs was derived and the model predictions were compared with execution-driven simulations of five concurrent programs for different number of processors and different block sizes.

Wen-Hann Wang talked on "Trace reductions and their applications to efficient trace-driven simulation for write-back caches." He approached the problem of the large time and space demands of cache simulations in two ways. First, the program traces are reduced to the extent that exact performance can still be obtained from these traces. Second, an algorithm is devised to produce performance results for many set-associative write-back caches in just one simulation run. The trace reduction and the efficient simulation techniques were extended to multiprocessor cache simulation. His simulation results show that this approach can significantly reduce the disk space needed to store the program traces. It can also dramatically speed up cache simulations and still produce the same results as non-reduced traces.

Wolf-Dietrich Webber presented his study on "Cache Invalidation Patterns in Shared-memory Multiprocessors." This work was done to study write invalidations behavior of parallel homogeneous applications. The results were extrapolated to see how they would affect a cluster-based shared memory multiprocessor with a directory based scheme. He observed that the write invalidation patterns were different for synchronization objects and data objects. This was a result of the coarse-grain process-based parallel programming model used for these applications. The study also showed that cache line size is an important factor in determining invalidation distributions.

Susan Eggers described her study of "The effect of Sharing on the Cache and Bus Performance of Parallel Programs." Susan's work is based on trace-driven simulations from traces taken on three parallel CAD applications. These applications are homogeneous applications using the coarse-grain process-based parallel programming model. Her studies showed that parallel programs incur significantly higher miss ratios and bus utilization than comparable uniprocessor programs. The sharing component of these metrics proportionally increases with both cache and block size. Some cache configurations determine both their magnitude and trend. The amount of overhead depends on the memory reference pattern to the shared data. Programs that exhibit good per-processor locality perform better than those with fine-grain sharing. This suggests that parallel software writers and better compiler technology can improve program performance through better memory organization of shared data.

Session 5: Synchronization, Virtual Address Caches and Hierarchy

James Goodman's talk was on "Synchronization, Serialization,and False Sharing". "False sharing" refers to the sharing of memory blocks by processes even in the absence of shared data in the block. It occurs when different words of a memory block are accessed by different processes. After demonstrating the effects of false sharing, James then presented a synchronization primitive called QOSB (Queue On Sync-Bit) which has been adopted in the Wisconsin Multicube multiprocessor.

Faye Briggs addressed the problem of "Virtual-Address Caches" in multiprocessors. Virtual-address caches have an advantage over physical address caches in that no time is lost to translation in accessing the cached data. However virtual caches cause problems due in part to synonyms, which are multiple virtual addresses pointing to the same physical address. In his talk, Faye compared several solutions based on their feasibility and their transparency to the software in both uniprocessor and multiprocessor systems. All these problems can be solved efficiently at the cost of more complex hardware and/or non-transparency from the software.

Hendrik Goosen talked on "The Role of A Shared 2nd Level Cache in a Scalable Shared Memory Multiprocessor." This work was done in the context of the VMP multiprocessor, a research project at Stanford. The original VMP design has been extended from a 2-level to a 3-level memory hierarchy of caches. This was done to allow a high degree of scalability by the addition of an intermediate shared second-level cache. The first level per-processor cache caches code and data local to the current execution context within a program. The third level cache is a virtual memory page cache, caching program files and data files between program executions. The talk outlined some possible roles of the second level cache, the design implications and open issues.

Session 6: Compiler-Aided Cache Coherence

Alex Veidenbaum talked on "Compiler-assisted Cache Management in Multiprocessors." He discussed three different software-assisted cache coherence enforcement schemes for large shared-memory multiprocessor systems using interconnection networks. All three schemes rely on a compiler to detect potential coherence problems and generate code to enforce coherence in a parallel program. The main goals are to maintain coherence without any interprocessor communication and to keep coherence enforcement overhead low. The former is achieved by using compile-time knowledge of the parallelism and data dependencies in a program.The latter is achieved by using special hardware to invalidate stale cache blocks in time independent of the number such blocks. Cache words are allowed to become inconsistent with memory as long as the compiler decides it is safe to do so. This allows invalidations to be delayed beyond the time a new copy of cache word has been generated until the time the word has to be invalidated. The three schemes differ in the complexity and power of the compiler detection algorithms, the complexity of the additional hardware, and the run-time support the hardware provides for deciding what to invalidate. Each scheme improves over the previous one in terms of the amount of unnecessary invalidations due to imprecision of compile-time detection, and achieves a higher hit ratio.

The last speaker of the workshop was Jean-Loup Baer who talked on "Self-invalidating cache coherence protocols." He reviewed briefly the cache coherence protocols that do not rely on a fast broadcast mechanism. He proposed a scheme based on compile-time marking of references and local hardware-based extensive tagging of cache entries.

The workshop was called to a close. The participants had enjoyed the informal discussions and got to know each other. This summary shows that several research studies are similar in goals and implementation. Through lively interactions, this workshop helped to clarify the various approaches adopted by different research groups. We hope to have a workshop on a similar theme soon based on the success at Eilat.

We wish to thank all the participants and the SIGARCH workshop organizing committee, for making this workshop possible.

# CACHE AND INTERCONNECT ARCHITECTURES IN MULTIPROCESSORS

# THE COST OF TLB CONSISTENCY

**Patricia J. Teller**

*IBM T. J. Watson Research Center*
*Yorktown Heights, NY 10598*

## Abstract

When paged virtual memory is supported as part of the memory hierarchy in a shared-memory multiprocessor system, *translation-lookaside buffers (TLBs)* are often used to cache copies of virtual-to-physical address translation information. This translation information is also stored in data structures called page tables. Since there can be multiple images of the translation information for a page accessible by processors, the modification of one image can result in inconsistency among the other images stored in TLBs and the page table. This *TLB consistency problem* can cause a processor to use stale translation information, which may result in incorrect program execution.

TLB consistency-ensuring management carries with it performance overhead. This cost is manifested in the processor time attributable, either explicitly or implicitly, to the adopted solution. Some solutions to this problem have been shown to be effective in small-scale multiprocessor systems but are not likely to be satisfactory for large-scale systems. In the absence of performance data, this paper examines performance costs associated with solutions to the TLB consistency problem and endeavors to delineate those characteristics of solutions that are desirable in terms of performance in large-scale systems.

It is likely that parallel programs targeted for large-scale systems will execute on large numbers of processors and that these processors will exhibit a large degree of data sharing. Therefore, as we describe in this paper, solutions for these systems should:

1. enlist the participation of a processor only when it will use inconsistent information,

2. place necessary locks on the smallest possible data entities,

3. not introduce serialization,

4. keep extra communication to a minimum, and

5. have an insignificant impact on network traffic.

Two solutions are described that meet the first four criteria but that may have an impact on network traffic.

## 1 INTRODUCTION

A *memory hierarchy* organizes the memory store of a computer system into levels, where more than one level can store an image of a data item. A shared-memory multiprocessor computer system provides multiple processors that can cooperate in the execution of a program and that may have access to the same data. Thus, in a shared-memory multiprocessor with a memory hierarchy, multiple images of a data item can exist both at different levels of the hierarchy and at the same level of the hierarchy. For example, if there are multiple general-purpose caches in a shared-memory multiprocessor computer system then images of a data item may be stored in the caches of more than one processor and may also be stored in main memory. Since one processor may access the cached image of a datum, while another accesses the image in main memory, the modification of one image can cause other images to become inconsistent with the modified version. This problem is known as the *cache consistency* or *cache coherency* problem. To ensure the correct execution of a parallel program, the processors must view data in the same way. Thus, the modification of one image of a datum must be reflected in all images of the datum [*cf.*, Tang, 1976; Censier and Feautrier, 1978].

When a paged virtual-memory system is supported as part of a memory hierarchy, a special case of the cache consistency problem arises. This restricted problem is called the *TLB consistency problem*. A *translation-lookaside buffer (TLB)* is a special-purpose, virtual-address cache that is used by a processor to translate the virtual address of referenced data to the location of the data in physical memory. The translation information stored in the TLB is also stored in a data structure called a *page table* that is often resident in main memory. Therefore, in a shared-memory multiprocessor architecture with more than one TLB, the modification of an image of translation information stored in either a TLB or page table entry can cause other images of the translation information to become inconsistent with the most up-to-date information. Since the use of stale translation information may cause incorrect program execution, consistency-ensuring TLB management must prevent the use of out-of-date copies of translation information.

The overhead associated with a solution may impact performance. This performance cost is manifested in the time processors spend participating in the algorithm used to ensure TLB consistency and the processor time that is attributable to side effects implicitly caused by the adopted solution, for example, increased page-fault or TLB-miss rates. One of the main goals of multiprocessor systems is to increase the speed with which application programs can be executed by allowing multiple processors to cooperate in the execution of programs. Therefore, the cost associated with a solution to the TLB consistency problem must not have a significant impact on performance. That is, the attainable speedup of application programs should not be significantly affected. This is especially true for scalable architectures, where it is desirable that one solution meet the needs of tens, hundreds, or thousands of processors.

Since small-scale systems and prototypes of large-scale systems have been built, it is possible to demonstrate the effectiveness of solutions that have been implemented on these architectures. Large-scale systems, however, are not yet available and some are in the design phase. In addition, factors that may determine the effectiveness of a solution have not been measured, for example, the frequency with which page table modifications are made, the rate at which TLB inconsistencies occur, the amount of sharing exhibited by parallel programs, and TLB miss rates. In the absence of performance data, it is important for computer architects designing large-scale systems to be able to evaluate the performance costs of solutions to the TLB consistency problem that may be effective on such systems, especially if hardware support is required.

Using a representative set of solutions to the TLB consistency problem that have appeared in the literature, this paper examines their performance costs. Then, assuming that parallel programs targeted for large-scale systems will execute on large numbers of processors and that the processors will exhibit a large degree of data sharing, we outline the characteristics that are desirable, from a performance point of view, for a solution in such an environment. As described in this paper, solutions for these systems should:

- enlist the participation of a processor only when it will use inconsistent information,

- place necessary locks on the smallest possible data entities,

- not introduce serialization,

- keep extra communication to a minimum, and

- have an insignificant impact on network traffic.

Two solutions are described that meet the first four criteria but that may have an impact on network traffic.

After presenting some background information in Section 2, we examine the costs associated with a solution to the TLB consistency problem in Section 3. Section 4 examines the costs associated with solutions that have been shown to be effective in small-scale systems, while in Section 5, we attempt to characterize solutions that may be effective in large-scale systems. We summarize our observations in Section 6, where we also discuss the need to carefully characterize, evaluate, and compare the solutions to the TLB consistency problem that have already been proposed in the literature.

## 2 BACKGROUND

First, we describe the milieu in which the TLB consistency problem arises, namely, a multiprocessor system that supports paged virtual memory and contains multiple TLBs.

A paged virtual-memory system organizes virtual memory as a set of virtual *pages*, each containing an equal number of contiguous virtual memory locations. The location of a page in virtual memory is defined by its virtual address. Accordingly, main memory is divided into physical pages or page *frames*, each the size of a page. The physical address of a page is defined to be the location of a frame.

By supporting a paged virtual-memory system, several processes can execute concurrently since only a portion of the instructions and data of each process need be stored in main memory. A process references data using its virtual address and, in doing so, references a page in its address space, where the *address space* of a process is the set of virtual addresses that can be generated by a process. In order for a process to access data stored in a page, the page must be resident in main memory and the processor on which the process is executing must translate the virtual address of the referenced page to the physical address of the frame in which the page resides. If a page is referenced and is not resident in physical memory, *i.e.*, a *page fault* occurs, main memory must be allocated to store the page. When all of physical memory is allocated, the referencing of nonresident data results in the eviction of another page.

Data structures, called *page tables*, are used to manage virtual memory. The status and location of each virtual page of a process is stored in a page table. Included in a page table entry (PTE) is the translation information for the page, which includes:

- the frame in which the page is stored,

- a bit that indicates if the mapping to the specified frame is valid,

- access permissions that protect the integrity of a page, and

- page use information.

To avoid accessing a PTE on each memory reference, a special-purpose cache, called a *translation-lookaside buffer (TLB)*, is used to cache recently used translation information. The purpose of a TLB is to increase performance by providing faster access to this information. A *TLB hit* occurs when the translation information for a referenced page is stored in the accessed TLB. Otherwise, a *TLB* miss occurs, which results in a *TLB reload* (or TLB fill) that loads the translation information for the page into the TLB. If the referenced page is not resident, a page fault is initiated by the TLB miss. The first processor to fault on a page causes the page to become physical-memory resident. This process is called a *page in*.

To affect a change in status of a page the translation information for the page stored in a page table is modified. This makes the following status changes visible to executing processes:

- physical-memory nonresident to resident,

- change of location in physical memory,

- modification of protection, or

- clearing or setting of page use bits.

Often the operating system allows processes to share pages. In addition, it may allow modifications to the address space of one process to be made by another process. Thus, in a multiprocessor computer system with multiple TLBs, a processor may change the status of a page while a TLB accessible to another processor contains an entry for the page. In this case, the translation information stored in the TLB becomes inconsistent with the PTE for the page and the use of such information may result in erroneous memory references. In addition, if TLB entries contain page use information, which may indicate whether a page was written or referenced while its translation information was TLB-resident, then a change to the page use information stored in a TLB entry can cause the translation information stored in the page table to become inconsistent with the TLB. To permit this paper to be concise, we do not address this latter issue. Instead, we assume that bits representing this information are implemented using software techniques. In order to record the modification of a page, when an entry is loaded into a TLB, the permission bits are set to read-only. When the first write occurs, a permission exception results in the execution of a trap routine which in addition to correctly setting the permission bits of the TLB entry, sets the dirty bit of the appropriate PTE. The consistency of reference bits are less critical, therefore, we assume that these bits are set when a TLB entry is invalidated or replaced.

Some PTE modifications can be made to result in TLB inconsistencies that are detectable by the operating system. Thus, consistency-ensuring TLB management is not required to prevent the use of TLB entries made inconsistent by such changes. An example of such a *safe change* is when the access permission for a page is increased from read-only to read-write.

On the other hand, *unsafe changes* to PTEs are not detectable by the operating system Explicit consistency-ensuring TLB management is, thus, needed to prevent the use of inconsistent TLB entries that result from unsafe changes. Below is a list of the unsafe PTE modifications:

1. virtual memory deallocation,

2. protection reduction,

3. page remapping, and

4. page eviction.

The circumstances under which unsafe changes occur depends upon the operating system and, in some cases, on the architecture as well. As a result, some solutions may be suitable for some systems and not others.

## 3 THE COST OF A SOLUTION

Now that the problem is defined, let us examine the performance overhead incurred by solutions to the TLB consistency problem.

The total cost of a solution may depend upon:

- the frequency with which unsafe PTE modifications occur,

- the number of TLBs affected by these changes,

- the amount of sharing exhibited by parallel programs, and

- TLB miss rates.

In turn, the behavior of these measures may change as the number of processors that are cooperating in the execution of a program increases.

The nature of this behavior is not yet known. Since we do not know how these measurements behave as the number of processors increases, the cost of a solution targeted for a scalable architecture is difficult to determine. Thus, we can examine the overhead associated with a solution and point out characteristics of a solution that may significantly impact performance, but we cannot predict the actual affect a solution will have on performance in large-scale systems. Many factors comprise the overhead associated with a solution to the TLB consistency problem. In this section we outline these factors.

A solution to the TLB consistency problem has two costs associated with it:

- processor execution and idle time incurred either explicitly or implicitly by the adoption of the solution and

- required hardware-support.

Since the hardware cost is a one-time cost, we do not address it in this paper except to say that it should scale with the architecture. Thus, when we refer to the cost of a solution, we mean its performance cost, *i.e.*, processor execution and idle time.

Since one of the main goals of a multiprocessor system is to decrease the execution of programs by allowing multiple processors to cooperate in their execution, it is important that a solution to the TLB consistency problem, as specified by the targeted system, does not cause a significant decrease in the attainable speedup of programs. The cost of a solution includes the overhead incurred by a processor as a result of its participation in the algorithm. In addition, processor execution and idle time may be attributable to side effects that result from adopting a particular solution. Thus, the costs associated with a solution are comprised of many factors, including the following:

- time expended by processors in order to ensure TLB consistency,

- communication among system components,

- changes in the frequency of page-ins, page faults, and TLB misses,

- inability to use time-saving optimizations, and

- the parallelism inherent in the adopted algorithm, *i.e.*, the number of consistency-ensuring TLB updates and the number of PTE modifications that can be done in parallel.

The processor time expended while participating in the algorithm includes the time spent executing the algorithm, synchronizing with other processors, and waiting for other processors to complete their portion of the algorithm.

In a multiprocessor system that allows more than one process to modify a PTE, the integrity of the page table must be ensured by implicit or explicit locking that guarantees the serialization of modifications to a PTE. The nature of the lock can reduce the amount of parallelism available to processors and, thus, can have a negative effect on performance.

Since some solutions have been implemented on small-scale multi-processor systems, we now take a look at the performance costs incurred by these solutions in an effort to recognize solution characteristics that may be amenable to large-scale systems.

## 4 SOLUTIONS FOR SMALL-SCALE MULTIPROCESSORS

Both hardware-dependent and hardware-independent solutions to the TLB consistency problem have been shown to be suitable for small-scale multiprocessor architectures.

Among the hardware-dependent solutions are ones that utilize bus-watching devices that work in conjunction with the general-purpose cache, for example, the solution of Wood, *et al.*, [1986]. In these solutions, the adopted cache consistency protocol solves the problem of TLB consistency because would-be TLB entries are stored in the general-purpose cache instead of a separate TLB. Virtual-to-physical address translation is accomplished by "in-cache translation" [Ritchie, 1985], *i.e.*, PTEs are accessed from the virtual-address, general-purpose cache, rather than from a TLB.

Since the implementation of these solutions rely upon a bus-watching devices, they are limited to bus-based architectures, where a shared bus interconnects the processors and memories. These solutions incur very little overhead. The reasons why this is so illustrate some desirable characteristics of solutions targeted for large-scale systems.

1. Processors are not interrupted to participate in the algorithm.

2. No additional communication is required. TLB consistency actions are triggered by the modification of a PTE.

3. Processor coordination or synchronization is not required.

The bus and the consistency protocol supply the locking necessary to ensure the integrity of the page table. But, in doing so, PTE modifications are serialized and the number of TLB consistency-ensuring actions that can occur in parallel are limited to those related to the same PTE modification.

A hardware-independent solution, called *TLB Shootdown*, has been proposed by Black, *et al.*, [1989]. This software solution serves an important function in that it provides a solution that does not require any hardware support and, therefore, can solve the problem in both bus-based and highly-parallel architectures which have not been designed with a particular solution in mind.

This solution interrupts the execution of processors that may use an entry in the page table being modified to participate in the algorithm. By linking processor synchronization with the modification of a page table, parallelism may be reduced for the following reasons:

1. only one entry of a page table can be modified at any one time,

2. scheduling of a process is delayed if a page table that it may use is being modified, and

3. processors may be caused to idle during page table modifications.

The possibly high performance cost of this solution stems from the goal of supplying a solution that works for a large set of multiprocessor architectures. However, Black, *et al.* report satisfactory results on small-scale systems and state that extrapolation of performance data predicts that their algorithm will not present performance problems on machines with a few hundred processors except perhaps with regard to kernel space.

Depending upon the targeted architecture, the impact of solutions that interrupt processors to participate in the algorithm might be reduced if instead of interrupting the execution of all processors using the page table being modified, only processors using the page table entry being modified or processors with TLBs containing a copy of PTE were interrupted.

# 5 SOLUTIONS FOR LARGE-SCALE MULTIPROCESSORS

As shown above, solutions that use bus-watching devices illustrate some characteristics that are desirable for solutions targeted for large-scale systems, while solutions akin to TLB Shootdown illustrate characteristics that may be detrimental to performance in large-scale systems. Using this as a guideline, in this section, we endeavor to delineate the characteristics that a solution should have in order to have an insignificant impact on performance in large-scale systems.

For a particular multiprocessor system, the nature of the operating system and the application programs that are targeted to run on the system will determine the frequency of unsafe changes and TLB inconsistencies, as well as TLB miss rates. In particular, the effectiveness of a solution can be affected by:

- the parallelism inherent in a program,

- the degree to which processes share pages, and

- the use of private vs. shared memory.

For example, the effectiveness of TLB Shootdown and other solutions that use broadcasting or multicasting to inform processors to execute consistency-ensuring TLB actions is dependent upon the behavior of the operating system and application programs. If a program is executed by a large number of processors and many pages are shared among these processors, the explicit interruption of processor execution may seriously degrade performance. Performance of these solutions scales linearly with the number of processors. Black, *et al.* agree but suggest that, with respect to the kernel, if the operating system restructures its use of memory then participation in the algorithm may be limited to groups of processors rather than all processors. Since parallel programs exist that exhibit the same degree of sharing as does the operating system, the predicted performance problems may be encountered by these programs as well.

Thus, solutions that do not interrupt processors to participate in ensuring TLB consistency may be better suited for large-scale systems. Teller, *et al.* [1988] presents solutions that have this characteristic. These solutions associate a lock with a page table entry rather than with a page table.  Parallelism both with respect to page table modifications and consistency-ensuring TLB actions is provided.

One of these solutions, *Memory-based TLBs* associates a TLB with each memory module, rather than with each processor.  Each TLB is designed similar to a snoopy-cache, and the TLBs of a cluster of memory modules and memory that stores the cluster page table are interconnected by a shared bus.  Modifications to the page table are transmitted on this bus and bus management, similar to a snoopy-cache protocol, is used to ensure consistency among the TLBs and the page table.  Thus, network traffic is not generated in order to maintain TLB consistency.

Another of these solutions, *Validation*, tags TLB entries in such a way that a stale entry can be detected upon its use.  When a memory request is generated, the tag accompanies the request.  While the access is taking place, the tag is compared to the latest tag associated with the referenced frame.  If the tags do not compare, the entry is considered stale and the processor is instructed to invalidate it.  An extra trip through the network results when a stale entry is used and the tags stored at the memory modules must be updated when a PTE is modified.

These solutions have some very positive characteristics but there is a negative side.  One of the main criticisms of these solutions is that memory requests are required to be larger than they might be otherwise.  Memory-based TLBs requires that the virtual, rather than the physical, address be transmitted with each memory request, while Validation requires that a tag be transmitted.  If the network does not provide sufficient bandwidth, then longer messages may results in network queueing delays.  As shown by Kruskal, *et al.* [1986], this most certainly can affect performance.

# 6 SUMMARY AND CONCLUSIONS

We have discussed the problem of TLB consistency and delineated the costs that are associated with a solution to this problem. In addition, we have illustrated which solution characteristics are desirable, and which ones may be detrimental to performance. It seems best that a solution for large-scale systems be designed so that:

1. the participation of a processor is only enlisted when it will use inconsistent translation information,

2. necessary locks are placed on the smallest possible data entities,

3. serialization of execution is not introduced,

4. extra communication is kept to a minimum, and

5. network traffic is not significantly impacted.

Two solutions were described that meet the first four criteria but that may have an impact on network traffic.

The picture certainly is not complete. A detailed description of each solution is needed to highlight important techniques that are being utilized. In addition, the solutions should be evaluated and compared in terms of the completeness with which they solve the problem and with respect to their expected performance on large-scale systems.

### Acknowledgement

I would like to thank Harold Stone for his review of this paper and his helpful comments.

### Bibliography

Black, D. L., R. F. Rashid, D. B. Golub, C. R. Hill, and R. V. Baron, "Translation lookaside buffer consistency: a software approach," *Proceedings of the Third International Conference on Architectural Support for Programming Languages and Operating Systems*, IEEE Cat. No. 89CH2710-2, pp. 113-122, April 1989.

Censier, L. M. and P. Feautrier, "A new solution to coherency problems in multicache systems," *IEEE Transactions on Computers*, C-25, 12, pp. 1112-1118, December 1978.

Kruskal, C. P., M. Snir, and A. Weiss, "The distribution of waiting times in clocked multistage interconnection networks," *IEEE Transactions on Computers*, **37**, 11, pp. 1337-1352, November 1988, and *Proceedings of the 1986 International Conference on Parallel Processing*, IEEE Catalog No. 86CH2355-6, pp. 12-19, August 1986.

Ritchie, S. A., "TLB for free: in-cache address translation for a multiprocessor workstation," Technical Report No. UCB/CSD 85/233, U. C. Berkeley, Computer Science Division, May 1985.

Tang, C. K., "Cache system design in the tightly coupled multiprocessor system," *Proceedings of NCC*, pp. 749-753, 1976.

Teller, P. J., R. Kenner, and M. Snir, "TLB consistency on highly-parallel shared-memory multiprocessors," *Proceedings of the 21st Hawaii International Conference on System Sciences*, IEEE Catalog No. 85TH0209-7, pp. 184-193, January 1988.

Wood, D. A., *et al.*, "An in-cache address Translation mechanism," *Proceedings of the 13th Annual International Symposium on Computer Architecture*, IEEE Catalog No. 86CH2291-3, pp. 358-365, June 1986.

# Virtual-Address Caches in Multiprocessors[†1]

### Michel Cekleov*
### Michel Dubois**, Jin-Chin Wang** and Fayé A. Briggs*

*Advanced Development Division
Sun Microsystems Inc.
2550 Garcia Avenue
Mountain View California 94043
(415) 960-1300

**Department of Electrical Engineering Systems
University of Southern California
Los Angeles, California 90089-0781
(213) 743-8080

## Abstract

*Most general-purpose computers support virtual memory. Generally, the cache associated with each processor is accessed with a physical address obtained after translation of the virtual address in a Translation Lookaside Buffer(TLB). Since today's uniprocessors are very fast, it becomes increasingly difficult to include the TLB in the cache access path and still avoid wait states in the processor. The alternative is to access the cache with virtual addresses and to access the TLB on misses only. This configuration reduces the average memory access time, but it is a source of consistency problems which must be solved in hardware or software. The basic causes of these problems are the demapping and remapping of virtual addresses, the presence of synonyms, and the maintenance of protection and statistical bits. Some of these problems are addressed in this paper and solutions are compared.*

## 1. INTRODUCTION

Cache memories are now used in practically all modern general-purpose computer systems to reduce the average latency of memory accesses. A

---

[†1] This paper is a condensed version of a technical report [3].

cache is a small, high-speed memory which is located between the processor and the main memory and which keeps the information currently in use [8].

When the processor architecture supports virtual memory, the cache can be accessed either directly with virtual addresses (virtual-address cache) or with physical addresses obtained after translation (physical-address cache). Because of the consistency problems caused by virtual-address caches, almost all computer systems use a physical-address cache. Although the translation of virtual addresses to physical addresses is supported by a special-purpose cache (usually called a Translation Lookaside Buffer or TLB) virtual memory tends to increase the memory access latency. With the advent of RISC technology [7] and the latest improvements in VLSI technology the cache access is becoming the critical path of most instruction pipelines. In physical-address caches, the TLB and cache accesses must be either pipelined or performed in parallel.

In virtual-address caches, consistency problems occur within the same cache whenever a virtual-to-physical mapping is changed or when different virtual addresses are mapped to the same physical address. The problems are even more complex in multiprocessors because these inconsistencies can occur in more than one processor. Nevertheless, a virtual-address cache has many attractive features. First and foremost, most accesses to data and instructions are satisfied in one cycle of the cache. Moreover, since virtual-to-physical address translations are primarily required on a cache miss, TLB access time is not critical. For low-cost systems, virtual-address caches can be used in conjunction with relatively slow, off-the-shelf MMUs (Memory Management Units) [4,5]. The TLB can be very large and therefore exhibit an excellent hit ratio.

In this paper, the problems related to virtual-address caches are exposed in the contexts of uniprocessor and multiprocessor systems. Some solutions are presented and discussed. To appreciate and understand these problems, we must first overview the relevant properties of virtual memory.

## 2. VIRTUAL ADDRESSING

### 2.1 Introduction

We consider a virtual memory system in which a distinct virtual space is allocated to each process and each space is paged. Virtual-to-physical mappings are characteristic of the running process and the kernel executes in the "context" of the process. Each process virtual space is divided in two main regions: the kernel or system space and the user space. The partition between the kernel and user spaces is fixed, and the user space is usually structured in three segments: the text (or code) segment, the data segment and the stack segment.

The virtual-to-physical address mapping of kernel pages is common to all processes while the mapping of user pages is different for each process. Although a single level of table is logically enough to translate a virtual page number (noted VPN) into a physical page number (noted PPN), two or three levels are usually provided to support sparse addressing more efficiently. Each entry of the last table, which is called a page table entry (noted PTE), contains a physical page number and various bit fields used by the kernel to implement demand paging and protection.

This addressing model implicitly provides part of the protection by confining the references of a process to its own virtual space. However, there are many cases where it is necessary to share some information among processes. The most common case is when a process creates another one. Usually, the parent and the child processes share the same text segment; therefore, distinct page table entries point to the same physical page frame. When two or more virtual addresses map to the same physical address they are said to by *synonyms* or *aliases*.

A virtual address is usually extended by concatenating a process identifier (noted PID); distinct mappings of otherwise identical virtual page numbers can then be present in the TLB at the same time, and the TLB does not have to be flushed at each context switch [8]. When the cache is a virtual-address cache the same benefit is gained by the PID extension.

## 2.2 Translation Lookaside Buffer

A TLB is a cache of translations which accepts a virtual page number and returns a physical page number or a signal indicating a missing translation. Besides providing an efficient way to translate virtual addresses, a TLB usually includes some hardware support for protection, and for the management of the data structures used by the kernel to implement the virtual memory system.

For systems with physical-address caches, the TLB is a mandatory access path for most memory references. Thus, the TLB is the ideal place for checking access rights. Some protection bits are generally associated with the physical page number and they are interpreted differently according to the current privilege level and the type of memory reference (Instruction fetch, Data write or read).

A TLB entry usually contains two additional bits to support demand paging: the *reference* bit, R, and the *modify* bit, M. These are copies of the R and M bits contained in the corresponding entry of the page table. The *reference* bit in the page table entry is used by the kernel to implement the page replacement algorithm. This bit is set whenever a process accesses the page and is reset by the page-stealer daemon [1]. When an entry is loaded into the TLB a copy of the R bit is also loaded. When the page stealer resets the *reference* bits in the page table entries it must also reset the copies present in the TLB. When the page has not been referenced for a while, the R bit remains reset, and the page becomes eligible for swapping. This algorithm is an approximation to the working set policy for replacing pages in main memory. The *modify* bit is used by the swapper process to decide if the page must effectively be copied back on disk when it is victimized by the page replacement algorithm. This bit must be set on the first modification of the page after it has been swapped in.

## 3. VIRTUAL-ADDRESS CACHES IN UNIPROCESSORS

In this section we identify three major problems with virtual address caches in uniprocessors.

## 3.1 Virtual To Physical Address Demapping / Remapping

Suppose that a virtual address VA is mapped to a physical address PA1 during a certain period of time. When the operating system decides to demap and then remap this virtual address VA to a new physical address PA2 an inconsistency can occur if some data associated with PA1 are kept in the cache. The CPU can access the data associated with PA1 instead of the data associated with PA2. This inconsistency happens if the access of the CPU is a read or a write and, in this sense, it is different from the inconsistency that can happen if two virtual addresses are synonyms as explained in the next section. In general, the demapping/remapping involves a subset of the virtual space.

In the case of write-through caches, all the blocks belonging to the page(s) being demapped and then remapped must be purged, i.e. invalidated. For example, when a page is reclaimed by the page stealer and becomes candidate for swap-out the cache needs to be purged. Invalidations in the cache should take place before the invalidations of the corresponding translations in the TLB because the cache controller needs the physical address of a block on a processor write.

A radical solution is to purge the cache whenever a translation is invalidated or displaced by the replacement algorithm in the TLB. This solution requires that the TLB hit ratio be very high to limit the resulting performance degradations.

In the case of a write-back cache the blocks of the demapped area must be flushed, i.e., entries with matching tags must be invalidated and main memory must also be updated if they have been modified. As for a write-through cache, blocks should be flushed before the corresponding TLB entries are invalidated since physical addresses are necessary to write dirty blocks to main memory. In general, flushing should be avoided when it is not necessary [2]; sometimes, a mere purge is sufficient, for example when the information in a demapped area is not going to be re-used.

## 3.2 Synonyms

Virtual addresses are said to be synonyms or aliases when they all map to the same physical address. Synonyms introduce consistency problems in a virtual-address cache because multiple copies of the same information can be present at the same time in different cache entries. For read-only information, there is no consistency problem because all the copies are identical; the only drawback is a pollution effect in the cache if aliasing is used extensively. For modifiable information, multiple, inconsistent copies may coexist in the memory hierarchy of the system and the CPU can later access a stale copy.

There are different ways to solve the aliasing problem in uniprocessors. The simplest solution is for the kernel to tag all pages known under several virtual addresses as non-cacheable. The only necessary hardware support is a cacheable/non-cacheable bit in each TLB entry. Another solution is to flush entries in the cache to guarantee data consistency when the access pattern to synonyms is totally predictable. Each time a mapping is discarded the cache can be purged or flushed. This solution is acceptable for mapping changes that are infrequent because of the large overhead and is applicable only for the kernel. Finally, if the hardware (the cache controller) systematically searches for synonyms of the missing block on each miss, then it can avoid the presence of multiple copies in the cache at any time. The problem remains of detecting the aliases on misses.

## 3.3 Support For Memory Management And Protection

Since the TLB is consulted at miss time only, the cache is the only mandatory access path for most memory references; thus, besides the virtual address of the block, the cache directory must also hold a copy of the access right fields found in the TLB entries to support protection.

Statistical bits needed to optimize memory management are the *modify* bit and the *reference* bit. In a write-back cache one can decide to set the *modify* bit of a TLB entry whenever the processor modifies a block of the page for the first time, as indicated by the *dirty* bit in the cache. In this scheme, there will be many redundant settings of the *modify* bits in the TLB entries. Another possible design is to maintain a copy of the *modify* bit in the cache tags. In this case, all the blocks that have been loaded before the first modification of the page trigger a redundant setting operation when they are later modified by the CPU.

With virtual-address write-back caches, the *reference* bits in the TLB entries are updated on a cache miss only. With a write-through cache the checking and possible setting of the *reference* bit in the TLB can also be done on each processor write. Therefore, with this implementation, the exact usage of the pages is not reflected in the *reference* bit. However, this approximation does not affect the overall performance of the virtual memory system noticeably.

## 4. VIRTUAL-ADDRESS CACHES IN MULTIPROCESSORS

### 4.1 Introduction

We consider shared-memory multiprocessors where the interconnection between the processors and the main memory is a single bus (Figure 1). A private cache associated with each processor can significantly increase memory bandwidth and reduce memory access time. The main issue in this type of architecture is to guarantee the coherency of the information stored in the *shared-memory image*. Many different solutions are possible [9].

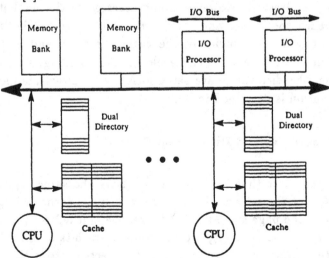

Figure 1 Single-bus shared-memory architecture

All the cache consistency protocols for single-bus multiprocessors suppose that every bus transaction is "watched" by all processors to check if their cache has a copy of the referenced information. For this reason, they are often designated informally as *snooping* protocols. To monitor bus transactions, it is necessary to duplicate the cache directory, at least in high performance systems. The copy of the cache tags is called the dual directory (Figure 1). It is used by the bus interface to "filter" the bus transactions without perturbing the activity of the local processor, except when the local cache has to be updated. Although a dual-ported cache directory is sufficient to support a snooping cache consistency protocol, we consider that for high-performance system (where virtual-address caches do make sense) the dual directory is absolutely required.

The bus must carry physical addresses, because of the synonym problem. When two processes running on distinct processors share information, they access it with different virtual addresses in general. Thus, it is not possible to snoop on the virtual addresses. Before accessing the bus the processor must translate virtual addresses in the TLB.

## 4.2 Virtual-To-Physical Directory Binding

In the usual operating mode, the cache is accessed by the processor with virtual addresses while the dual directory is accessed from the bus with physical addresses. However, some accesses to the dual directory must also reach the cache, and vice versa. Therefore, a binding must be defined between the entries in the cache directory and in the dual directory pointing to the same cache block. This binding is particularly tedious when the directories are set-associative or direct-mapped. The following solution is described in [6].

### 4.2.1 Set-Associative and Direct-Map Directories

Let suppose first that both directories have the same organization. When the size of the set-associative (or direct-map) cache is larger than the product of the page size by the set size, the indexed set (or entry) of each directory can be different, because some of the bits used for indexing are translated. However, we know that both selected sets in the case of a set-associative cache or entries in the case of a direct-map cache belong to the same *superset* [6]. The superset is illustrated in Figure 2.

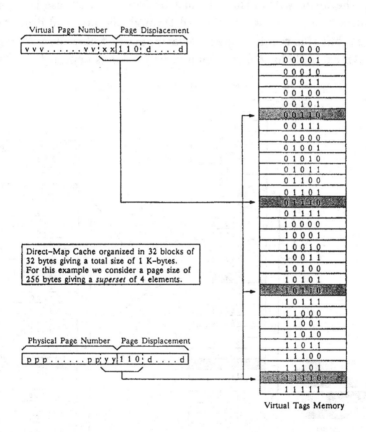

Figure 2 Superset Example

To access the entry holding the physical address of a block in the dual directory it is necessary to keep a pointer in the cache tags. This pointer is made of the bits of the physical address indexing the set inside the *superset*. Some bits locating the block within the set must also be kept. Conversely, in each entry of the dual directory a pointer made of the bits of the virtual address indexing the set inside the *superset* and some bits locating the block within the set must be kept. With these pointers, the virtual directory can now be accessed through the physical directory and vice versa, but this requires one associative access followed by a "random" access. An example for a direct-map organization is depicted on Figure 3.

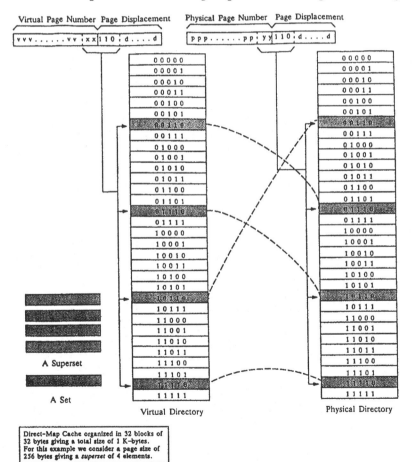

Figure 3 Virtual-to-Physical Directory Binding

When there is a miss in the cache, one of the blocks of the selected set must be victimized. In the dual directory a distinct entry must also be victimized if the physical address of the displaced block and the physical address of the missing block do not index in the same set. Therefore in some cases two blocks of the cache must be allocated to a missing block. To choose a victim in the selected set of the dual directory a simple, purely random selection algorithm can be applied. Another block may have to be displaced in the cache due to this second allocation. If the main memory is updated with a write-back policy it can happen that the two victim blocks have to be copied back. It therefore appears that the logic of the cache controller and the bus interface are more complex with a virtual-address cache than with a physical-address cache in a multiprocessor system.

Moreover, with the above organization, the occupancy ratio of the cache in some cases is less than 100% and this under-utilization affects the hit ratio.

### 4.2.2 Critical Associativity

The deleterious effect on the occupancy ratio can be eliminated provided the degree of associativity of at least one of the two directories is equal to or greater than the *critical associativity*.

For a given cache size the *critical associativity* is defined as: [Cache Size] / [Page Size]. In this case, the set selection is done only with bits belonging to the page displacement and all blocks that are synonyms map in the same set. Since timing constraints are usually less stringent at the bus interface, the best solution is to increase the associativity of the physical directory. A pointer must still be kept inside each entry of both directories. The size (in bits) of these pointers depends on the particular organization of the directories.

This solution can be extended up to the point where both directories are fully-associative. In this case, a full pointer to address "randomly" the cache blocks must also be held in each entry of the dual directory. If both CAM arrays implementing the directories and the RAM array implementing the data memory, are integrated on the same chip these pointers are not necessary. The match lines of the CAM can directly feed the RAM array decoders. Then, the binding of the two directories is guaranteed by the hardware implementation.

### 4.2.3 Cache Occupancy Ratio

We consider in first approximation that there is no correlation between the bit fields selecting the set inside the *superset* in the VPN and in the PPN. This is a reasonable assumption because the page replacement algorithm is oblivious to page frame addresses. Figure 4 presents results of simulations done for various organizations of cache and the dual-directory. The various graphs display the cache occupancy ratio as a function of the superset size. The superset size is expressed in number of sets.

In all cases, the replacement algorithm takes the following steps to allocate an entry when a missing block is loaded into the cache:

- If invalid entries are found in the selected set of both directories they are allocated and linked.

- If an invalid entry is found in only one of the directories, this entry is allocated and an entry is picked at random in the other directory.

- If no invalid entry is found in the selected sets of both directories, the replacement algorithm tries to find a pair of entries which are linked together.

- Finally, when there is no other alternative, the replacement algorithm picks an entry at random in both directories.

This replacement algorithm is optimal relative to the cache occupancy. It displaces two blocks only when there is no other alternative. However, it is not optimal for the cache hit ratio as valid entries are picked at random.

The graphs of Figure 4-a depict the occupancy ratio for an architecture where both directories have the same set size. It is important to note that the occupancy ratio remains 100% until the superset size is strictly larger than the set size. This effect can be explained simply. After a transient period where the cache is filled up, all entries of any set are linked with entries of all sets of the superset. At this point, the replacement algorithm

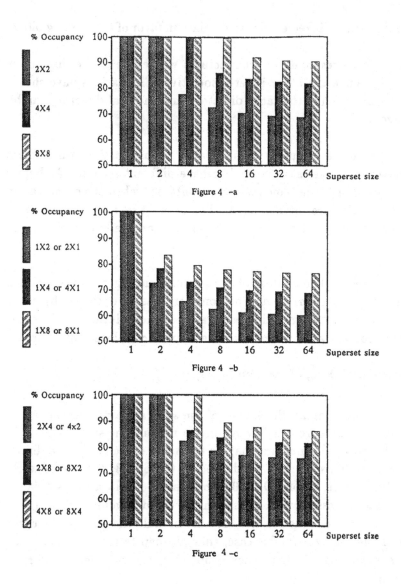

Figure 4 -a

Figure 4 -b

Figure 4 -c

Figure 4 Cache Occupancy

always find a pair of linked entries to displace in favor of the missing block.

Figure 4-b corresponds to architectures where one of the directories is direct-map while the other is set-associative. Simulations have shown that the organization of the cache directory and the dual directory can be interchanged.

Finally, Figure 4-c displays the occupancy ratios of architectures where both directories are set-associative but have different set size. As before there is a symmetry: the same results are obtained when the organization of both directories are interchanged. The occupancy ratio departs from 100% when the superset size is strictly larger than the lowest of the two set sizes.

Because the implementation of the replacement algorithm is complex the results presented here should be considered as an optimum by cache designers. In the following section, we examine other solutions to the cache occupancy problem which do not require a specific replacement policy.

### 4.2.4 Virtual Indexing of the Dual Directory

To avoid exploring all the entries of the *superset*, a restriction can be imposed on the software to allow synonyms modulo the size of the cache only. In this way, all synonyms map to the same cache entry in a direct-mapped cache. This solution is adopted in the Sun 3/200 line of workstations [10] and the Apollo DN4000 workstation [4]. In a set-associative cache, virtual addresses which are synonyms could be allocated such that they select the same cache set, i.e. they are modulo the ratio of the cache size and of the set size. In this case, they all map to the same cache set and the *snooping* cache consistency protocol can always detect information sharing.

All bus transactions must pass with the physical address the bits of the virtual address selecting the set inside the *superset*. The dual directory still contains the physical addresses but the set is selected with the same bits as those used to index in the cache. With this scheme, the virtual and physical addresses of the cache blocks are always in the same set and there is no more need to victimize two blocks on a replacement. Moreover, now the binding of the two directories is very simple because only the bits selecting the block inside the set are necessary.

## 4.3 Synonyms

A check for the presence of a synonym in the cache must be made whenever a missing block is fetched from the shared-memory image. In a multiprocessor, a *reverse translation* through the physical directory is the right approach to detect the presence of a synonym when a miss occurs in the cache. The cache controller must access the dual directory with the virtual address derived from the PPN obtained from the TLB and the displacement in the page.

Different courses of action are possible after the detection of a synonym. With a write-through cache the missing block can be either loaded from main memory or recopied from the existing copy in the cache. If both synonyms index in the same set, which is always the case when there is a restriction on synonyms to avoid cache under-utilization (Section 4.2.4), the tag can be changed to the new virtual address. In this case no block needs to be displaced. With a write-back cache if the synonym block present in the cache is not dirty the same approach is applicable. However, if the displaced block is dirty it must be recopied to the new entry when both synonyms do not index in the same set (again, only the tag must be changed when they do). When the block is moved from one set to the other, only one block must be displaced because the entry in the dual directory does not need to be moved. Only the pointer to the cache entry must be changed.

## 4.4 Virtual To Physical Address Demapping/Remapping

As in a single processor system, when a virtual-to-physical address translation is invalidated some actions must be taken to maintain the consistency in the virtual-address cache of each processor.

In a shared-memory multiprocessor, when a portion of the virtual address space (page, context, segment) is demapped, it is still necessary to purge the caches (i.e. to invalidate but not to discard the entries) and

TLBs of the system which were holding blocks and page translations contained in the demapped area. However, it is no more necessary in the case of a write-back cache to recopy the modified blocks to main memory (i.e. flush) because the consistency protocol ensures that dirty blocks are always part of the *shared-memory image*. The valid bit in the entry of the dual directory can remain set to indicate that the data contained in the block are still valid while the valid bit in the corresponding entry of the cache directory can be cleared to indicate that the address mapping has been modified. More than one cache can hold copies of blocks within the demapped memory area and more than one TLB can hold the virtual-to-physical translation(s) of any page located in the demapped area. Thus, the purge operation requires the intervention of all processors that were previously accessing data in the demapped area.

The matching criterion for the purge operations for the cache can be (part of) the physical address or (part of) the virtual address. However, the invalidation of the page address translations in the TLBs must still be made through the virtual addresses unless a dedicated comparison logic for the physical page numbers is added. In general, it is preferable to use the virtual address as matching criteria for purge operations but there is an implication on the PIDs. To be able to perform the cache and/or TLB purge on virtual addresses, the PIDs must be system wide identifiers. When a process migrates it must keep the same PID.

One can find an advantage of doing the purge on the physical address if the cause is a reallocation of the page frame. A purge "command" must be sent on the bus for each synonym (if there are any) of the page being demapped if the matching criterion is based on the virtual address. If the purge operations are based on the physical address, it is not necessary for the kernel to keep a special data structure linking all the virtual page numbers that are synonym.

The decision to demap a portion of the virtual space is taken by the operating system kernel. Hence, purge operations are under the control of software but some hardware support is required. To inform the other processors, the processor executing the kernel must be able to send/receive interrupt signals to/from other processors. The interrupt is physically issued by the bus interface when it receives a specific command sent out by its attached CPU. When receiving an interrupt, the attached handler can retrieve the data specifying the range of addresses to demap at a conventional memory location and the CPU can issue the purge commands to the cache, dual directory and TLB.

There must be an explicit **synchronization** so that the kernel knows when all the purge operations are completed. This synchronization can be done in software with a regular synchronization primitive. For example, a common counter could be decremented by each processor when it has completed all the purge operations in its cache, dual directory and TLB. The kernel knows it can safely do the remapping when the counter has reached the minimum value.

The scenario described above for the demapping and remapping of a portion of a virtual space in a multiprocessor assumed the presence of a very minimal hardware support; namely the ability for a processor to interrupt another one plus the ability to send out purge commands to its own cache, dual directory and TLB. However, the purge operations in the caches and TLBs of the system can be made more or less transparent to the software with more sophisticated hardware.

Many variations are possible and the level of sophistication of the hardware support must be driven exclusively by the frequency of demapping and remapping operations in the system. This frequency depends on the organization of the kernel and the virtual addressing scheme. More performance studies are needed to clarify these design tradeoffs.

## 4.5 Support For Memory Management

Although each process has its own page tables for virtual-to-physical address translation, there are many cases where a page table entry (noted PTE) can be shared by different processors. For example, in **UNIX** System V, when a parent process *"forks"* a child process, the resulting processes share access to the page table for the shared text region [1]. If the child process is scheduled on a separate processor, multiple copies of the information contained in a PTE are cached in distinct TLBs and possibly cache tags.

When the kernel supports the notion of threads or lightweight processes, distinct processors can also dynamically share page table entries. Because the threads or lightweight processes share the same virtual space and can be scheduled on separate processors multiple copies of the information held in PTEs can be present in the system.

These multiple copies of the same information lead to a classical coherence problem when one of them is modified. For example, when the page stealer clears the *reference* bit of a page table entry in the shared memory image, all copies in the TLBs of the system should also be cleared. In a uniprocessor, the kernel runs on the same processor as user processes, thus all *reference* bits in the TLB are accessible and can be cleared easily. In a symmetric multiprocessor system, the kernel can run on any processor. Without any special hardware support the page stealer cannot clear the other copies of the *reference* bit held in the TLBs of other processors.

Hardware support for clearing *reference* bits can lie between the use of an interrupt mechanism and a dedicated bus transaction which clears the *reference* bit in TLB entries where a given virtual-to-physical translation is contained. This bus transaction could be interpreted and executed by the bus interface of each processor transparently to the processor (i.e. to the software). A good tradeoff is to use a TLB purge transaction because these invalidations are infrequent. In this case, only the TLB is invalidated but not the caches.

Since distinct processes can share a page table, they can use distinct entries inside the same TLB to store the virtual-to-physical translation. This is due to the fact that a different PID is allocated to each process in order to be able to share the TLB. In this case, virtual addresses are "synonyms" although they come from the same page table entry. If the organization of the TLBs is direct-map or set-associative, an access to clear the *reference* bit must be done for the PID values of all processes sharing the page table entry.

In a multiprocessor system the *reference* bit stored in the PTE should be updated in a write-through manner. Hence, if multiple processes running on distinct processors are sharing a page table, some redundant updates of *reference* bits can occur. However, the traffic on the bus due to these extra updates (if the PTEs are not cached) or to the consistency protocol (if the PTEs are cached) is expected to be very small.

Processes can share information with synonyms coming from distinct page table entries. Thus, the kernel must keep track of the number of processes which reference a page. For example, in **UNIX** System V, this is done with a reference counter associated with each physical page frame in the *page frame data table* (noted *pfdata*) [1]. However, the page stealer takes into account only the value of the *reference* bit in the PTEs to determine if a page is eligible to be swapped out. The physical page frame is never reallocated until the reference counter is null. Thus, the page remains in the shared memory image as long as the page stealer has not victimized all the synonyms.

With this implementation of the page replacement, there is no need to maintain the consistency of the *reference* bits at the physical page frame level.

As for the *reference* bit the updating of the *modify* bit in the page table entries must be done in a write-through fashion. Hence, there will be some redundant attempts to set the copy of the *modify* bit in the PTEs corresponding to pages shared and modified by processes running on distinct processors. Because the copy of the *modify* bit in each PTE is updated only on the first modification done by each process referencing the page, the induced traffic on the bus is very small and does not affect the overall performance.

## 5. CONCLUSIONS

In this paper, we have shown that problems related to virtual-address caches could be solved at acceptable hardware cost and/or with acceptable restrictions on the software. Software transparency is highly desirable for complex programs. However, hardware cost and overall performance are the basic factors affecting the cost effectiveness of a design.

To maintain the coherence within and among virtual-address caches in both uniprocessor and multiprocessor systems the hardware is much simplified and the machine is more efficient when synonyms are restricted to map into the same cache entry (case of modulo synonyms). If synonyms are not restricted, then the only solutions are to search through the *superset* on each miss (uniprocessor) and to bind the entries in the cache and the dual directories (multiprocessor). This later solution either under-utilizes the cache or requires a very high degree of associativity.

When a virtual to physical mapping is changed, this change must be reflected in the cache and even in the cache of other processors in a multiprocessor. A mechanism to purge the cache(s) must be included in the design of virtual address caches.

The consistency of the *reference* bit and the *modify* bit for each page table entry must also be maintained. The handling of these bits can be greatly simplified with some cooperation from the software.

## Bibliography

1 Maurice J. Bach. The design of the UNIX operating system. *Prentice-Hall*, 1986.

2 Ray Cheng. Virtual address cache in UNIX. *Proc. 1987 summer usenix conference*, pages 217-224, 1987.

3 Michel Cekleov, Michel Dubois, Jin-Chin Wang and Faye' A. Briggs, *Virtual-Address Caches,* U.S.C. Technical Report No. CENG 89-701.

4 Craig R. Frink and Paul J. Roy. The cache architecture of the Apollo DN4000. *Proc. 1988 Compcon, IEEE*, pages 300-302, 1988.

5 Borivoje Furht and Veljko Milutinovic. A survey of microprocessor architectures for memory management. *Computer*, pages 48-67, Mar., 1987.

6 James R. Goodman. Coherency for multiprocessor virtual address caches. *Proc. 2nd International Conference on Architecture Support*

*For Programming Languages and Operating Systems, ACM*, 1987.

7 David A. Patterson. Reduced instruction set computer. *Communications of the ACM*. 28, 1, pages 8-21, Jan., 1985.

8 Alan J. Smith. Cache memories. *ACM Computing Surveys*, 14, 3, pages 473-530, Sept., 1982.

9 Paul Sweazey and Alan J. Smith. A class of compatible cache consistency protocols and their support by the IEEE Futurebus. *Proc. of the 13th Annual International Synmposium on Computer Architecture*, pages 414-423, June, 1986.

10 William Van Loo. Maximize performance by choosing best memory. *Computer Design*, pages 89-94, Aug., 1987.

# A Critique of Trace-Driven Simulation for Shared-Memory Multiprocessors

*Philip Bitar*

Aquarius Project
Computer Science Division
University of California
Berkeley, CA

## ABSTRACT

Trace-driven simulation of a multiprocessor system faces serious validity issues since *multiprocessor trace-driven simulation generally cannot represent interacting processes correctly:* the interactions represented by multiprocessor trace-driven simulation generally do not correspond to correct execution of the algorithm in the hypothetical architecture. Consequently, *multiprocessor trace-driven simulation must generally be validated by other modeling/simulation techniques.* Low-level modeling/simulation provides low-level accuracy, while high-level modeling/simulation provides high-level insight and the ability to generalize.

**Key Words:** Trace-driven simulation

## CONTENTS

# 1 HARDWARE AND SOFTWARE MODELS

A critical issue in computer architecture today is how to evaluate the performance of a hypothetical multiprocessor system. The system must be modeled in some way, and then performance under the model evaluated. There are two parts to such a model: a model of the *hardware* and a model of the *software*. A model of the hardware is generally straightforward and justified by intuition. Modeling the software that generates the processor activity, however, is a serious problem, more so for multiprocessor systems than for uniprocessor systems since the processes in an multiprocessor system will, in general, interact and their behavior will be interdependent.

Let us examine validity issues in trace-driven simulation of a multiprocessor system, and then examine the general issue of low level *vs.* high level modeling.

# 2 TRACE-DRIVEN SIMULATION

**2.1   Overview**
**2.2   Basic Concepts**
**2.3   Validity Issues**

## 2.1   Overview

A processor simulator that represents the execution of actual program code, instruction by instruction, holds intuitive justification. However, such a simulator is expensive to build and slow to run, so trace-driven simulation is often adopted for uniprocessors where possible. Trace-driven simulation (TDS) holds intuitive validity if the trace represents *a sequence of instructions and memory references that is independent of the architecture being evaluated;* that is, the sequence depends only on its internal consistency. Thus, as the architecture is changed from simulation to simulation, the trace would not be expected to change as well, allowing the original trace to remain a valid representation of processor activity in each architecture.

More recently, trace-driven simulation has been used for modeling multiprocessor (MP) program behavior. However, the above independence property generally does not hold for a set of multiprocessor traces, so *trace-driven simulation is generally invalid for a multiprocessor system.* This is true since the behavior of a process in a multiprocessor system will, in general, depend on concurrent interactions with other processes, and hence will depend on the architecture being evaluated, since it will affect the intertrace, or inter-processor, concurrency relationships.

Put differently, *MP trace-driven simulation generally cannot represent interacting processes correctly: the interactions represented by MP trace-driven simulation generally do not correspond to correct execution of the algorithm in the hypothetical architecture.* The basic reasons for this are easy to see: interacting processes are dynamic — their intertrace concurrency relationships and their actions generally change during the interactions based on the results of the ongoing interactions. However, trace-driven simulation is generally unable to change the intertrace concurrency relationships and/or trace content to represent these dynamic dependencies correctly.

Since the above observation places the validity of MP trace-driven simulation in question, MP trace-driven simulation must generally be validated — by analytic argument, if that is sufficient, otherwise by low-level simulation. Let us now consider three basic concepts, and then the validity issues in detail.

## 2.2   Basic Concepts

The three basic concepts are these.

- *Interprocess sharing:* access control algorithms and operations
- *Intercache sharing:* critical behavior in MP performance evaluation
- *Intertrace concurrency relationships:* two types of trace-driven simulation

Let us consider each in turn.

Regarding interprocess sharing, generally one process communicates with another in a shared-memory system by writing a shared data object that the other subsequently reads. Communicating processes in a shared-memory system *control each other's accesses* to such shared, writable data objects for either of *two purposes:* correctness or contention control. Examples of access control operations that insure *correctness* include locking a queue on an access that may enqueue or dequeue an entry, and implementing a ready-queue algorithm so that work that is ready (and only work that is ready) is made available for execution. An example of a *contention control* algorithm is an algorithm to distribute interprocessor contention among several work queues, instead of concentrating it all on one queue.

Access control operations may be ordered according to *abstraction level.* The lowest level operations, which may be called *primary,* are *hardware operations,* such as test-and-set, atomic increment/decrement, compare-and-swap, and hardware-implemented barrier wait. Higher level, or *n-ary operations* ($n > 1$), are *software algorithms* of various levels of abstraction, such as multiple-reader/single-writer sharing, a ready-queue algorithm determining when work should be put on a ready queue, and a priority queue algorithm determining when entries should be taken off the queue.

Intercache sharing, the second basic concept, is a *critical behavior of interest in assessing MP performance.* Intercache sharing has these three causes:

- *Interprocess sharing:* multiple processes share the same data object

- *Block sharing:* multiple data objects share the same memory block

- *Process migration:* one process accesses the same data on different processors

Finally, the concept of intertrace concurrency relationships creates two types of trace-driven simulation: synchronous and asynchronous. Under *synchronous trace-driven simulation (STDS)* the intertrace concurrency relationships that occurred under original execution are maintained, as the traces are cranked through the simulator processors in lock-step fashion (Figure 1). STDS, hence, has *fixed* intertrace concurrency relationships and *fixed* trace operations (trace content). In contrast, under *asynchronous trace-driven simulation (ATDS)* the intertrace concurrency relationships and the results of certain access-control operations are allowed to change according to dynamic conditions in the architecture (Figure 2). Table 1 summarizes these features of synchronous and asynchronous TDS.

Having considered the basic concepts relevant to trace-driven simulation, let us now turn to the validity issues.

## 2.3   Validity Issues

We will first consider asynchronous TDS, and then synchronous TDS.

**Asynchronous TDS.** There are two fundamental ways in which an access-control operation may be violated in ATDS: *allowing access* when it should not be allowed, and *disallowing — delaying — access* when it should not be delayed. In addition, ATDS may violate other software algorithms by basing the action that follows an access-control algorithm on the protected

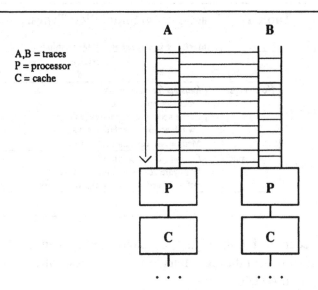

**Figure 1. Synchronous Trace-Driven Simulation.**

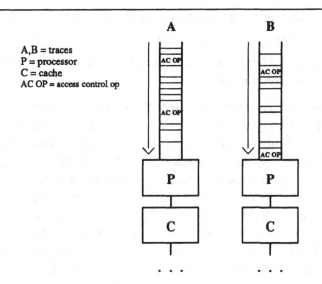

**Figure 2. Asynchronous Trace-Driven Simulation.**

### Table 1.    Trace-Driven Simulation Types.

| | | Intertrace Concurrency Relationships | |
|---|---|---|---|
| | | Fixed<br>(STDS) | Variable<br>(ATDS) |
| **Trace**<br><br>**Operations** | Fixed | No changes | *Reasons for Variability:*<br>Processor operation times<br>Cache access times/misses/waits<br>Switch access times/misses/waits<br>Memory access times/misses/waits |
| | Variable | Not Applicable | *Reasons for Variability:*<br>Hardware access-control operations ($1°$)<br>Software access-control algorithms/operations ($n°$) |

result that occurred during original execution rather than on the protected result that should occur during simulation. This creates *three violation types* that may occur in ATDS.

- Violation of access-control algorithm/operation

  □ *Allowing access* when it should not be allowed

  □ *Disallowing (delaying) access* when it should not be disallowed

- Violation of other software algorithm

  □ *Consequence of protected result* based on original result rather than on correct simulation result

The violations of access-control algorithms may, of course, alter sharing metrics that may be of interest, as well as other kinds of metrics. But resulting violations of other software algorithms may cause even more extensive inaccuracies that, in general, will not be easy to comprehensively identify.

One solution for these violations may be to annotate the traces by identifying access-control operations as such, and then by executing the access-control operations during simulation. This generates access-control results that are correct during simulation, rather than merely repeating the results that are contained in the trace and were correct during original execution but may not be correct during simulation. However, an access-control operation or algorithm, such as a ready queue algorithm, may have its code spread throughout the program, so that it may not be possible to identify it in a trace and then execute it dynamically during simulation, as it would be possible to do for test-and-set, for example. Furthermore, it may be that the results of the operations protected by an access-control operation should be different during simulation than during original execution, but it would, in general, be possible to simulate this correctly only by simulating the entire software algorithm.

Before looking at specific examples of these violations, let us briefly note the following. We can easily imagine violations of incorrectly allowing or disallowing access for hardware access-control operations based on mutual exclusion, such as test-and-set, atomic increment/decrement, and compare-and-swap: an access that violates the mutual exclusion property, or a control operation that disallows an access that would not violate mutual exclusion. With respect to software access-control algorithms, a multiple-readers/single-writer algorithm would be violated by a writer having concurrent access with a reader or another writer, or by a control operation that disallows an access that would not violate the multiple-readers/single-writer property. A ready-queue algorithm would be violated by the removal of a work-queue entry that is not yet ready hence has not yet been inserted in the queue. A priority-queue algorithm would be violated by the removal of an entry is not the highest priority entry in the queue, or in the case of linked entries, by inserting a new entry by linking it to an entry that has not yet been inserted.

Now let us look at specific examples of violations. Figure 3 shows how test-and-set could be violated if ATDS did not explicitly represent the lock bit and execute the test-and-set and clear operations on the bit during the simulation. The figure shows that under original execution, trace A accessed the lock bit before trace B, while the reverse is true under ATDS. The consequence is that under ATDS trace B executes an unnecessary delay (because it was necessary during original execution). The figure also shows that mutual exclusion may be violated, access to trace A being incorrectly allowed (because it was correctly allowed during original execution). Finally, the figure also shows that the action that follows from the access protected by test-and-set is the action that was appropriate during original execution, in which trace A made its protected access before trace B made its protected access. This action may not be appropriate during simulation since it may be that the value of the protected object should be different during simulation since trace B accessed the protected object first during simulation. Hence the resulting action is potentially a violation of the encompassing software algorithm.

Figure 4 shows how a multiple-readers/single-writer algorithm could be violated if ATDS did not explicitly represent the controlling data structure and execute the respective control algorithm using the data structure. In contrast to Figure 3, the lock bit for the controlling data structure is explicitly

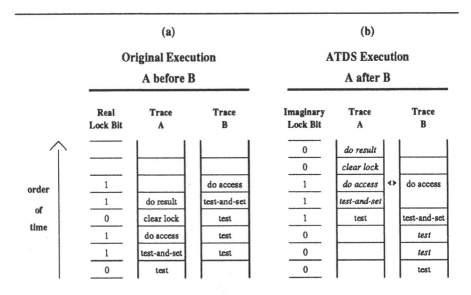

|  | (a) | | | | (b) | |
|---|---|---|---|---|---|---|
|  | **Original Execution** | | | | **ATDS Execution** | |
|  | **A before B** | | | | **A after B** | |
|  | Real Lock Bit | Trace A | Trace B | Imaginary Lock Bit | Trace A | Trace B |
|  |  |  |  | 0 | *do result* |  |
|  |  |  |  | 0 | *clear lock* |  |
| order | 1 |  | do access | 1 | *do access* | do access |
| of | 1 | do result | test-and-set | 1 | *test-and-set* |  |
| time | 0 | clear lock | test | 1 | test | test-and-set |
|  | 1 | do access | test | 0 |  | *test* |
|  | 1 | test-and-set | test | 0 |  | *test* |
|  | 0 | test |  | 0 |  | test |

*Note:* Time units indicate order only, not magnitude of time.
Italics in (b) indicate potential errors under ATDS.

**Figure 3.   Potential Algorithm Violations Under ATDS:** *Test-and-Set.*

represented and manipulated, so the test-and-set algorithm is not violated. However, as in Figure 3, under original execution, trace A accessed the data structure before trace B, while the reverse is true under ATDS. Accordingly, trace B executes an unnecessary delay, and later trace A violates the multiple-readers/single-writer algorithm. And finally, the action of trace A that follows from the access protected by the multiple-readers/single-writer algorithm is the action that was appropriate during original execution, and may not be appropriate during simulation.

Figure 5 shows how a ready-queue algorithm may be violated by the simulated removal of an entry before it has been inserted. If a barrier can be added to separate the insertion phase of all processors from the removal phase of all processors, then this violation can be prevented — at the cost of lower concurrency — as shown in Figure 5a.

The studies of Eggers (1988, 1989 [5-8]) provide examples of the use of ATDS. In her simulator there are caches, a bus, and memory, and the metrics evaluated include bus utilization and number of busy-waiters at a

**(a)**                                **(b)**

**Original Execution**                 **ATDS Execution**

**A before B**                         **A after B**

| order of time | L | R | W | Trace A Reader | Trace B Writer | L | R | W | Trace A Reader | | Trace B Writer |
|---|---|---|---|---|---|---|---|---|---|---|---|
| | | | | | | | | | *do result* ⋮ | | |
| | 0 | 0 | 1 | do result ⋮ | do access ⋮ | 0 | *1* | *1* | *do access* | ‹› | do access |
| | 0 | 1 | 0 | · | clear lock | 0 | *1* | *1* | clear lock | | |
| | 1 | 1 | 0 | do access | writer wait | 1 | *1* | *1* | *inc R* | | |
| | 1 | 1 | 0 | | test-and-set | 1 | *0* | *1* | test-and-set | | |
| | 0 | 1 | 0 | clear lock | test | 0 | 0 | *1* | test | | |
| | 1 | 1 | 0 | inc R | test | 0 | 0 | 0 | | | clear lock |
| | 1 | 0 | 0 | test-and-set | | 1 | 0 | 0 | | | *writer wait* |
| | 0 | 0 | 0 | test | | 1 | 0 | 0 | | | test-and-set |

*Note:* Time units indicate order only, not magnitude of time.
L = lock bit, R = # readers, W = # writers; L,R,W are all real in (a); R,W are imaginary in (b)
Italics in traces of (b) indicate potential errors under ATDS.

**Figure 4.** **Potential Algorithm Violations Under ATDS:** *N Readers, 1 Writer.*

test-and-set — metrics that synchronous trace-driven simulation cannot measure, since it maintains the original intertrace concurrency relationships.

The traces came from four multiprocessor CAD programs that all follow nearly the same simple paradigm. Each process in a program executes the same code, and begins by accessing a shared queue containing work (busy-waiting if necessary) and then takes an entry from the queue. The process does the work corresponding to the entry, places the entry back on the queue (busy-waiting if necessary), and then waits at a barrier synchronization point for the rest of the processes. After they all arrive, they iterate the above loop. One program does no queue locking, and another program has no barrier.

Due to trace annotation, the processors in Eggers' simulator can detect and execute the only two low-level synchronization operations that occur in the traces, namely, test-and-set and barrier wait, which allows her simulation

46

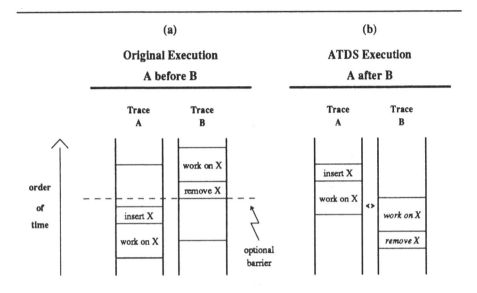

*Note:* Time units indicate order only, not magnitude of time.
Italics in traces of (b) indicate potential errors under ATDS.

**Figure 5.** **Potential Algorithm Violations Under ATDS:** *Queuing.*

to avoid violating the respective access-control algorithms. It appears to me that her simulation will not compromise her metrics, except in the case of the study that has no barrier, making the violation of the ready-queue algorithm, shown in Figure 5, possible.

**Synchronous TDS.** Under STDS, the intertrace concurrency relationships that held during original execution are maintained during simulation. Consequently (assuming that original execution was correct), STDS will not violate access-control algorithms or other software algorithms. However, it still turns out that systematic inaccuracies in the representation of intercache sharing may still occur. Let us illustrate this by an STDS paradigm.

Let us consider an STDS paradigm in which cache size is varied and the resulting miss ratio is measured over all processors (Figure 6). The key concept underlying the potential inaccuracy is the systematic effect that *working set size* — which may differ from processor to processor — can have on *intertrace concurrency relationships* — which STDS does not alter to accommodate dynamic conditions that occur during simulation. Intertrace concurrency relationships, in turn, can systematically alter *intercache sharing,* an effect that STDS will not be able to detect.

Figure 7 provides an example of this. Suppose there are two processes $P_1$ and $P_2$ that regularly access the same work queue but have different working set sizes $w_i$, with $w_2 \ll w_1$. Suppose also that there are two cache sizes in the simulation, a large size greater than $w_1$ and a small size between $w_1$ and $w_2$. Suppose, finally, that under the large cache size the times between $P_1$'s successive accesses to the queue tend to be about the same as the times between $P_2$'s accesses to the queue (Figure 7a), whereas under the small cache size, the interaccess times for $P_1$ tend to be about three times those for $P_2$ due to the additional misses that the small cache will cause $P_1$ to have

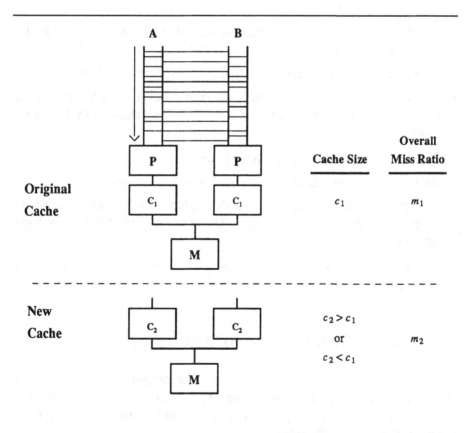

Figure 6. STDS Paradigm.

(Figure 7b). Then as shown in Figure 7b, $P_2$ will have several queue accesses not interleaved with $P_1$'s queue accesses, giving $P_2$ hits on any queue structure that it must access on each queue access. This affect will decrease the overall miss ratio somewhat. Although this affect may be insignificant compared to other effects on the miss ratio, STDS will be unable to detect the effect no matter how large it is. Therefore, we see that STDS can entail systematic inaccuracies in measuring the miss ratio as a function of cache size in this paradigm.

Thompson (1987, 1989 [9,10]) developed a one-pass trace-driven simulation technique following the above STDS paradigm. Consequently, data collected by Thompson are subject to the validity issue raised here.

**Conclusion.** The solutions to the ATDS validity issues appear to be as follows.

- Identify all access-control algorithms and other algorithms that may be violated in the simulation.

- Determine how these violations may affect the metrics of interest.

- If the effect on the metrics cannot be determined or if it can be determined to invalidate the metrics, then the TDS must be validated by low-level simulation.

The solution to the STDS validity issue is similar.

- Identify all possible inaccuracies on the metrics of interest.

- If the effect on the metrics cannot be determined or if it can be determined to invalidate the metrics, then the TDS must be validated by low-level simulation.

In general, the respective analyses will be impossible; however, they may be possible in very restricted cases.

## 3   LEVEL OF MODELING AND SIMULATION

Let now us consider the continuum of abstraction in the domain of modeling and simulation by focusing on the extremes: low-level modeling/simulation and high-level modeling/simulation. Each approach has its strength, which the other lacks:

- *Low-level modeling/simulation:* low-level accuracy

- *High-level modeling/simulation:* high-level insight, ability to generalize

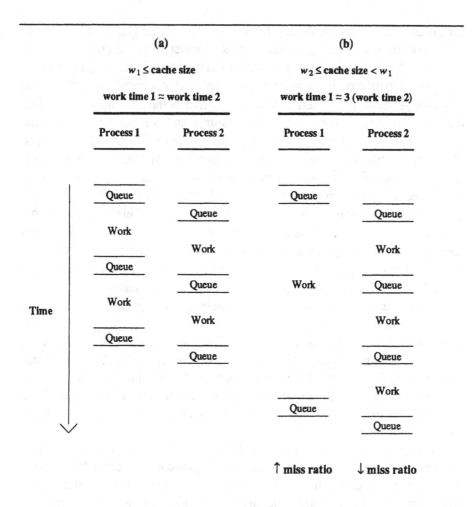

**Figure 7.   Potential Inaccuracy Under STDS.**

That is, the major advantage of *low-level modeling/simulation* is that it offers low-level accuracy, which may be intuitively justified if it is sufficiently low. High-level modeling/simulation, on the other hand, offers high-level insight, and accordingly allows generalization to the class of objects/programs represented by the high-level abstraction. Both are needed in order to understand the behavior of programs executing in an architecture of interest.

To illustrate, suppose that uniprocessor simulations are run on a set of programs and the hit ratio is reported as a function of cache set associativity for given cache sizes, producing respective asymptotes (Figure 8). Now, to what other programs can these asymptotes be generalized? None!

In order to generalize observed behavior from a set of programs to unobserved behavior from another program it is necessary to identify *the program features* that determine the respective behavior, and to determine *the causal relationships* between the features and the behavior. Then the behavior can be generalized to the programs that have the respective features. The identification of features and the determination of causal relationships is simply *high-level modeling*, and may range from simple, imprecise to complex, precise characterizations: from qualitative relationships to back-of-the-envelope formulas to refined analytic models to simulation models that provide detail that would make an analytic model intractable. Note that causal relationships can only be determined through controlled experimentation, in which independent variables (program features) are manipulated and dependent variables (program behavior metrics) are measured.

As an example of the insight available from high-level modeling, in 1986 there were two studies of broadcast (snooping) cache protocols that were based on an analytic model by Dubois and Briggs (Archibald, Baer 1986 [1]; Vernon, Holliday 1986 [11]; Dubois, Briggs 1982 [3]). These studies showed that under intense write-sharing of cache blocks, when a word that may have a copy in another cache is written, it is better for the cache to update other caches with the word rather than invalidating the respective block in those caches.

However, in Bitar and Despain (1986 [2]) I pointed out that better perspective on intercache sharing is needed. In particular, in order to represent intercache sharing accurately, it is necessary to keep in mind that write-shared objects, or *atoms*, are generally synchronized by the software and that it would be a good strategy to allocate one atom per block where possible to avoid unnecessary contention for the block between caches. It follows, then, that the advantage of update over invalidate, referred to above, should generally be reduced. In fact, Dubois has since updated his model along these lines and is currently studying broadcast protocols in this context, although update and invalidate protocols have not yet been compared (Dubois, Wang 1988 [4]).

This example illustrates that due to the high-level modeling, I was able to generalize the results of the 1986 studies — a negative generalization in this case — observing that the results should not generalize to typical program behavior.

In conclusion, low-level modeling/simulation is needed for low-level accuracy, while high-level modeling/simulation is needed for high-level insight and ability to generalize.

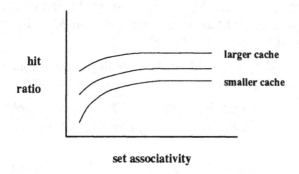

**Figure 8. Hit Ratio as Function of Set Associativity and Cache Size.**

# 4 SUMMARY

We have seen that trace-driven simulation of a multiprocessor system faces serious validity issues since multiprocessor trace-driven simulation generally cannot represent interacting processes correctly: the interactions represented by multiprocessor trace-driven simulation generally do not correspond to correct execution of the algorithm in the hypothetical architecture. Consequently, MP TDS must generally be validated by other modeling/simulation effort. Low-level modeling/simulation provides low-level accuracy, while high-level modeling/simulation provides high-level insight and the ability to generalize.

## ACKNOWLEDGEMENTS

I appreciate the support of Al Despain and Vason Srini through the Aquarius Project. I thank Michel Dubois for his encouragement, his insights, and his criticisms, which have proved crucial to the development of this paper. This research was partially funded by the Defense Advanced Research Projects Agency (DoD) and monitored by Office of Naval Research under Contract No. N00014-88-K-0579.

# REFERENCES

[1] **Archibald, J., Baer, J-L. 1986.** "An evaluation of cache coherence solutions in shared-bus multiprocessors," *ACM Trans. on Computer Systems*, 4(4), Nov. 1986, 273-298.

[2] **Bitar, P., Despain, A.M. 1986.** "Multiprocessor cache synchronization: issues, innovations, evolution." *13th ISCA*, 1986, 424-433.

[3] **Dubois, M., Briggs, F.A. 1982.** "Effects of cache coherency in multiprocessors." *IEEE Trans. Computers*, C-31(11), Nov. 1982, 1083-1099.

[4] **Dubois, M., Wang, J-C. 1988.** "Shared data contention in a cache coherence protocol." *14th ICPP*, August 1988, 146-155.

[5] **Eggers, S.J. 1989.** "Simulation analysis of data sharing in shared memory multiprocessors," March 1989, Ph.D. dissertation, Tech. Report UCB/CSD 89/501, Computer Science Division, U. of Calif., Berkeley, CA 94720.

[6] **Eggers, S.J., Katz, R.H. 1988.** "A characterization of sharing in parallel programs and its application to coherency protocol evaluation," *15th ISCA*, 1988, 373-383.

[7] **Eggers, S.J., Katz, R.H. 1989a.** "The effect of sharing on the cache and bus performance of parallel programs," *3rd ASPLOS*, 1989, 257-270.

[8] **Eggers, S.J., Katz, R.H. 1989b.** "Evaluating the performance of four snooping cache coherency protocols," *16th ISCA*, 1989, 2-15.

[9] **Thompson, J.G. 1987.** "Efficient analysis of caching systems," Oct. 1987, Ph.D. dissertation, Tech. Report UCB/CSD 87/374, Computer Science Division, U. of Calif., Berkeley, CA 94720.

[10] **Thompson, J.G., Smith, A.J. 1989.** "Efficient (stack) algorithms for analysis of write-back and sector memories," *ACM Trans. on Computer Systems*, 7(1), February 1989, 78-117.

[11] **Vernon, M.K., Holliday, M.A. 1986.** "Performance analysis of multiprocessor cache consistency protocols using generalized timed petri nets." *ACM SIGMETRICS*, 1986.

# Performance of Symmetry Multiprocessor System

**Shreekant S. Thakkar**

*Sequent Computer Systems*
*15450 S.W. Koll Parkway*
*Beaverton, Oregon 97006*

*Abstract*

*This paper presents the performance characteristics of three members of the Sequent Symmetry series of parallel processors. The performance of two homogeneous parallel applications, Butterfly Network Simulator and Parallel Linpack is described here. The system performance was also observed on a large multi-user software development environment. Performance is measured in terms of bus utilization, cache miss-rate, and application speed. The Symmetry system gives us a unique opportunity to measure system performance with two different cache coherence protocols with the same hardware.*

## 1. INTRODUCTION

Sequent's Symmetry Model A and Model B systems are variations of a shared-memory multiprocessor using up to 30 Intel 80386 microprocessors. The significant difference between the two machines is in the cache coherency protocol they use. Model A machines support a write-through cache protocol. Model B systems support a copyback protocol. There are small hardware differences, but Model B systems can support either protocol by selecting appropriate cache control software.

This situation presents a unique opportunity to study and compare the performance of two different multiprocessor cache coherence protocols on identical hardware. The system is also instrumented to provide access to measure detail hardware and system software behavior.

We were able to evaluate and compare the performance of several different applications on Symmetry systems using both write-through and copyback modes.

The major observations here were that cache miss-rate dominates the performance of the system. If the miss-rate gets higher than some number than the processor accesses can saturate the bus. This saturation point of course depends on the number of processors in the system.

The copyback system performance show significant reduction in the cache miss-rate compared to the write-through system. This allows significantly higher scaling (i.e., number of processors) of the system than possible for write-through system.

The write-sharing is not a problem in a system such as Symmetry since the parallel programming model used here is medium or large grain process model. In this model, the real hot-spots are highly contested locks and not the shared data structures.

The effect of process migration was observed in a multi-user environment. The cache-to-cache traffic caused by process migration increases as the number of processors are increased.

## 2. SYMMETRY MULTIPROCESSOR SYSTEMS

Sequent's Symmetry Series is a bus-based shared-memory multiprocessor system [LOVTHA88]. A diagram is shown in Figure 1. A system can contain from two to thirty CPUs with a total performance of around 120 MIPS. Each processor subsystem contains a 32-bit microprocessor, a floating point unit, optional floating point accelerator, and a private cache.

The system features a 53.4 MB/sec pipelined system bus, up to 240 MB of main memory, and a diagnostic and console processor. Symmetry systems can support five dual-channel disk controllers (DCCs), with up to 8 disks per channel. Each channel can transfer at 1.8 MB/sec.

The DYNIX operating system is a parallel version of UNIX, designed and implemented by Sequent for their Balance and Symmetry machines. It provides all services of ATT System V UNIX as well as Berkeley 4.2 BSD UNIX.

We evaluated the performance of applications on three different configurations of Sequent Symmetry systems: on standard processor subsystems using both write-through cache mode and copyback cache mode; and on a system using the copyback cache protocols with larger processor caches and a faster processor clock rate.

Model A Symmetry systems used the Symmetry write-through cache coherency protocol. Model B Symmetry Systems uses the Symmetry copyback cache coherence protocol. Each processor in Model A and B system has 64 Kbytes two-way set associative caches.

We also evaluated performance of several applications on a variant of model B (called Model B' here) using a 2X larger cache and a 25% faster processor.

## 3. SYMMETRY CACHE COHERENCE AND BUS PROTOCOLS

The Symmetry cache and bus protocols work together to support cache coherency in the system. The cache coherence protocol is a *write invalidate* and *ownership* based protocol. That is, a write by a processor will first invalidate all copies in the systems before the write is completed. To complete a write the cache must first gain ownership of the cache block in question. This action is described below.

### 3.1 The Protocols

The Sequent System Bus (SSB) in Symmetry Model A systems used the following cycles to support the write-through protocol:

| | |
|---|---|
| RA | Read Address cycle |
| WAI | Write Address with Invalidate cycle |
| RDF/RDL | Read data first and last cycles |
| WDF/WDL | Write data first and last cycle. |

The SSB protocol was extended in Model B to support the copyback cache coherency scheme by adding the following cycles:

| | |
|---|---|
| RAI | Read Address with Invalidate |
| WA | Write Address |
| IA | Invalidate Address Cycle |

Two additional cycle type bits were added to the Symmetry bus to extend the bus protocol to support the Symmetry copyback cache coherence protocol. The first bit is used to identify transactions using the extended 64-bit width of the bus. The second bit allows an address to be tagged to show whether or not it should cause an invalidation. This can be used with a read address if a cache needs to insure that it holds the only copy of a block (i.e., gain ownership).

In addition, in Model B systems two status lines were added to the bus to support the protocol. They are SHARED and OWNED. The first, SHARED, indicates that an RA cycle on the bus has hit a block that exists in another cache. This lets a requester know whether to install a new block as PRIVATE or SHARED. The second, OWNED, indicates that an RA or RAI cycle on the bus has hit a block that is held MODIFIED by another cache. This lets the memory subsystems know that a cache will respond to the request.

The Symmetry copyback cache coherence protocol [LOVTHAK88] makes use of four cache states: INVALID, PRIVATE, SHARED, and MODIFIED.

These states are defined as follows:

INVALID     Block is not currently valid in the cache.

PRIVATE     Block has been read and does not exist in any other cache in
            the system.

SHARED      Block has been read and may exist in another cache.

MODIFIED    Block has been modified and does not exist in any other cache
            in the system.

The coherence protocol, in general, works as follows:

READ HIT

No bus activity is required and requested data is supplied to the processor.

READ MISS

An RA type cycle is issued on the bus. If any cache has a copy of the block of data in
PRIVATE or SHARED state it changes the state of the block to SHARED, and asserts
the SHARED line on the backplane.

If any cache has the data in MODIFIED state it asserts the OWNED line, responds to the
request, and changes its local state to INVALID. The state could have been changed to
SHARED instead of INVALID, but our implementation does not allow this. The memory
subsystem observes this transaction, noting the assertion of the OWNED signal, and takes
a copy of the data as it is being passed from one cache to the next (called "implied"
copyback operation). This process allows the responding cache to relinquish ownership.

If no cache signals ownership then the memory responds to the request with its copy of
the requested block. The receiving processor sets his tags to PRIVATE, if SHARED was
not asserted, or SHARED otherwise.

WRITE HIT

If the block is in MODIFIED state then this implies that this cache already owns the
block and can complete the write. No bus activity is necessary. If the block is in the
PRIVATE state, then the cache changes the state to MODIFIED and completes the write.
If the block is in the SHARED state then the cache issues an IA cycle on the bus, causing
all other caches to invalidate their copies (i.e. write invalidate operation), and changes its
state to MODIFIED.

WRITE MISS

An RAI cycle is issued on the bus to obtain the current copy of the block and to signal all other caches to invalidate their copy. If any cache has the copy of the block in MODIFIED state then it responds to the request. Any cache which holds the block in PRIVATE or SHARED state invalidates its copy. If no cache holds the block MODIFIED then memory will respond to the request. The receiving cache installs the block as MODIFIED and completes the write.

### 3.2 I/O Devices And Symmetry Cache Coherence

I/O devices do not participate in the caching protocol and therefore can issue writes to blocks that caches hold MODIFIED. These WAI cycles are absorbed by the caches which own the block being written.

### 3.3 Response Latency

In general, caches in multiprocessor systems serve two masters, the processor and the bus. A cache has to respond to bus requests when it owns a dirty block, and also to processor requests. The memory only responds to a single processor access at a time, hence it can respond much faster. Thus a cache-to-cache transfer is usually slower than a memory-to-cache transfer. The Symmetry multiprocessor system follows this pattern especially since the interface between cache and bus is asynchronous.

The Sequent System Bus is an unpended (split-transaction) bus. A fixed number of requests are allowed on the bus, and responses to requests are strictly ordered. Responses to earlier requests have to come back before responses to later requests can be allowed on the bus.

The number of requests allowed on the bus is optimized for the number of cycles required by a memory response, because memory responds to the majority of bus requests. Cache responses, having longer latency, require more bus cycles than memory responses. The additional bus cycles spent waiting for non-optimal, slower-than-memory responses are wasteful of bus bandwidth because they prevent further requests from being put on the bus. These additional cycles can be classified as "hold" cycles. Thus if a cache responds to a bus request, potentially useful bus cycles are wasted as hold cycles. One of the performance characteristics discussed in this evaluation is the effect of cache traffic on bus utilization.

### 3.4 Synchronization Mechanism

The synchronization mechanism on the Symmetry Model A uses global interlocks. Only one processor is allowed to access the bus with locked access. Other processors subsequently read the locked variable after failing to complete their atomic access. These processors continuously read this value waiting for it to change. This action is called *spinning* in cache since it does not involve any bus accesses. The write on the bus of the atomic access invalidates copies of the lock variable the other processors are spinning on. The whole activity of accessing a locked variable restarts after this invalidation. This mechanism is costly in terms of bus utilization beyond 10 processors [GRATHA89].

The synchronization mechanism on the Symmetry Model B uses cache-based locks. The locks are ownership based. That is, the cache controller treats a locked read from a processor like a write operation.

Assuming a cache miss, the cache controller performs an exclusive read operation on the bus to gain ownership of the block. The atomic lock operation is then completed in the cache. These locks are optimized for multi-user systems where locks are lightly contested and the critical sections are short. They do not work well in some parallel applications where a lock is heavily contested. The heavy contention for locks produces lot of cache-to-cache transfers. On Symmetry Model B systems these transfers generate hold cycles as mentioned earlier.

Several software synchronization schemes can be used to reduce contention for the locks in the hardware [ANDERSON89] [GRATHA89]. These schemes are orthogonal to the hardware based locks and are implemented using them. The queue-based software synchronization scheme reported by Graunke and Thakkar [GRATHA89] eliminates the contention entirely for these locks. Thus the cache-to-cache traffic in Model B systems due to these locks is eliminated. The queue locks also work well in Model A systems.

## 4. PERFORMANCE MONITORING

Symmetry systems incorporate performance monitoring hardware that can be accessed by special system software. The hardware includes counters, masks and multiplexing logic. The mask can be set and appropriate events of interest selected before the counters are started. The counters can be stopped and read by system software. This action is non-intrusive on system performance.

The types of events that can be measured include all types of accesses to the cache controller by the processor, accesses from the bus to the cache controller (i.e owned and invalidate operations), and state changes. This allows us to detect the accesses to shared blocks, etc. Other events that can be measured include the different types of bus cycles and other aspects of bus protocol. These features give us a unique opportunity to study this architecture and its behavior under different applications.

System performance was evaluated in terms of bus utilization, miss-rate, and application speed.

## 5. PERFORMANCE EVALUATION

We have evaluated performance of more than 12 different parallel applications on Symmetry systems using both cache coherence modes. We are reporting here on the most interesting of these applications. We will discuss two parallel applications:

> Butterfly Network Simulator
> Parallel Linpack

The parallel applications we examined are all based on medium- and large-grain parallelism. These types of applications run efficiently on shared memory system such as the Symmetry because they mask out the overhead of synchronization costs. These applications also exhibit little or no write-sharing. The contention is for the lock rather than a medium or large data structure. This attribute has been observed for all the parallel applications we have monitored.

We will also discuss performance of a multiuser workload in an engineering environment.

### 5.1 Butterfly Network Simulator Application

The butterfly network simulator [BROOKS89] is an integer intensive application. It is the one application which used team splitting [BROOKS89] to improve load balance for small problem sizes.

The network being simulated has two concurrent halves of exactly the same size, so team splitting is particularly effective. Each half of the network being simulated has roughly NlogN transfers between the switch nodes on each step of the simulation.

The communication pattern between the switch nodes resembles the FFT butterfly pattern, so locality is minimized and the decoupling of the processors performing the simulation is very slow (logarithmic) as the problem size N is increased.

It is expected that this sort of communication behavior is the worst case for real applications, that is applications which are not contrived benchmarks designed specifically to stress the memory subsystem. As long as N is not much larger than the processor count of the machine being used to perform the simulation, the entire data set of the application will fit in the individual processor caches and the cache-to-cache data traffic will be high.

We evaluated the performance of the Butterfly simulator using write-through cache mode and copyback cache mode. Two problem sizes were used, we will distinguish these by small (order 7 network) and large sizes (order 10 network) for our explanation. A thirty processor Symmetry system was used for monitoring the behavior of this application.

Speedup

In write-through mode, the speedup achieved as processors were added reached about 7.5x with 14 processors, then goes down with addition of more processors (Figure 2).

In copyback mode, the speedup of this program is dependent on the problem size. The speedup for problem size 1 is over 14 with 30 processors. The speedup for problem size 2 is around 20 with 30 processors (Figure 3).

The single processor Model B performance is around 22% better than single Model B processor. This shows that the overhead of parallelization is high. This overhead has to be overcome by the parallelism in the application.

The degradation in performance of this application in Model B is due to the application behavior and not due to operating system behavior. The user time is a major contributor to the loss in performance for the application both in write through and copyback system. However the user time rises much more in the write through system than in the copyback system (400% as opposed to 40%). This indicates that there is significant overhead in the write-through system. This degradation in performance of this application on Model A is due to the synchronization mechanism as mentioned earlier.

An experiment was conducted in copyback mode to see if resident set size and operating system paging mechanisms played any role in limiting the performance of this code. The results indicated that these factors had no significant impact on the performance of this program.

Bus Utilization

In write-through mode, the bus utilization (Figure 4) goes up rapidly to 8 processors. At 8 processors the bus is about 75% utilized. The bus utilization increases to 80% for 16 processors and then goes down to 63% with 28 processors. This fall of bus utilization is related directly to the synchronization mechanism on the write-through system. The synchronization mechanism on the write-though system inhibits bus utilization as number of processors participating for this application increases. Unfortunately the number of cycles lost due to synchronization on the write-through system cannot be measured directly. The roll-off starts to happen around 10 processors.

The write invalidates dominate the bus utilization (Figure 5) in the write-through system. The roll-off results because synchronization activity inhibits greater bus utilization. Read cycles continue to increase at a slow rate and are caused by normal cache miss and synchronization activity. The bus holds are asserted as processor writes swamp the bus write pipes.

The bus utilization (Figure 4) in copyback mode with 28 processor is 40% less than the peak bus utilization in write-through mode. The write-through system's peak traffic goes over 80% with 14 processors. For 8 processor system, copyback system bus traffic is less than half of the write-through system.

In copyback mode, the bus traffic is dominated by non-exclusive read cycles (Figure 6). These read cycles increase with the number of processors. The read cycles increase for three reasons. First, there are cache misses due to the cold start by each processor, and these contribute to the read cycles on the bus. Second, the read invalidate cycles cause invalidation in other caches and these processor's later request for same word will be a cache miss. These misses also contribute additional read cycles. Third, the read misses caused by the size of the cache. As the cache size increases these read misses will decrease.

The cache miss-rate decreases per cache in copyback mode as more processors are added, because of the increase in total cache space. This is indicated by the decrease in write (copyback) cycles beyond 18 processors for large problem size. The miss-rate is measured per second instead of per reference. This reason for this is that only sampling of performance counters for a given period is possible with the present instrumentation. In anycase the miss-rate per second and per reference are similar for the parallel application since the miss-rate has been observed to vary by little over the execution of the application.

The IA cycles on the bus in copyback mode are less than 1% of the traffic with a 28-processor system. This indicates that there is little write sharing activity. This confirms what we have seen on the Balance [THAK87] and what other researchers have reported since then [EGGERS89], [WEBGUP89].

There are hold cycles (Figure 7) on the bus caused by the synchronization or by other cache-to-cache traffic. The cause of the hold cycles is likely to synchronization with cache based locks. This degradation in bus performance will contribute to the loss in speedup for this application. The hold cycles rise exponentially which fits the roll-off seen in the speedup.

Cache Miss-rate

In write-through mode for small problem size, the cache miss-rate (Figure 8) is around 13% (these numbers include all the processor writes) with a single processor. The miss-rate falls to under half that with 28 processors. The read miss-rate is low, as the number of read cycles on the bus show small increases with addition of more processors.

In copyback mode the cache miss-rate is about 1.9% with a single processor and falls to around 1.3% with 14 processors. The miss-rate stays around 1.3% beyond 14 processors.

The copyback miss-rate for large problem size (Figure 9), as expected, is much higher than for small problem size. The miss-rate for large problem size falls lower when a larger cache is used as in Model B' (Figure 9). This corresponds to the reduction in the bus utilization between the two systems (Figure 10)

Coherence Protocol Traffic

The Symmetry cache coherence protocol behavior indicates the amount of read sharing, owned and memory traffic. Figures 11 and 12 show that the percentage of owned traffic doubles when the number of processors are increased from 10 to 24. The amount of read sharing shows 3% increase when number of processors are increased from 10 to 24. The memory to cache response ratio is around 7:3 for 24 processor system. Increasing the cache size has similar results as increasing the number of processors, that is, the owned traffic doubles.

Summary

The write pipe in the write-through system is a limiting factor for most applications that use more than 8-10 processors. This application suffers from the system degradation caused by the write-pipe filling up. The application also suffers from degradation caused by the global interlock bus synchronization scheme when number of processors participating increases beyond 10 processors.

In copyback mode there seem to be several slopes in the speedup curves. These slopes indicate roll-off in the speed-up. Some of the roll-off can be attributed to the increase in cycles lost through ownership-based locks. However a another component in the roll-off is the problem size, really the grain size of computation.

**5.2 Parallel LINPACK**

LINPACK is library package that is used for comparing the performance of different computer systems solving dense systems of linear equations [DONG88]. LINPACK is floating point intensive benchmark. It measures the performance of two subroutines SGEFA and SGESL. SGEFA factors a matrix by gaussian elimination. SGESL solves the real system

$$Ax = b$$

using the factors computed by SGEFA. Both subroutines call a third subroutine, SAXPY, which computes a constant times a vector plus a vector.

There are two versions of LINPACK, a single and a double precision floating point version. The double precision version of the above subroutines are called DGEFA, DGESL and DAXPY.

This study used a C-version of the parallel LINPACK program written by Jack Dongarra. The program uses static allocation of work using the Sequent microtasking library. The purpose in this study was to understand the behavior of the architecture rather than get the best performance for LINPACK. The study also used a dynamic allocating version of parallel LINPACK. However, very little difference was observed in the behavior of the architecture.

Speedup

Figure 13 shows the speedup of parallel LINPACK on write-through and copyback systems. The speedup is just under 5 for both systems. The reason for this small speedup is that the problem size is too small. The overheads of parallelization overwhelm the parallelization. However, the speedup for the write-through systems rolls-off more than speedup on copyback system. This can be attributed to the writes generated in the write-through system as described below.

Figure 14 shows that speedup improves considerably in the copyback system as the problem size is increased. The roll-off in this version is attributed to large cache miss-rate since the problem no longer fits in the cache. The routines can be restructured in LINPACK so that better miss-rate can results. This has been done at Sequent and other places. However, the objective here was not to pursue tuning effort.

Bus Utilization

The bus utilization for small problem size on the write-through system is 4 times that of copyback system (Figure 15). The write-through system bus utilization is dominated by write invalidates (Figure 16). The copyback system bus utilization is dominated entirely by read cycles. Interesting to note is that the read cycles for both system are the similar (Figure 17).

Figure 18 shows how the bus utilization increases as the problem size is increased. This increase is caused by increase in the cache miss-rate (Figure 22) as the problem cannot be contained in the cache. The bus utilization comprises of non-exclusive read and write (copyback) cycles (Figure 19). Both types of cycles increase as the problem size is increased. Like the previous application, there are very little Invalidate Address cycles. This indicates very little write sharing.

There is degradation in performance due to synchronization mechanism. The hold cycles rise as more processors are added. They consume less than 18% of the bus bandwidth for large problem size with 29 processors (Figure 20). These cycles can be eliminated by using queue-based locks which the new version Sequent Parallel Library supports.

Miss-Rate

The write-through system for small problem size has significantly large cache miss-rate since it also includes all the writes (Figure 21). Symmetry uses non-allocating policy on write misses in write-through system. The miss-rate for the write-through system drops significantly as numbers of processors participating is increased. The cache miss-rate also drops in the copyback cache system. The bus utilization for copyback system is small since the cache miss-rate is small. This miss-rate is essentially due to cold start since the data for the small problem fits in the cache.

The cache miss-rate (Figure 22) rises as the problem size is increased. It increases by 6 times for 10 fold increase in the problem size.

Cache Coherence Traffic

Figure 23 shows that 99% of responses for read request comes from memory in a 24 processor copyback system. There is little read sharing (10%). Only 1% of responses come from the caches.

Summary

The speedup for parallel Linpack in both the write-through and copyback system is small for the small problem size. This is entirely due to the high overhead of parallelization. As the problem size is increased the speedup gets better till the traffic cause by high miss-rate and hold cycles caused by synchronization mechanism saturates the bus. The miss-rate can be reduced by restructuring the computation. The hold cycles due to the synchronization mechanisms can be eliminated by using the queue-based locks.

**5.3 Multi-user Application**

Sequent's CRG2 computer system (Symmetry Model B with 20 processors) supports over 100 software engineers working on the development of operating systems and software tools. This experiment monitored the bus and cache performance of CRG2 during normal working hours. In addition to normal load, a source level UNIX build was started using the parallel make facility.

Every effort was made to keep the load average stable during the monitoring process by taking processors on- and off-line during the monitoring process. The minimum number of processors online during this experiment was 4. Performance numbers for fewer than four processors are extrapolated.

Bus Utilization

The bus utilization (Figure 24) reached a peak of 50% utilization with 16 processors. The UNIX load average statistic (Figure 25) goes lower as more processors are added because more computing resource is available. System throughput increases because there are less context switches per processor. Less context switching means less cache misses which translates into fewer bus cycles. Also, the addition of more caches causes fewer cache misses in the system.

Bus utilization is dominated by non-exclusive read cycles (Figure 26). The read cycles at peak comprise 35% of the total cycles. The remaining bus cycles (Figure 26) are divided between exclusive read cycles and write cycles (copybacks). The read cycles are caused by cold starts, the size of the cache and process migration. These read cycles increase as more processors are added. The number of exclusive read operations also increases as more processors are added because of process migration. The number of write cycles increases because of the cumulative rise in cache replacements.

Figure 27 shows that hold cycles rise exponentially as number of processors are increased. These cycles arise from increase in cache-to-cache traffic. This traffic arises as a result of two different activities. First, as the load on the system increase there are more context switches happening in the system. Since little account is taken of scheduling the context switched process back on to the same processor, process migration occurs. As context switches happen more frequently in a loaded system, there is likelihood of process contexts migrating from the previous cache to the current cache. This traffic as described earlier produces hold cycles on the bus. Second, a hot-lock in the operating system can also produces cache-to-cache traffic which causes Hold cycles on the bus [LOVTHA88]. However, the first cause here is suspected to cause majority of the Hold cycles on the bus since the synchronization activity here is light when compared to the one in homogeneous parallel application such as Butterfly.

Cache Miss-rate

Cache miss-rate (Figure 28) varies from about 4.5% with 1 processor (extrapolated) to 1.6% for 20 processors. The miss-rate falls essentially because there are fewer context switches per processor, due to the larger processing resource and total cache space.

Cache Coherence Traffic

Figure 29 shows that 9% of the total read responses come from other caches (owned responses) and 91% come from main memory in a 10 processor system. The figure also indicates that there is high read sharing in the system (40%). The owned response rate doubles as the cache size is doubled or as number of processors are increased.

Summary

The Symmetry copyback system performance in terms of throughput in a multi-user environment increases as more processors are added. The environment is different to the two previous application environment in that total system time is more than half of total real time. This environment represents a heterogeneous parallel processing system where the grain of parallelism is large user and system UNIX processes.

The striking observation here is the effect of process migration. Even with relatively small caches (64 Kbytes), some process migration was observed. A favored-processor scheduling algorithm would reduce bus utilization for this kind of multi-user environment.

Contention for operating system resources can be reduced by distributing resources, thus semaphore-locking the resources. Enhanced software synchronization mechanisms can also reduce bus traffic due to synchronization.

## 6. CONCLUSIONS

The performance of Symmetry Multiprocessor System has been presented for parallel and multi-user environments. The Symmetry copyback cache coherence and bus protocol have shown to perform well for both parallel and multi-user applications.

The copyback systems have significantly superior performance over the write through systems. The copyback policy allows the scaling of system which would have otherwise been impossible. This scaling is primarily achieved through the reduction in bus writes generated by each processor. Further reduction in the bus traffic is also achieved through reduction in miss-rate by the adoption of the copyback policy.

All the application environments show that they would benefit if the cache size were increased. However, a balance has to be reached here. The size of caches should not be increased so as to make them the primary responders. This can have detrimental affect on the performance as the observations indicate.

The traffic due to write sharing is almost non-existent on the system. This is because the parallel applications on this type of system uses a medium or large grain parallelism process model. The real hot-spot in this type of environment is the synchronization mechanism and not the shared data structures.

*References*

[LOVTHAK88 ]          Lovett, T., and Thakkar, S. S., "The Symmetry Multiprocessor System", Proceeding of ICPP, 1988.

[ANDERSON89]       Anderson, T., "The Performance Implications of Spin-Waiting Alternatives for Shared-Memory Multiprocessors", Technical Report, Department of Computer Science, University of Washington, 1989

[GRATHA89]         Graunke, G., and Thakkar, S. S., "An Analysis of Synchronization Algorithms for Shared-Memory Multiprocessors", Sequent Computer Systems, Submitted For Publications.

[THAK87]        Thakkar, S. S., "Performance of Shared Memory Multiprocessor System", Proceedings of ICCD, 1987.

[EGGERS89]      Eggers, S., and Katz, R., "The Effect of Sharing on the Cache and Bus Performance of Parallel Programs", Proceedings of ASPLOS II, 1989.

[WEBGUP89]      Weber, W., and Gupta, A., "The Effects of Sharing on the Cache and Bus Performance of Parallel Programs", Proceedings of ASPLOS II, 1989.

[BROOKS89]      Brooks III, E. D., Axelrod, T. S. and Darmohray, G. A, "The Cerabus Multiprocessor Simulator", G. Rodrigue, editor, Parallel Processing for Scientific Computing, pp384-390, SIAM, 1989.

[DONG88]        Dongara, J. J., "Performance of Various Computers Using Standard Linear Equations Software in a Fortran Environment. Technical Report, Argonne National Laboratory, September 1988.

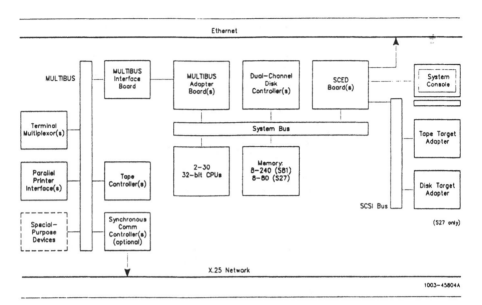

**Figure 1**

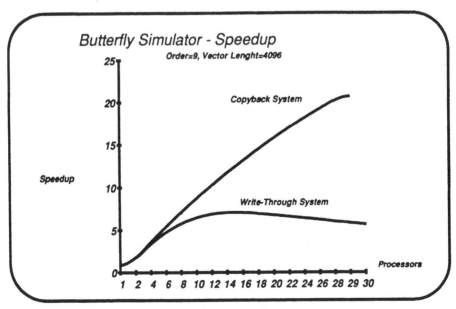

**Figure 2**

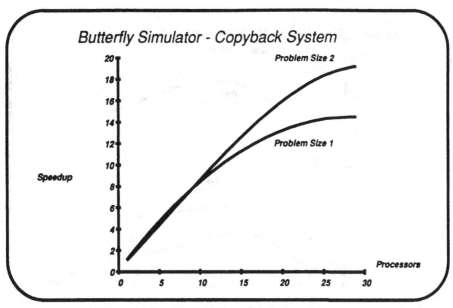

**Figure 3**

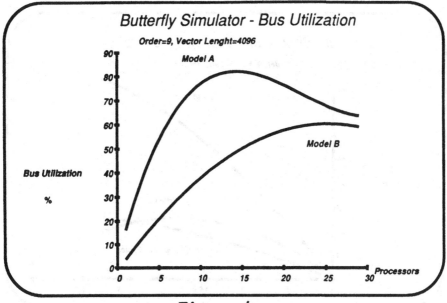

**Figure 4**

70

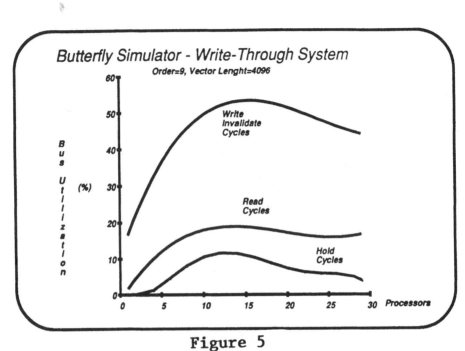

**Figure 5**

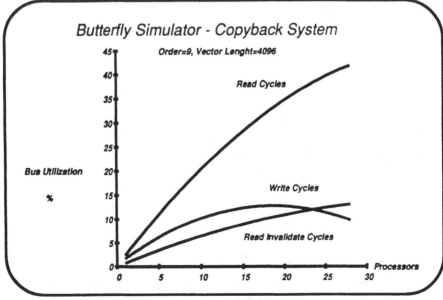

**Figure 6**

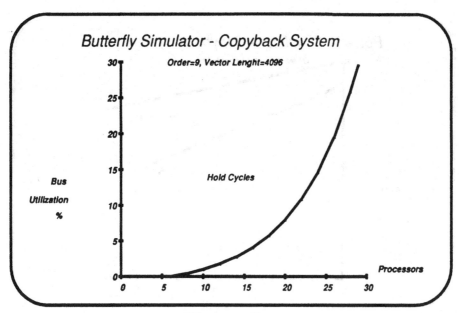

Figure 7

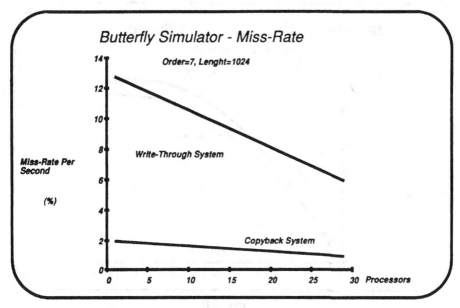

Figure 8

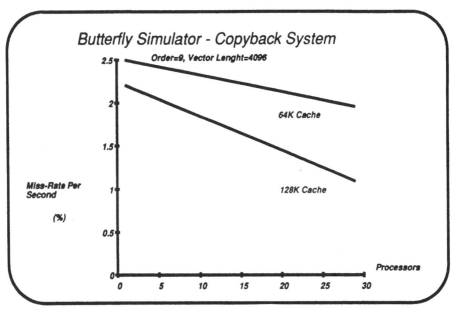

Figure 9

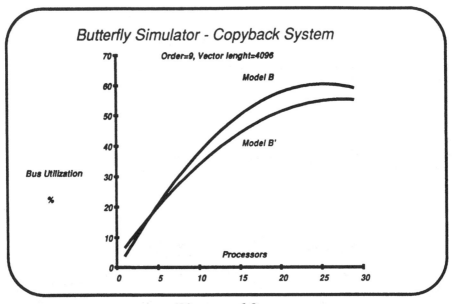

Figure 10

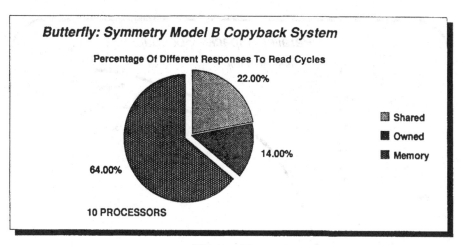

Figure 11

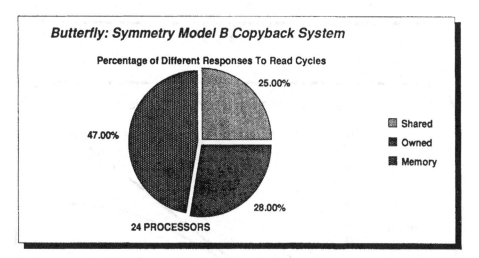

Figure 12

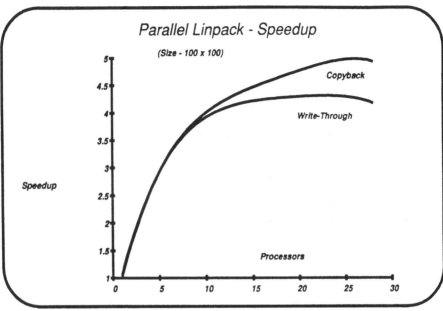

**Figure 13**

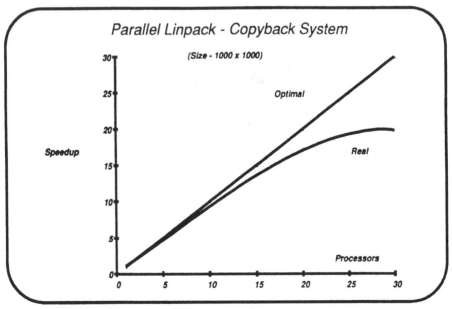

**Figure 14**

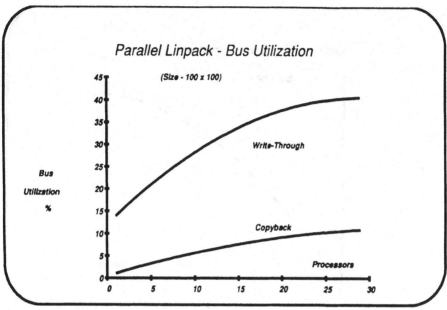

**Figure 15**

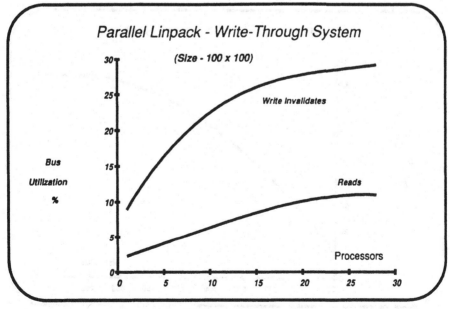

**Figure 16**

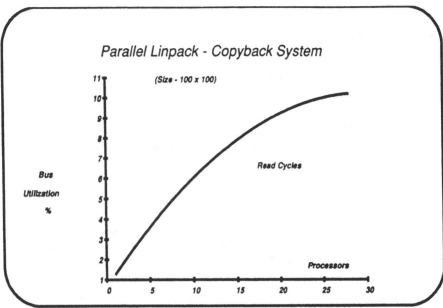

Figure 17

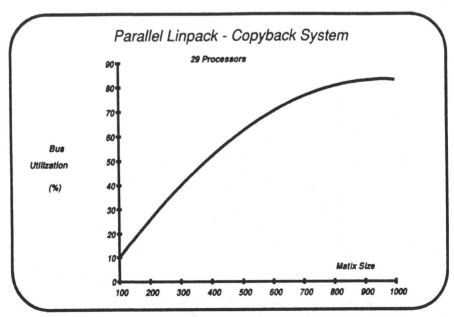

Figure 18

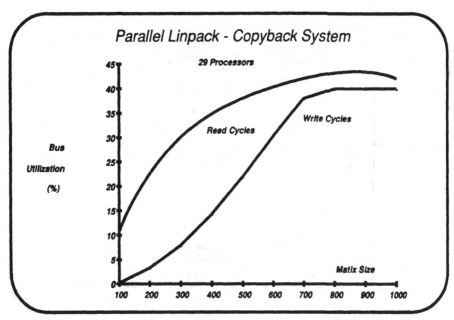

Figure 19

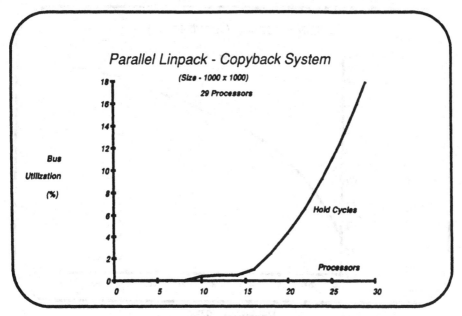

Figure 20

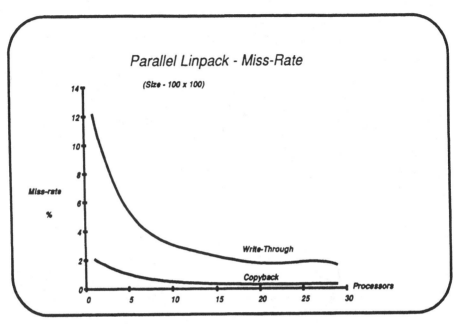

Figure 21

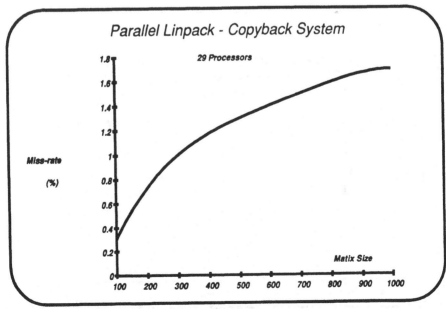

Figure 22

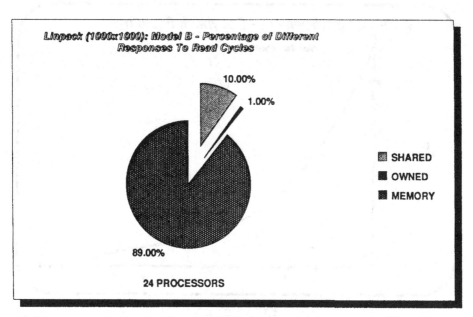

Figure 23

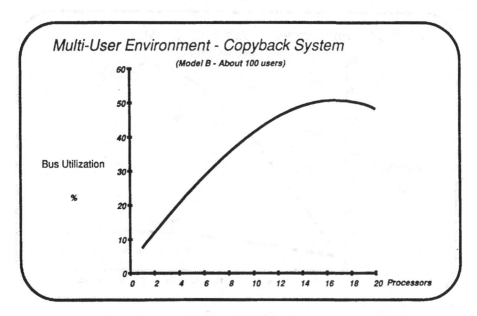

Figure 24

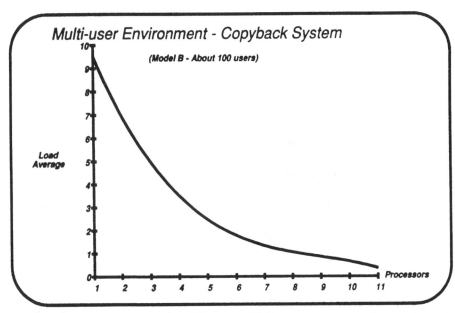

Figure 25

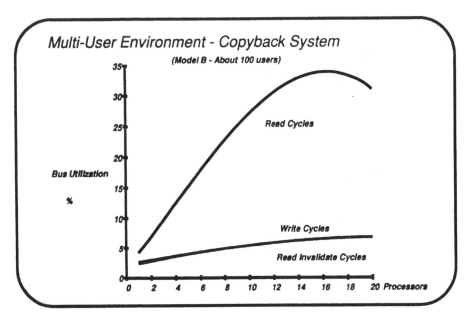

Figure 26

81

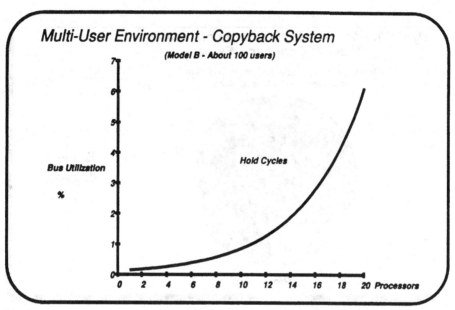

Figure 27

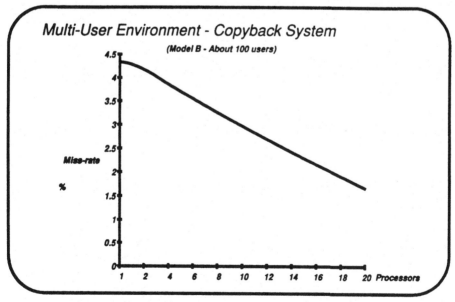

Figure 28

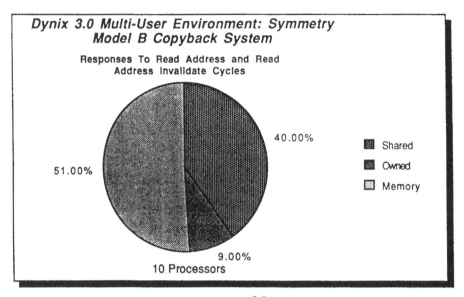

**Figure 29**

# Analysis of Cache Invalidation Patterns in Shared-Memory Multiprocessors

**Anoop Gupta and Wolf-Dietrich Weber**
Computer Systems Laboratory
Stanford University, CA 94305

### Abstract

To make shared-memory multiprocessors scalable, researchers are now exploring cache coherence protocols that do not rely on broadcast, but instead send invalidation messages to individual caches that contain stale data. The feasibility of such directory-based protocols is highly sensitive to the cache invalidation patterns that parallel programs exhibit. In this paper, we analyze the cache invalidation patterns caused by several parallel applications and investigate the effect of these patterns on a directory-based protocol. Our results are based on multiprocessor traces with 4, 8 and 16 processors. To gain insight into what the invalidation patterns would look like beyond 16 processors, we propose a classification scheme for data objects found in parallel applications and link the invalidation traffic patterns observed in the traces back to these high-level objects. Our results show that synchronization objects have very different invalidation patterns from those of other data objects. We point out situations where restructuring the application seems appropriate to reduce the invalidation traffic, and others where hardware support is more appropriate. Our results also show that it should be possible to scale "well-written" parallel programs to a large number of processors without an explosion in invalidation traffic.

## 1   Introduction

One of the most critical issues in the design of shared-memory multiprocessors is the cache coherence strategy. Most multiprocessors [7, 12, 18, 25] rely on a shared bus and use a broadcast-based protocol to keep the caches coherent [9, 19, 21]. However, such multiprocessors are not very scalable, as the shared bus soon becomes a bottleneck. As an alternative, researchers have started exploring cache coherence protocols that do not rely on broadcast, a common example being directory-based protocols [2, 4]. In directory-based protocols the system maintains state about which caches contain a particular piece of data. On a write, invalidation messages are sent only to these specific caches. The number of pointers in each directory entry determines how many other caches can be kept track of. In order to determine the performance of directory-based protocols we need to answer several questions. We would like to know the distribution of the number of remote caches that need to be invalidated on shared writes. We would like to know how these distributions scale as the number of processors is increased. We are interested in knowing what types of data objects in the applications result in what kind of invalidation patterns. This paper attempts to answer some of these questions for directory-based protocols.[1]

We analyze the patterns of invalidation traffic produced by a set of five application programs. Three of the five applications selected are "real" parallel programs, in the sense that they solve real-world problems and that a lot of effort has gone into obtaining good processor efficiency with them. The remaining two applications are smaller, but they are still interesting in that they could form the kernels of larger applications. Our study is based on memory reference traces obtained for the applications when simulating 4, 8, and 16 processors.[2] The traces were generated using software-traps on a $\mu$VAX-II running MACH. In addition to presenting the invalidation patterns as observed directly from the traces, the paper links the invalidation patterns to the high-level program data structures (objects) that cause them. A classification of such shared objects on the basis of their expected invalidation behavior is given. Linking the invalidation patterns to the high-level objects helps us predict how the invalidation traffic would change as the number of processors is increased. It is far more accurate to extrapolate the behavior of each class of data object than to simply extrapolate the composite behavior. For the application types we have considered, our results indicate that it is quite possible to write parallel programs that do not create an enormous amount of invalidation traffic. Thus directory-based schemes with just a few pointers per entry could efficiently execute well-designed parallel programs.

The next section explains the methodology used in generating the traces and explains how the traces were analyzed. Section 3 introduces the five applications used in this study and gives a brief overview of their computational behavior. In Section 4 we present some basic trace characteristics. Section 5 presents the proposed classification of shared data objects in parallel programs. In section 6 we give a detailed analysis of the invalidation behavior of each application and relate these patterns to specific data objects in the applications. Section 7 presents results obtained from experimenting with different cache line sizes. Finally, Section 8 assembles the results from the various applications and presents conclusions.

# 2   Methodology & Assumptions

## 2.1   Traces

The traces were collected using a combined hardware/software method [8]. The process creation is modified to have one master process, which controls the actual tracing, and a number of slave processes, one for each "virtual processor". Once the desired start position for tracing is reached, each of the slaves stops itself and is then single-stepped by the master. The stepping takes place in a round-robin fashion. The stepping employs the UNIX *ptrace* system call which uses the T-bit on the VAX. While stepping, the master process records data in the trace file. For each reference, the type (ifetch, read, or write), the address, and the CPU number are recorded. Trace lengths used were 20Mbytes for 4-processor traces, 30Mbytes for 8-processor traces, and 50Mbytes for 16-processor traces. This corresponds to about 2.5, 4 and 7

---

[1]This paper is an updated version of our ASPLOS-III paper [26]. It contains results obtained with pre-loaded caches and investigates the effect of varying the cache line size.

[2]Previous studies [1, 2] presented results using traces with only 4 processors. This study uses a more extensive set of applications, a larger number of processors, and goes more deeply into the causes of invalidation patterns.

million references respectively, or around 0.5 million references per processor. The traces were gathered on a $\mu$VAX-II running the MACH operating system. It took about 24 hours to obtain 20Mbytes of trace.

The main advantage of the software scheme of gathering traces is that we can get traces for an arbitrary number of processors, which is not possible with hardware schemes like ATUM [22]. However, there are some disadvantages too. For example, the *ptrace* call does not trace operating system calls, but rather treats them as a single reference. This is not a major problem in this study, since there are not many operating system calls in the sections traced. Also, each instruction takes one time unit to complete, regardless of the complexity of the instruction. This is clearly an oversimplification, but we have no reason to believe that it significantly distorts our results.

## 2.2   Cache Simulator

Once the traces were gathered, they were used as input to a program that simulates multiprocessor cache behavior and gathers statistics. Infinite caches were used for simplicity of the cache simulator. The cache coherence protocol used was an invalidation scheme similar to the Berkeley Ownership scheme [19].

For each shared write, the cache simulator writes a record containing the CPU number, the data address, the most recent instruction address and the number of other caches actually invalidated. The data and instruction addresses are later used to associate the invalidation with the high-level program object that caused it. Several post-processing programs are used to gather statistics from the invalidation traces.

One of the problems of using address reference traces of finite length to obtain cache invalidation patterns is that during a large part of the simulation run the caches are in a transient state, and their contents have not stabilized. For example write references in the beginning of the trace will hardly ever cause invalidations as the rest of the caches are almost empty. To simulate a warm-start of the caches, we run the traces through the simulator twice. After the first run, the cache state is saved and then used as the initial cache state for the second run. We realize that this pre-loading of caches with the same short trace is not as accurate as using a very long trace, but it nonetheless captures and eliminates many of the start-up effects. The applications commonly access their shared data in cyclic patterns. Some outer loop will cause the program to pass over the data several times during the course of a run. Pre-loading of caches is a particularly effective method of simulating larger traces for this type of application.

Pre-loading has no significant effect for Maxflow and SA-TSP. MP3D, P-Thor and LocusRoute, on the other hand, exhibit different behavior when the caches are pre-loaded. There are more invalidations and larger invalidations.[3] We note that in general, the discrepancy between cold-start and warm-start results will be largest in programs with a large amount of shared data, where each data object is accessed relatively infrequently. Pre-loading the caches assures that each data object is present in at least one cache, and may thus result in invalidations on the very first write to that data object.

---

[3] Throughout the paper *large invalidations* refers to shared writes causing invalidations in many caches.

## 2.3 Directory-based Schemes

In this paper we study invalidation patterns in the context of a directory-based cache coherence scheme. This sort of scheme employs a directory consisting of several pointers for each memory line [2]. The pointers are used to keep track of which caches have a copy of a given line, thus allowing point-to-point messages for consistency traffic instead of requiring broadcast. A $Dir_iB$ scheme has $i$ pointers per memory line and employs broadcast when it runs out of pointers. In a $Dir_iNB$ scheme, on the other hand, no broadcast is allowed, and there can only be $i$ copies of a given memory line in various caches.

# 3  Application Programs

In this section we describe the data structures and computational behavior of the applications. This is important background for Section 6, where we relate invalidation traffic to high-level objects. The applications used for tracing were selected to represent a variety of algorithms used in an engineering computing environment. All of the applications were written in C. The Argonne National Laboratory macro package [13, 14] was used to provide synchronization and sharing primitives. The synchronization primitives used include spin locks, barriers and distributed loops.

## 3.1  Maxflow

Maxflow [3] finds the maximum flow in a directed graph. This is a common problem in operations research and many other fields. The program is a parallel implementation of an algorithm proposed by Goldberg and Tarjan. The bulk of execution time is spent picking off nodes from a task queue, adjusting the flow along each node's incoming and outgoing edges, and then placing its successor nodes on to a task queue. Maxflow exploits parallelism at a fine grain.

Maxflow does not assign the nodes of the graph to processors statically. Instead, task queues are used to distribute the load. Each processor has its own local task queue and need only go to the single global task queue when its local queue is empty. Tasks are put on to the global queue only when processes are waiting there, and on to the local queue otherwise. Note that the task queues are made up of the nodes themselves, linked together with appropriate pointers. Locks are used to serialize access to each node element, but contention for these is fairly low as there are many more nodes than processors. In Section 6 we will see that most cache invalidations are related to the global task queue and the migration of node data from one processor to another.

The traces were collected while solving Maxflow for a set of nodes arranged as a 10-ary 2-cube. Tracing was started as the program entered the main loop after completing the initial distance labeling. The implementation provides speedups of about 8 with 12 processors.

## 3.2  SA-TSP

SA-TSP [23] solves the traveling salesperson problem using simulated annealing
[11]. A linear array contains the cities in tour order. At each step, a processor
selects a pair of cities to swap. The swap is performed if it results in a shorter tour
or if the increase in tour distance is within the margin prescribed by the cooling
function. The tour is locked *only* during the actual swap, which means that the
cities swapped may not be the ones originally selected for swapping. This trades
off quality of solution for greater speedup. Note that there is only one global lock
for all the tour data which becomes a major bottleneck as the number of processors
increases. This is particularly true during the initial annealing phase – which is the
section we traced – where most moves are accepted and contention for the lock is
very large. While the program achieves an overall speedup of 7 with 8 processors,
no more than 4 processors can be kept busy during this initial portion.

## 3.3  MP3D

MP3D [16, 17] is a 3-dimensional particle simulator for rarified flow. It is used to
study the shock waves created as an object flies at high speed through the upper
atmosphere. MP3D is a good example of scientific code that is vectorizable and can
be parallelized using distributed loops. A version of MP3D that runs on the Cray-2
is being used extensively at NASA for research.

The overall computation of MP3D consists of evaluating the positions and veloci-
ties of molecules over a sequence of time steps. During each time step, the molecules
are picked up one at a time and moved as governed by their velocity vectors. Collisions with the boundaries and with each other are resolved. The simulator is well
suited to parallelization because each molecule can be treated independently at each
time step. The work is spread over the processors with the help of a distributed loop,
consisting of a lock and a global index variable. Each processor obtains the lock,
reads the index, increments it, and releases the lock. In this manner the processes
pick up the index of the next particle to be moved. The traces cover several time
steps, i.e. each particle is moved several times. No locking is employed in the
various arrays that keep track of the particles and the physical space in which they
are located, because collisions are impossible in the particle arrays and very rare in
the space arrays. Thus, the distributed loop is the only synchronization seen in this
trace.

## 3.4  P-Thor

P-Thor [24] is a parallel logic simulator developed at Stanford University. It is based
on the Chandy-Misra simulation algorithm [5], which is specially designed for highly
parallel machines — unlike event-based algorithms, this algorithm does not rely on
a single global time during simulation.

The primary data structures associated with the simulator are the logic elements
(e.g., AND-gates, flip-flops), the nets (the wires linking the elements) and the task
queues which contain activated elements. Each processor has as many task queues
as there are other processors. This ensures that there is no contention when adding
elements to some other processor's queue. Each processor executes the following

loop. It removes an activated element from one of its task queues and determines the changes on the element's outputs. It then looks up the net data structure to determine which elements are affected by the output change and potentially schedules those activated elements on to other processors' task queues. Newly activated elements are assigned to other processors in a round-robin fashion.

## 3.5 LocusRoute

LocusRoute [20] is a global router for VLSI standard cells. It has been used to design real integrated circuits, and it is also highly tuned to run well on a shared-memory multiprocessor. LocusRoute represents the class of parallel programs that apply combinatorial optimization and can tolerate some data inconsistency.

The LocusRoute program exploits parallelism by routing multiple wires in a circuit concurrently. Each processor executes the following loop: (i) remove a wire to route from the task queue; (ii) explore alternative routes; and (iii) pick the best route for the wire and place it there. The central data structure used in LocusRoute is a grid of cells called the *cost array*. Each row of the cost array corresponds to a routing channel for standard cells. LocusRoute uses the cost array to record the presence of a wire at each point, and the congestion of a route is used as a cost function for guiding the placement of new wires. No locking is needed in the cost array, which is accessed and updated simultaneously by several processors, because the effect of occasional collisions is tolerable. Each routing task is fairly large grain, which prevents the task queue from becoming a bottleneck.

## 4  Trace Characteristics

Table 1 gives an overview of the traces of the five applications. For each application, we give the trace length in number of references and the breakdown in terms of ifetches, reads and writes. We also show the proportion of shared reads, shared writes, and the average number of invalidations caused by each shared write. In addition to absolute numbers, the columns also list the number of references in each category as a fraction of all references in the trace.

In all of the programs, with the exception of MP3D, about 45-50% of the references are ifetches. MP3D has a larger proportion of ifetches because there are a lot of array references which require several instructions to compute the effective address of the reference. A typical line of code from MP3D requires 15 ifetches, 5 reads and 1 write. These numbers correspond to 71% ifetches, 24% reads and 5% writes, which is close to the actual distribution found.

The proportion of read references varies from about 30% in MP3D to over 45% in SA-TSP. In SA-TSP there are a lot of simple integer reads when determining the effect of a swap on tour distance. There is also an increasingly large amount of spinning on the global tour lock. The read fraction is low in MP3D because of the larger proportion of ifetches.

Writes hover around 10-15% of all references. MP3D again stands out with a very low write fraction (about 6%), again due to frequent array references. The number of writes in SA-TSP stays virtually constant (at about 0.43 million) even though the number of references increases greatly as we move from 4 to 16 processors. This is

Table 1: General Trace Characteristics.

| Application | num of CPUs | refs mill | ifetch % | read % | write % | sh-read % | sh-write % | avg invals per sh-wrt |
|---|---|---|---|---|---|---|---|---|
| Maxflow | 4 | 2.62 | 46 | 40 | 13 | 14.2 | 2.81 | 0.32 |
| | 8 | 4.15 | 46 | 41 | 13 | 14.5 | 2.93 | 0.51 |
| | 16 | 8.36 | 46 | 41 | 12 | 15.7 | 3.29 | 1.09 |
| SA-TSP | 4 | 2.65 | 42 | 42 | 16 | 4.5 | 0.74 | 1.27 |
| | 8 | 4.16 | 44 | 45 | 11 | 12.1 | 0.90 | 2.29 |
| | 16 | 7.11 | 46 | 47 | 6 | 18.3 | 1.08 | 2.93 |
| MP3D | 4 | 2.60 | 64 | 30 | 6 | 10.5 | 3.97 | 0.77 |
| | 8 | 4.51 | 63 | 31 | 6 | 11.2 | 3.90 | 0.96 |
| | 16 | 7.38 | 60 | 34 | 5 | 13.8 | 3.27 | 1.27 |
| P-Thor | 4 | 2.61 | 49 | 39 | 12 | 4.3 | 0.33 | 0.60 |
| | 8 | 4.13 | 49 | 39 | 12 | 5.9 | 0.48 | 0.77 |
| | 16 | 7.09 | 50 | 39 | 11 | 8.1 | 0.60 | 0.92 |
| LocusRoute | 4 | 2.68 | 52 | 37 | 12 | 1.2 | 0.16 | 0.65 |
| | 8 | 4.12 | 52 | 37 | 12 | 3.2 | 0.15 | 1.36 |
| | 16 | 7.05 | 51 | 37 | 12 | 3.2 | 0.17 | 1.77 |

explained by the fact that writes are only used when a swap is accepted. Contention for the lock in the portion of SA-TSP traced is so large that no more swaps are accepted in the 16-processor trace than in the 4-processor trace. This portion of SA-TSP was chosen to demonstrate the effects that a poorly written program segment may have on directory-based coherence schemes. Details are presented in Section 6.2.

In our study, we define *shared blocks* to be those that are referenced by more than one process in the trace. Thus *shared reads* are read references to shared blocks and *shared writes* are write references to shared blocks. Note that some locations that really are shared in the application are considered non-shared in our study, because within the limited length of the trace multiple processes do not reference those locations.

The proportion of shared reads varies widely from application to application. As we go from 4 to 16 processors, the proportion of shared reads generally increases. There are two reasons for this. In SA-TSP there is more spinning on locks which sharply increases the number of shared reads. Also, as more processors are added, the chances of a data item being accessed by more than one processor increases,[4] resulting in a larger fraction of shared reads.

The second to last column in Table 1 presents the proportion of shared writes in the applications. Note that it is important to study shared writes because in the absence of process migration, they are the only references that can cause remote invalidations. There is a general trend towards an increasing percentage of shared writes as the number of processors increases. Normally one would expect the fraction of shared writes to be constant, because the number of shared writes should be a

---

[4]This is partly because we get a longer trace for a run with more processors, and partly because with a larger number of processors, there is a higher probability that subtasks sharing data get scheduled on different processors rather than on the same processor.

function of the application code and not the number of processors used. The reasons for a larger proportion of shared writes are similar to those presented above for shared reads. Instead of more spinning on shared test-test&set locks, however, there are more writes when a lock is *freed*. All processors waiting on that lock fall through the test portion of the lock and issue the test&set, which is a shared write.

An important metric of invalidation traffic is the average number of invalidations per shared write. A high average value indicates that a large number of directory pointers is needed. The values are shown in the last column of Table 1. We see that the average goes up with increasing number of processors. One would like this increasing trend to be very slow if the machine is to be scalable. Average invalidations per shared write is largest for SA-TSP, mostly due to invalidation traffic caused by the single global spin-lock. In fact, the average number of invalidations increases steeply with more processors due to the increased contention for this global lock. The number of invalidations per shared write grows most slowly for P-Thor. This is mainly because there are no synchronization objects in the portion of P-Thor traced. Averages, however, do not carry all of the interesting information. Consequently, the detailed invalidation distributions and their analysis are presented in Section 6.

Note that a good indicator of the traffic due to invalidations is the product of percent-of-shared-writes and avg-invals-per-shared-write (the last two columns of Table 1). How directory-based architectures scale is to a large extend determined by how this product scales as the number of processors is increased.

# 5  Classification of Data Objects

When trying to extrapolate invalidation behavior to a larger number of processors, it is important to explain the invalidation patterns in terms of the underlying high-level structures which cause the invalidations. We distinguish several types of shared objects on the basis of their significance in parallel programs and their expected invalidation behavior:

1. Code and read-only data objects.

2. Migratory objects.

3. Synchronization objects.

    - low contention synchronization objects
    - high contention synchronization objects

4. Mostly-read objects.

5. Frequently read/written objects.

Code and read-only data objects do not pose a problem to the directory schemes that allow broadcast because they do not cause invalidations at all. Read-only data *can* cause invalidations in directory schemes without broadcast, if the number of processors sharing the data exceeds the number of pointers per entry. A fixed database such as the matrix that contains the distances between cities in SA-TSP is a good example of such read-only data.

Migratory data objects are those that are manipulated by only a single processor at a time. Shared objects protected by locks often exhibit this property. While such an object is being manipulated by one processor, the object's data resides in the associated cache. When the object is later manipulated by some other processor, the cache entry of the previous processor needs to be invalidated.[5] Migratory data usually causes a high proportion of *single* invalidations. The nodes in Maxflow are a good example of migratory data. Each node is looked at by several processors over the complete run, but there is only one processor manipulating each node at any one time.

Examples of synchronization objects are the locks and barriers used in parallel programs. When used improperly, they can cause a very large number of invalidations. For example, when locks are implemented as test-test&set and there are processors waiting on a lock, invalidations are caused each time the lock changes hands. As a lock is freed, all waiting processors fall through the test part of the test-test&set. They then attempt the test&set, but only one of them succeeds, causing invalidations in all other waiting processors' caches. We divide synchronization objects into two categories: low and high contention locks. Distributed locks that protect access to a collection of shared data objects are a good example of a low-contention locks. A task queue lock is an example of a high-contention lock. High-contention can further be classified by the number of processors waiting when an unlock occurs. For barriers, the number of processors waiting will be large and a very large invalidation will result. A task queue lock, on the other hand may only have a few processors waiting each time it is unlocked, thus causing relatively small invalidations. Depending on the number of pointers available in a directory based cache consistency scheme, frequent large invalidations can have a severe impact on machine performance. Special hardware will probably be required to support high-contention synchronization objects.

An example of mostly-read data is the cost-array of LocusRoute. Most of the time it is just read, but every now and then, when the best route for a wire is decided, the array is written. It is a candidate for large invalidations because many reads by different processors occur before each write. Thus the data is cached by many processors, and a write causes many invalidations. However, since only the writes cause invalidations and writes are infrequent, the overall number of invalidations will be quite small.

Finally, there is frequently read/written data.[6] An example is the variable that counts how many processors are waiting on the global task queue in Maxflow. Like synchronization objects, frequently read/written objects also have bad invalidation behavior. Unlike mostly-read objects, this data is written quite frequently. Although each write may only cause 3 or 4 invalidations, this may exceed the number of pointers per entry in a directory scheme, thus causing frequent broadcasts.

# 6    Application Case Studies

In this section we present the results of the detailed analysis of the invalidation traces produced when running the cache simulator over the multiprocessor traces. For each application, we show the overall invalidation patterns, the high-level objects causing

---

[5] Cheriton discusses a programming model based on such objects, called *"workforms"* in [6].

[6] Frequently read/written should be interpreted as both frequently read *and* frequently written.

the invalidations, the expected broadcast behavior of directory-based cache coherence schemes [4, 2], and the scalability of the application beyond 16 processors.

The overall invalidation behavior is presented in terms of an invalidation distribution graph as shown in Figure 1. The graph shows the fraction of shared writes that caused no invalidations, single invalidations and so on. Ideally these graphs will contain a large proportion of small invalidations, as these can be handled efficiently by directory-based cache schemes. By comparing the invalidation distributions for 4, 8 and 16 processor traces, we can begin to get a feeling for how the invalidations scale with a larger number of processors. Note that the x-axes for the 4, 8 and 16 processor graphs are identical. Naturally we do not expect larger than triple invalidations for 4-processor runs and no larger than 7 invalidations for 8-processor runs.

For each application, we also present another kind of graph that shows the fraction of broadcasts required as a function of the number of pointers per entry in the directory (see Figure 6). This graph is only given for the 16-processor trace. A directory-based scheme such as $Dir_i B$ [2] needs to use broadcast when a shared write is to a location that is contained in more caches than there are directory pointers for that entry. The data is plotted for directories with pointers varying from 1 to n, where n is the number of processors in the trace. We do not show directory schemes with 0 pointers as these require a broadcast for every shared write. Obviously, a directory with n pointers can keep track of all processors and broadcast is never required.

## 6.1   Maxflow

Figures 1, 2 and 3 show the invalidation distributions for Maxflow with 4, 8 and 16 processors respectively. Note that the distribution shifts to larger invalidations as the number of processors is increased. While at 4 processors only about 2% of shared writes cause more than one invalidation, this figure moves up to 18% with 16 processors. Analysis shows that the bulk of this increase is due to synchronization traffic involving the global task queue. Figures 4 and 5 show the invalidation distribution broken down by global queue traffic and all other invalidation traffic respectively. The global queue traffic includes all writes to the queue locks as well as the count of the number of processors blocked and the queue head pointer. It is clear that most of the spreading of the invalidation distribution is due to global-queue related traffic.

A large fraction of the invalidations in Figures 1, 2 and 3 are single invalidations. They are caused by the manipulation of nodes and edges, which are good examples of migratory data objects. One processor picks up an active node and pushes flow through it. Later, when the node is reactivated some other processor will pick it up and start processing it.

Some parameters of the nodes, such as its distance label, behave like mostly-read objects. Distance labels only get changed in the infrequent relabeling steps. Between relabeling, many processors may read a node's distance label causing relabeling to generate a large number of invalidations. In the 16-processor trace, an average of 4.6 invalidations occur for each relabeling write. Although 4.6 invalidations per shared write is large, the effect of these writes on the total number of invalidations is small since the writes are infrequent (only 1.7% of all shared writes).

The locks for the global task queue cause a large number of invalidations. Not only are they accessed and written frequently, but they also cause an average of

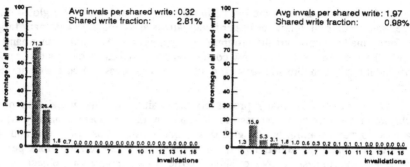

Figure 1: Maxflow 4

Figure 4: Maxflow 16 (Global Queue)

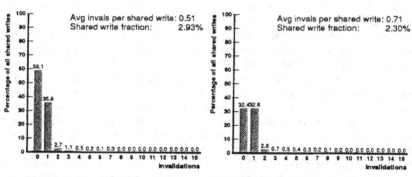

Figure 2: Maxflow 8

Figure 5: Maxflow 16 (Data)

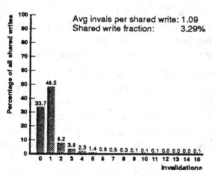

Figure 3: Maxflow 16

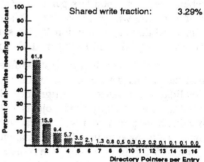

Figure 6: Maxflow 16 Directory Performance

about 2 invalidations per shared write in the 16-processor trace. The global queue is the major source of double or larger invalidations and should be a primary target for efforts aimed at improving the program. The per-node locks, on the other hand, work well. They are an example of low contention synchronization objects that cause few invalidations. There are so many more nodes than processors that contention is very limited.

The count of how many processors are waiting for the global task queue is checked frequently by all processors. It is also written frequently, namely whenever a process starts waiting on the global task queue. It is thus often read and written and causes many invalidations. It has an average of 2.8 invalidations per shared write and the highest number of shared writes to any single data object except for the global task queue locks (2.5% of all shared writes are to this single variable) .

We now discuss a pattern of double invalidations that frequently occurs when dealing with queues, as observed in Maxflow and several other applications. In Maxflow, one processor puts a node on to the global task queue, thus writing its link pointer. That processor's cache now has a dirty copy. A second processor may add another node, having to read the previous link pointer. Thus the object becomes read shared in two caches. Later the node may be placed on some other queue, and the link pointer is written again. This write causes a double invalidation. Many variations of this basic theme exist. Another example was found in POPS [10], a parallel rule-based expert system, where a single buffer is used for a task queue. An item is written into the buffer by one processor and read by another. Later, a third processor overwrites that item with some new data, thus invalidating the caches of both previous processors. The conclusion from this section is that one needs at least two pointers per line in the directory for this pattern, if an excessive number of broadcasts is to be avoided. The other choice is to allow a special flush operation, that removes the object from the cache of the first processor after placing it on the queue.

Figure 6 shows the proportion of shared writes that need to be broadcast for directory-based schemes with a varying number of pointers per entry. Although a scheme with two pointers per entry ($Dir_2B$ in [2]) only needs to broadcast 1.8% of shared writes with 4 processors, this figure jumps up to 15.9% for 16 processors. The invalidation distribution keeps spreading out as the number of processors is increased, mostly due to the invalidations associated with the global queue.

Let us now use the object classification to see how the invalidation distributions will change as the number of processors is scaled. We expect little change in the invalidations produced by migratory objects which will continue to produce single invalidations. Mostly-read objects will have a slightly higher average number of invalidations per shared write because more processors are likely to have cached the data. Note though that for this category the average number of invalidations per write (4.6 for 16 processors) may already be beyond the number of pointers stored in the directory, so no additional broadcasts will result. Synchronization objects and frequently read/written objects, on the other hand, are expected to have a higher average number of invalidations per shared write. In addition, we expect to see *more* shared writes due to synchronization. Since both synchronization objects with high contention and frequently read/written objects exist in Maxflow, we will see a continued spread of the invalidation distribution towards larger invalidations per shared write. If the program is to be scaled successfully, we will have to reduce synchronization contention and eliminate frequently read/written objects.

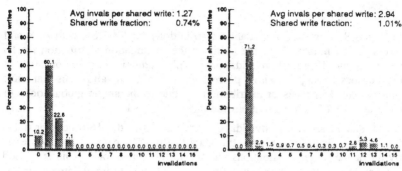

Figure 7: SA-TSP 4

Figure 10: SA-TSP 16 (Lock)

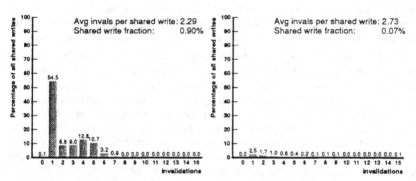

Figure 8: SA-TSP 8

Figure 11: SA-TSP 16 (Data)

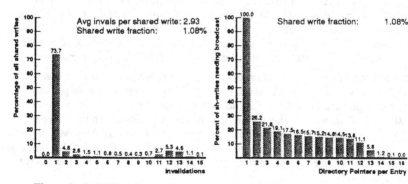

Figure 9: SA-TSP 16

Figure 12: SA-TSP 16 Directory Performance

## 6.2   SA-TSP

Figures 7, 8 and 9 show the invalidation distributions for SA-TSP with 4, 8 and 16 processors. Most noticeable is the hump in the invalidation distribution for 16 processors at around 12 to 13 invalidations. This hump is less obvious with 8 processors and does not appear with 4 processors. All of the invalidations that make up this hump in the 16-processor distribution are due to the single global lock. In fact as many as 94% of all invalidations are due to that lock.

Figures 10 and 11 show the invalidation distribution for the 16-processor trace, broken down into lock traffic and all other data traffic. These graphs show clearly that nearly all of the large invalidations are due to the single lock. This is a good example of how a poorly-used lock can flood a machine with invalidations. In the initial annealing phase (the portion that was traced), most moves get accepted. Thus all of the processors want to update the global tour, which requires the lock. This results in very high contention for the lock. We found that with 12 to 13 processors waiting for the lock to be released, this phase of the program could use no more than about 4 processors. As the cooling function progresses, fewer and fewer moves are accepted, contention for the lock subsides and the program achieves good speedup.

The invalidations due to the shared data range between 0 and 9. All of these are from the array that holds the order of the cities in the tour. The large average of shared-write invalidations is due to the mostly-read nature of this data. A processor needs to look at two cities and their four neighbors to determine whether a swap is to occur, and only if the swap meets certain annealing criteria does it actually take place. This means that for each proposed swap, at least four cities are only read, not written. Each successful swap thus invalidates a large number of caches. Another reason why the average shared write results in a large number of invalidations is that there are relatively few data objects (36 in this case, as the program was solving a tour with 36 cities), especially when compared to LocusRoute or MP3D, where there are thousands of objects. Hence the chances of several other processor caching an object before it is written are much larger.

Figure 12 shows that even directory schemes with large number of pointers per entry perform poorly in the face of SA-TSP's invalidation traffic. After an initial lowering in the number of broadcasts with increasing number of directory pointers, the graph basically flattens out until we reach the hump. In the 16-processor case, a 10-pointer scheme would perform essentially as poorly as a 5-pointer scheme.

Further scaling of the number of processors would result in even larger contention for the global lock. This would move the invalidation hump to a larger number of invalidations per shared write. Essentially no additional useful work would be accomplished. A distributed locking scheme could reduce contention for the elements of the global tour. Even if the synchronization traffic is eliminated, however, we will still have a fair amount of shared data invalidation traffic. This is due to the fact that there are only a small number of data objects that are continuously read and written by several processors.

## 6.3   MP3D

Figures 13, 14 and 15 show the invalidation distributions for MP3D with 4, 8 and 16 processors respectively. The distributions are dominated by zero and single invali-

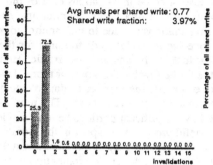

Figure 13: MP3D 4

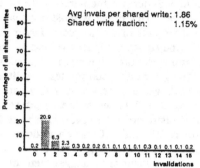

Figure 16: MP3D 16 (Synchronization)

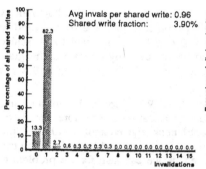

Figure 14: MP3D 8

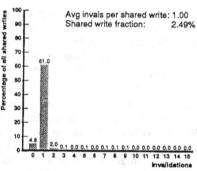

Figure 17: MP3D 16 (Data)

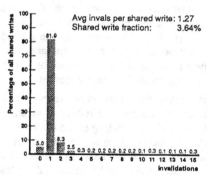

Figure 15: MP3D 16

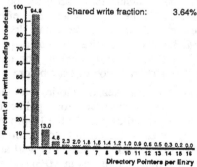

Figure 18: MP3D 16 Directory Performance

dations. As we increase the number of processors, some invalidations of 2 or more start to appear. This effect is most noticeable with 16 processors. Further analysis shows that the bulk of the double or larger invalidations are due to the monitor lock of the distributed loop. Figures 16 and 17 give the invalidation distribution for the 16-processor trace, broken down into monitor lock traffic and all other traffic. Here we note that shared data contributes very little to the invalidations of 2 or more. Unlike SA-TSP, where there are very few data elements, the number of data elements is very large in MP3D and so we do not see many large invalidations. The monitor lock traffic distribution, however, is seen to have significant portions beyond single invalidations. The ratio of time spent doing useful work to time spent in the monitor was found to have an average value of about 16. If there are fewer than about 16 processors, they manage to stagger themselves in the first round of contention. Contention in subsequent rounds is very limited because staggering has occurred. This means that with any more than about 16 processors, we will see a step-increase in invalidations for each processor added. In this manner, a well-behaved program can suddenly produce a very large number of invalidations as it is being scaled.

It is interesting to note that a much faster implementation of the distributed index is possible with some hardware support. This would shift the ratio of unlocked to locked time to a much higher value and would enable the program to be scaled beyond 16 processors. A similar result could be achieved by increasing the grain size — for example by letting each processor extract and move five molecules at a time instead of one at a time.

The monitor lock illustrates another phenomenon. When contention for a critical section is low, the lock references cause few invalidations. As more processors are added, the critical section becomes a bottleneck and contention for the lock increases. This in turn raises the number of invalidations caused by lock references. By changing the program to remove the bottleneck we can also fix the problem of generating a large number of invalidations. In conclusion, synchronization objects themselves are not a problem unless contention for them is high.

Most accesses to shared data by MP3D consist of a read followed immediately by a write. This will allow at most one other cache to be invalidated, unless two processors are accessing the exact same portion of data at the same time. Chances of such a collision are very low and their effect can be tolerated in MP3D, hence no locks are required for the shared data. Update-type data objects such as the shared data of MP3D, can be considered to be a special case of migratory objects, and their invalidation behavior is very similar. The only difference is that each data object is kept for only a short period of time before it moves on to the next processor.

As Figure 18 indicates, directories with just three or four pointers per entry would do extremely well with MP3D. For 4-pointer directory schemes we reduce broadcasts to 2.3% of shared writes, even in the 16-processor case. A recoding of the distributed loop as suggested above could hold the broadcast percentage to below 1%, even if the number of processors is scaled to well above 16. Since shared writes are only a small fraction of all references in MP3D, a broadcast fraction of 1% of shared writes corresponds to 0.33 broadcasts per thousand references, which is low enough to be supportable in fairly large machines.

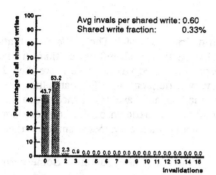

**Figure** 19: P-Thor 4

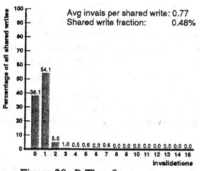

Figure 20: P-Thor 8

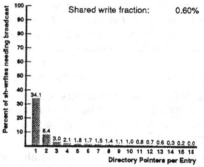

Figure 22: P-Thor 16 Directory Performance

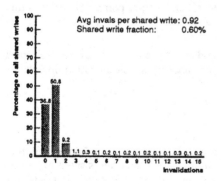

Figure 21: P-Thor 16

## 6.4 P-Thor

Figures 19, 20 and 21 give the invalidation distributions of P-Thor. We note that the number of shared writes is a much smaller fraction of all references than in the previous three applications. Furthermore, very few shared writes cause more than 2 invalidations. Note that synchronization is very infrequent in P-Thor and that our traces cover sections of program execution that do not have any synchronization references. This is why we do not show a further breakdown of the 16-processor distribution. The distributions we see are for shared data only. Most shared writes cause only zero or single invalidations.

The basic data objects of P-Thor are the element and net structures. Some parts of these structures behave like mostly-read data (e.g., the activation flags) and some parts like migratory data (e.g., next input event pointers). The invalidation patterns vary accordingly.

The activation flag of an element is set as a processor changes one of the element's input values. If the element has a large number of inputs, many processors may check this flag to see whether an element is already activated. Later, the element is evaluated and the activation flags are reset. While the *setting* of the activation flag causes only one invalidation, the *resetting* can cause many because many processors may have read and cached the flag in the meantime. The resetting of the activation flags causes about 60% of the shared writes that result in more than single invalidations.

The next-input-event-pointers, on the other hand, are used when an element is being evaluated, and are thus only read and written by one processor while it is updating the element. Hence we see mostly single invalidations – the pattern typical for migratory data.

Another factor that affects the number of invalidations is the connectivity of the circuit being evaluated. Nets that are connected to many elements, clock lines for example, are more likely to cause large invalidations when they are updated. The small concentration of 15-invalidations is caused by nets of this sort.

Figure 22 shows that P-Thor is well suited for directory-based cache schemes. A two-pointer directory requires 8.4% broadcasts and a third pointer diminishes this fraction to 3.0%. Further reduction of broadcasts could only be achieved if the program exploited processor locality in some way.

A scaling in the number of processors would result in a larger invalidation average per shared write, but not in more shared writes, since no synchronization objects are present in this portion of P-Thor.

## 6.5 LocusRoute

Figures 23, 24 and 25 show the invalidation distributions for LocusRoute. We note that the fraction of shared writes is very small as most of the time is spent exploring alternative routes for each wire. This activity involves frequent shared reads, but shared writes only occur once the best route is found and the wire is actually placed. In the 16 processor trace, there were 227,000 shared reads but only 12,000 shared writes.

The single largest source of invalidations in LocusRoute is the global cost array. It is a good example of mostly-read data. It is frequently read while testing different

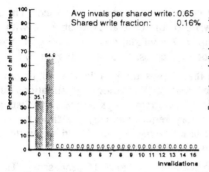

Figure 23: LocusRoute 4

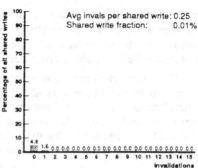

Figure 26: LocusRoute 16 (ShMalloc lock)

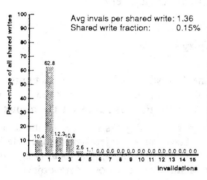

Figure 24: LocusRoute 8

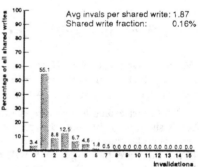

Figure 27: LocusRoute 16 (Data)

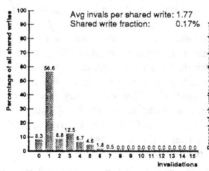

Figure 25: LocusRoute 16

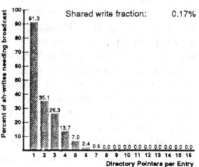

Figure 28: LocusRoute 16 Directory Performance

routes for a wire, but is written only when the wire route is decided. The average number of invalidations per shared write of the cost array is about 2 with 16 processors, but some writes can cause up to 7 invalidations, depending on how many processors have cached a given portion of the cost array (see Figure 27).

The only synchronization object that shows up is a lock used to control the access to the shared memory allocation routine (ShMalloc). Invalidations due to the ShMalloc lock are very infrequent, as the program keeps its own free lists and will have allocated most of its shared memory requirement by the time the trace was gathered. As contention for the lock is non-existent, all shared writes to the lock cause only zero or single invalidations (see Figure 26).

LocusRoute would be expected to scale well beyond 16 processors. The shared data is mostly-read and shared writes are very infrequent. As more processors are added, the average number of invalidations per shared write will increase slightly (because more processors are likely to have cached a given portion of the cost array), but the fraction of shared writes is expected to stay very low.

# 7  Effect of Cache Line Size

We now investigate the effect of cache line size on invalidation patterns. All the data supplied so far used the minimum line size of 4 bytes per cache line. We now look at line sizes of 16 and 64 bytes. Refer to Figures 29-33 for the results.

The most effective line size is one that is as large as the size of the data objects being shared. If the lines are smaller, accessing an object will cause references to several cache lines; i.e. the pre-fetch effect gained from spatial locality is diminished. If the lines are too large, they will contain more than one data object. This may lead to *false sharing* where a line appears to be shared between two processors, even though each processor is really only accessing its own private object in that line.

In terms of invalidation patterns, incorrect line size can have an effect both on *number* of invalidations and on *size* of invalidations. A higher frequency of invalidations results if the line sizes are either too large or too small. If the lines are too small, as is the case for LocusRoute with a line size of 4 bytes (see Figure 33), a large number of invalidations result as the relevant portion of the cost array moves piece by piece from one processor's cache to another. Recall that routing a wire involves frequent reads from a limited portion of the cost array and that there is significant spatial locality in the accesses to the cost array. When the line size is increased to 64 bytes, the relevant portion of the cost array moves to the new processor in significantly fewer transfers, thus causing fewer invalidations. Since the cost array is a mostly-read object where each write causes a large invalidation, we would expect the number of large invalidations to go down with an increasing line size, and this is indeed the case for LocusRoute.

On the other hand, if the lines are too large, as is the case for P-Thor with a line size of 64 bytes (see Figure 32), we get false sharing and the number of invalidations also increases. In the case of P-Thor, the total number of invalidations goes up from 42,000 to 67,000 when the line size is increased from 4 to 64 bytes.

While in some cases a large cache line can decrease the number of large invalidations (as discussed above for LocusRoute), it can also have the opposite effect. This is the case for MP3D with a line size of 64 bytes (see Figure 31). We get false

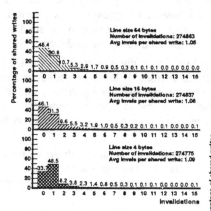

Figure 29: Maxflow 16

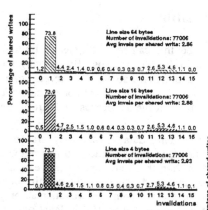

Figure 30: SA-TSP 16

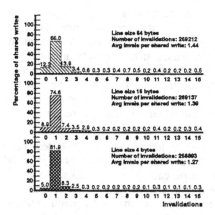

Figure 31: MP3D 16

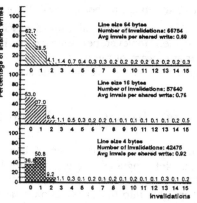

Figure 32: P-Thor 16

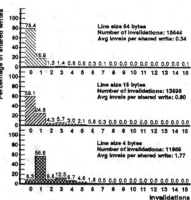

Figure 33: LocusRoute 16

sharing and unnecessarily large invalidations. Recall that most of the shared data in MP3D is in the form of arrays that are not referenced sequentially, i.e. there is no spatial locality in the reference patterns. Decreasing the line size to the smallest possible size (4 bytes) reduces the number of double and larger invalidations.

The decision of which cache line size is best for a given system depends on the cost of invalidations besides all the traditional factors. If large invalidations are expensive, such as they would be in a directory scheme with few pointers, smaller cache lines are better as they will reduce the frequency of large invalidations. If large invalidations are acceptable, a larger line size could be more favorable as it can reduce the total number of invalidations.

It is clear that no particular line size will be optimal for all applications running on a machine. However, performance can be enhanced if the programmer and/or the compiler are aware of the effect of cache line size on invalidations, and use objects that match or fit in the available line size.

# 8  Generalizations and Conclusions

We have proposed several classes of data objects that can be distinguished by their use in parallel programs and by their invalidation traffic patterns. By merging the invalidation behavior found in the applications as discussed above, we can gain more general insights into the invalidation patterns of certain high-level constructs. We also have the opportunity to predict behavior beyond the 16 processor limit of the case studies.

Little needs to be said about code and read-only data. Since they are never written, they never cause invalidations. Some directory schemes do not allow a memory location to be present in more caches than there are entries (for example $Dir_iNB$ schemes in [2]). We would normally expect such schemes to recognize code and handle it differently, thus alleviating part of the problem. However, read-only data is much harder to detect, especially since it is usually written at least once at initialization time.

Migratory data objects move from processor to processor as execution progresses, but they are never manipulated by more than one processor at any one time. The node structures of Maxflow and the global particle arrays of MP3D are good examples of this data type. Migration of the data object causes at most single invalidations, because each processor writes to the object before relinquishing control of it. Single invalidations are expected, even as the number of processors is scaled. We note that a large number of these invalidations could be avoided if the processors were smart enough to flush the data items out of their cache when they are no longer needed. Hardware or compiler support for this feature seems desirable.

Synchronization primitives were found in all applications. In "well-designed" applications contention for the critical sections protected by the locks is minimal and this effectively reduces the invalidation traffic caused by the locks. As multiprocessors are scaled, it may not always be possible to avoid high contention synchronization objects. An example is the barrier construct that is frequently used in numerical applications. Invalidation traffic can then be reduced by means of various hardware/software support features. For example, high contention locks with many processes waiting can be implemented with a queuing lock mechanism that releases waiting processes one by one without causing large invalidations. Similarly, if the directory has only a few pointers per memory line, the compiler may construct fan-in and fan-out trees for implementing barriers, thus reducing both the latency and the number of broadcasts.

Mostly-read data such as the global cost array in LocusRoute has potential for causing a large number of invalidations, since each write is preceded by a number of reads from various processors. The average number of invalidations caused by each write is thus high. The good news is that writes to this kind of data tend to be relatively infrequent and hence the total invalidation traffic is not very large. With more processors, we expect an increase in the average number of invalidations per shared write, because it is likely that more processors will have touched the data object before a write to it takes place. Some of this effect may be mitigated by taking advantage of locality, i.e., assigning work in a local area of the problem to a relatively small section of the processors available. We are currently exploring such issues of locality, which we think will be critical in the design of highly scalable machines [15].

Frequently read and written data presents a big problem in terms of invalidations. Not only does each write cause several invalidations, but writes are also frequent. A good example of this type of data is the variable in Maxflow that keeps track of how many processors are waiting on the global queue. Frequently read/written data are expected to show increased invalidations as more processors are used, because more reads and more writes to the data item will take place. If possible, this type of data object should be avoided for parallel applications with large number of processors. However, as in the case of high contention synchronization objects, some hardware support can reduce invalidation traffic. For example a hardware fetch&op operation can reduce invalidation traffic caused by such high contention objects as distributed loop indexes.

Experiments with various cache line sizes indicate that it is important for the cache line to match the size of the data objects being shared. Both line sizes that are too small and line sizes that are too large can cause more invalidations. In addition, large line sizes can cause a greater proportion of *large* invalidations. Compiler support can aid in the selection and placement of data objects with respect to cache lines.

In summary, in this paper we have presented data about the invalidation patterns of five applications using 4, 8 and 16 processor traces. By classifying data objects, we are able to predict invalidation behavior beyond the number of processors currently traced. Such extrapolation suggests that directory-based cache schemes with just three or four pointers per entry can work in scalable multiprocessors, if the applications are well-designed. In particular, effort has to be put into limiting contention over synchronization objects, exploiting locality and reducing frequently read/written data objects. Hardware support features such a queue-based locks and fetch&op primitives can also help reduce invalidation traffic.

# 9  Acknowledgments

We would like to thank Roberto Bisiani for letting us use his VAX-8350 at CMU and David Black, Robert Baron, and Mary Thompson for helping us with the inner details of the MACH operating system. We wish to thank Larry Soule, Jeff

McDonald, Jonathan Rose, Mike Smith and Francisco Carrasco for letting us trace their applications, and for patiently explaining the details of the data structures used by them. We are grateful for the useful feedback given by members of the multiprocessor project at Stanford. We would like to thank Richard Sites of Digital Equipment Corporation, Hudson MA, for providing the VAX-8350 used for tracing at Stanford and for supporting Wolf-Dietrich Weber. Anoop Gupta is supported by DARPA contract N00014-87-K-0828 and by a faculty award from Digital Equipment Corporation.

# References

[1] Anant Agarwal and Anoop Gupta. Memory Reference Characteristics of Multiprocessor Applications under MACH. In *ACM SIGMETRICS*, 1988.

[2] Anant Agarwal, Richard Simoni, John Hennessy, and Mark Horowitz. An Evaluation of Directory Schemes for Cache Coherence. In *15th International Symposium on Computer Architecture*, 1988.

[3] Francisco Javier Carrasco. A Parallel Maxflow Implementation. CS411 - Final Project Report, Stanford University, March 1988.

[4] M. Censier and P. Feautier. A New Solution to Coherence Problems in Multicache Systems. *IEEE Transactions on Computers*, C-27(12):1112–1118, December 1978.

[5] K. M. Chandy and J. Misra. Asynchronous Distributed Simulation via a Sequence of Parallel Computations. In *Communications of the ACM*, April 1981.

[6] David Cheriton. Workform Processing: A Model and Language for Parallel Computation. Stanford University, Computer Science Technical Report, 1986.

[7] Encore Corporation. *Multimax Technical Summary*.

[8] Stephen R. Goldschmidt. Simulating Multiprocessor Memory Traces. EE390 Report, Stanford University, December 1987.

[9] J.R. Goodman. Using Cache Memory to Reduce Processor-Memory Traffic. In *Proc. Tenth International Symposium on Computer Architecture*, pages 124–131, June 1983.

[10] Anoop Gupta, Milind Tambe, Dirk Kalp, Charles Forgy, and Allen Newell. A Parallel Implementation of OPS5 on the Encore Multiprocessor: Results and Analysis. In *International Journal of Parallel Programming*, volume 17, 1988.

[11] S. Kirkpatrick, C.D. Gelatt, and M. P. Vecchi. Optimization by Simulated Annealing. *Science*, 220(4580):671–680, May 1983.

[12] Tom Lovett and Shreekant Thakkar. The Symmetry Multiprocessor System. In *Proceedings of the 1988 International Conference on Parallel Processing*, pages 303–310, August 1988.

[13] Lusk, Overbeek, et al. *Portable Programs for Parallel Processors*. Holt, Rinehart, and Winston Inc., 1987.

[14] Lusk, Stevens, and Overbeek. *A Tutorial on the Use of Monitors in C: Writing Portable Code for Multiprocessors*. Argonne National Laboratory, Argonne, Illinois 60439, 1986.

[15] Margaret Martonosi and Anoop Gupta. Shared Memory vs. Message Passing Architectures: An Application Based Study. Stanford University: Computer Systems Lab, Technical Report, 1989.

[16] Jeffrey D. McDonald. A Direct Particle Simulation Method for Hypersonic Rarified Flow on a Shared Memory Multiprocessor. CS411 - Final Project Report, Stanford University, March 1988.

[17] Jeffrey D. McDonald and Donald Baganoff. Vectorization of a Particle Simulation Method for Hypersonic Rarified Flow. In *AIAA Thermodynamics, Plasmadynamics and Lasers Conference*, June 1988.

[18] Louis Monier and Pradeep Sindhu. The Architecture of the Dragon. In *Proc. Thirtieth IEEE Int. Conference*, pages 118–121. IEEE, Februrary 1985.

[19] R. Katz, S. Eggers, D. Wood, C. Perkins, and R. Sheldon. Implementing a Cache Consistency Protocol. In *12th International Symposium on Computer Architecture*, 1985.

[20] Jonathan Rose. LocusRoute: A Parallel Global Router for Standard Cells. In *Design Automation Conference*, pages 189–195, June 1988.

[21] Larry Rudolph and Zary Segall. Dynamic Decentralized Cache Consistency Schemes for MIMD Parallel Processors. In *Proc. 12th Int. Symp. on Computer Architecture*, pages 355–362. ACM SIGARCH, June 1985. also SIGARCH Newsletter, Volume 13, Issue 3, 1985.

[22] Richard L. Sites and Anant Agarwal. Multiprocessor Cache Analysis using ATUM. In *Proc. 15th Annual International Symposium on Computer Architecture*, May 1988.

[23] Michael Smith and Wolf-Dietrich Weber. Parallel Simulated Annealing. CS411 - Final Project Report, Stanford University, March 1988.

[24] Larry Soule and Tom Blank. Parallel Logic Simulation on General Purpose Machines. In *Design Automation Conference*, pages 166–171, June 1988.

[25] C. Thacker and L. Stewart. Firefly: A Multiprocessor Workstation. In *2nd Int. Conference on Architectural Support for Programming Languages and Operating Systems*, pages 164–172. ACM, October 1987.

[26] Wolf-Dietrich Weber and Anoop Gupta. Analysis of Cache Invalidation Patterns in Multiprocessors. In *ASPLOS III*, April 1989.

# Memory-Access Penalties in Write-Invalidate Cache Coherence Protocols[†][1]

## Jin-Chin Wang and Michel Dubois

*Department of Electrical Engineering-Systems*

*University of Southern California*

*University Park, Los Angeles, CA 90089-0781*

## Abstract

*Using an analytical program model, we compare the memory-access penalty of five write-invalidate cache coherence protocols. The memory-access penalty is the average time that a processor is blocked per memory reference to shared writable blocks because of a miss or of coherence activity. The protocols are compared for two systems with different cache-to-cache and memory-to-cache transfer times. The model permits rapid evaluation of protocols for different environments.*

Keywords: **cache coherence protocols, program model, trace-driven simulations, multiprocessors, multitasking.**

## 1 Introduction

Cache protocols can be classified into two categories, *write-invalidate* protocols [4, 10, 11, 12, 14], and *write-broadcast* protocols [13, 15]. The first type of protocols maintains consistency by invalidating all copies in other caches on a write. The Basic [6], the Write-once [11], the Synapse [10], the Illinois [14] and the Berkeley [12] protocols fall into this category. In write-broadcast protocols such as the Firefly [15] and the Dragon [13] protocols copies are updated instead of being invalidated.

In this paper, we apply an analytical program model called the *access burst model*, to compare the effectiveness of different coherence protocols in handling shared writable blocks. The access burst model was introduced in [7, 17] and is based on the observation that shared writable blocks are

---

[1][†]This research is supported by an National Science Foundation under Grant No DCCR-8709997.

accessed in critical or semi-critical sections [5]. It is an extension of the program model used in [6, 19]; this program model does not capture the locality of accesses to shared blocks. The predictions of the access burst model were compared with trace-driven simulation results of five algorithms, for the Basic coherence protocol [7].

In our studies, caches have infinite sizes and models are derived for computations in steady-state. This simplification drastically reduces the number of parameters in the models. The results obtained are an indication of protocol efficiency for very large caches and compute-intensive, iterative algorithms. Many such algorithms exist for asynchronous multiprocessors [3]. An example of such an algorithm is given at the end of the paper. These two restrictions on the system were also assumed in the paper by Eggers and Katz [9] and in the paper by Agarwal *et al.* [1], in which some trace-driven simulations are presented, but no analytical model is proposed.

The remainder of this paper is organized as follows. In Section 2, we briefly describe the access burst model. In Section 3, the model is applied to the analysis of five write-invalidate protocols. In Section 4, we compare the prediction of the model with trace-driven simulations in the case of a specific algorithm. Finally, the efficiencies of the protocols are compared in the light of the models in Section 5.

# 2   Program Model

In multiprocessor systems, we distinguish between two classes of shared variables, namely, synchronization variables and shared writable operands, accessed in *critical sections* [5] (only one process can access the data at a time either on a Read or on a Write) or in *semi-critical sections* [5] (multiple processes can read a data item at the same time, but only one process can modify the data item at a time). If a block can be read and modified by different processors then we call the block an S-block; otherwise, it is a P-block. Accesses to synchronization variables are not considered in this paper.

The $P$ processors generate homogeneous streams of references to P- and S-blocks. S-blocks may belong to different *sets*, based on the reference patterns. In any multitasked implementation of an algorithm, it is possible to identify sets of S-blocks shared by given groups of processors. *In the following, we analyze the coherence overhead for a given set of S-blocks.* In practice, the contributions of each set must be added [7]. A great advantage of the infinite cache assumption is that a set of S-blocks can be analyzed in isolation. Only the access pattern to the S-blocks in the set need be specified. Also, the infinite cache result for a given set of S-blocks is independent of all cache parameters besides the block size.

While a processor accesses a shared writable datum, no other processor is able to *interleave* accesses to the same datum. Accesses to a shared writable datum by one processor therefore occur in uninterrupted bursts. When a cache block can contain more than one data element, the locality of accesses also contributes to access bursts. If $q_s \cdot p_i$ is the fraction of references to an S-block $i$ shared by $J$ processors and if $ls$ is the average number of references to S-block $i$ in each access burst – when the block size is one datum, then $ls$ is also the number of accesses to the datum in the critical section– the probability of starting an access burst for S-block $i$ is $q_s \cdot p_i/ls$. In the semi-critical section model, there may be isolated Read accesses while multiple processors are allowed to read the data; we can consider those as access bursts of size one. The processor starting the next burst of accesses to S-block $i$ is chosen at random in the model. The probability that at least a Write occurs in an access burst is $W$ and the probability that only Reads occur is $1 - W$. An access burst in which a Write occurs is called a Write access burst.

In the access burst model, the outcome is different when a Write access burst starts with a Write or with a Read [7]. Therefore, we have to define the parameter, $f$, the fraction of Write access bursts such that the Write occurs first; $(1 - f)$ is the fraction of access bursts such that there is at least a Read before the first Write.

# 3    Cache Coherence Protocols

In this section, we describe five different cache coherence protocols, analyze them, and present closed-form formula for the overhead of each coherence event based on the access burst program model.

## 3.1    The Basic Coherence Protocol

This coherence protocol was described in detail in [6, 7]. A block may exist in one of three states in a cache, INVALID (no copy of the block in the cache), RO (Read-Only; an arbitrary number of caches can have this block, and all the copies are identical), and RW (Read-Write; the block has been locally modified since it was brought into the cache and the main memory copy is stale).

### 3.1.1 Protocol Description

The Basic coherence works in steady state as follows:

1. *Read hit*: The block may be accessed locally without delay.

2. *Read miss*: If a remote cache has an RW copy of the block, the modified block must first be written back to shared memory, and then shared memory supplies the block to the requesting cache. Otherwise, the block comes directly from shared memory. Each cache with a copy of the block sets the state of its copy to RO.

3. *Write hit*: If the copy of the block is in state RO an invalidation signal must be sent to all other caches. The state of the local copy is changed to RW.

4. *Write miss*: A Write miss is treated like a *Read miss* with the following difference. If copies existed in other caches, they are invalidated and the state of the local copy is set to RW.

We can denote the state of a block in the system by $1\_RW$, $2\_RO$,..., $J\_RO$, where $1\_RW$ means that the block is owned by one cache and is an RW copy; $k\_RO$ means that there are RO copies of the block in $k$ caches. In steady-state the state $1\_RO$ cannot be reached. State transitions occur at the end of each access burst; the protocol can be modeled as a discrete Markov chain illustrated in Figure 1.

### 3.1.2 Coherence Analysis

Four possible cache coherence events can occur:

1. **Miss**: this event, denoted $M$, occurs when a block is referenced and is not present in the cache. When a miss occurs, the block always comes from shared memory. When there are $k$ copies of the block in $k$ caches, a miss occurs at the beginning of a new access burst only if the processor starting a new access burst is one of the $(J - k)$ processors without a copy of the block in their caches. Hence, $P(M)^2$ is equal to $[(P_{1\_RW} \cdot (J-1)/J) + \sum_{j=2}^{J-1} P_{j\_RO} \cdot (J-j)/J]/ls$. All misses occurring as a result of the following events are accounted for as $M$ events.

---

[2]In this paper, we denote by $P_{state}$ the stationary probability of a given state in the Markov chain and by $P(event)$ the fraction of accesses causing a given event.

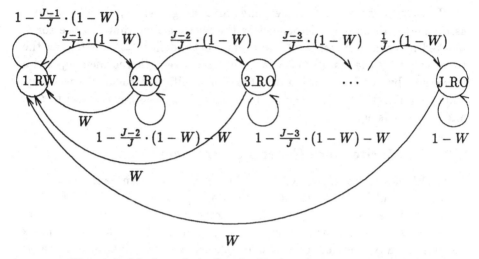

Figure 1: Markov chain for the Basic coherence protocol

2. **Transition from RO to RW**: this event occurs when a processor needs to modify a block already present in another cache as RO. We denote this event as $IN\_RO$ (INvalidation of RO copy(ies)). An invalidation of RO copies occurs whenever an access burst modifies the block in an RO state. It also occurs in a transition from 1_RW to 1_RW, provided the second access burst is executed by a different processor and starts with a Read [7]. Therefore, $P(IN\_RO)$ is equal to $[\sum_{j=2}^{J} W_{\scriptscriptstyle |} \cdot P_{j\_RO} + W \cdot (1 - f) \cdot P_{1\_RW} \cdot (J - 1)/J]/ls$.

3. **Transition from RW to RO**: this event occurs whenever a burst leaving a block in state 1_RW is followed by a burst starting with a Read access by a different processor. This RW copy has to be written back to shared memory before shared memory supplies the block to the requesting cache. We denote this event as $CS\_RW$ (Change State of a RW copy). Therefore, $P(CS\_RW)$ is equal to $[P_{1\_RW} \cdot (1 - W) \cdot (J - 1)/J + P_{1\_RW} \cdot W \cdot (1 - f) \cdot (J - 1)/J]/ls$;

4. **Transition from RW to RW** in a different cache: this event occurs when an access burst leaving a block in state 1_RW is followed by a Write from any other processor. This RW copy has to be written back to shared memory before shared memory supplies the block to the requesting cache. Thus, $P(IN\_RW)$ is equal to $[W \cdot f \cdot P_{1\_RW} \cdot (J - 1)/J]/ls$.

To each of these events corresponds an average penalty, $\lambda$. The penalty associated with an event is defined as the average time that a processor is blocked at each occurrence of the event. Let's define $t_{mc}$ and $t_{inv}$ as the times taken by the transfer of a cache block between shared memory and a cache and by the invalidation of a block in a different cache, respectively. Thus, $\lambda_M$ is equal to $t_{mc}$, $\lambda_{IN\_RO}$ is equal to $t_{inv}$, $\lambda_{CS\_RW}$ is equal to $t_{mc}$, and $\lambda_{IN\_RW}$ is equal to $t_{mc}$.

## 3.2 The Write-Once Coherence Protocol

In the Write-Once protocol [11, 18], a block in a cache can be in one of four states: INVALID, VALID (as RO in the Basic protocol), RESERVED (data in the block has been locally modified exactly once since it was brought into the cache and shared memory is updated), and DIRTY (data in the block has been locally modified more than once since it was brought into the cache and the shared memory copy is stale).

### 3.2.1 Protocol Description

The Write-Once coherence works in steady state as follows:

1. *Read hit*: The block may be accessed locally without delay.

2. *Read miss*: If a remote cache has the copy of the block in state DIRTY, the remote cache supplies the block to the requester and updates shared memory at the same time. Otherwise, the block is loaded from shared memory. All caches having a copy of the block set its state to VALID.

3. *Write hit*: If the block is already in state DIRTY or RESERVED, the Write can be processed locally without delay and the state of the block is always set to DIRTY. If the block is in state VALID, the word being modified is written through to shared memory, block copies in other caches are invalidated and the state of the block is set to RESERVED.

4. *Write miss*: If one remote cache owns a copy of the block in state DIRTY, the block is loaded from the remote cache and the remote cache invalidates its own copy; otherwise, the block is loaded from shared memory. Upon detecting the write miss signal on the bus, all caches with the copy of the block invalidate their copies at the same time. Once the block is loaded, the Write takes place and the state of the block is always set to DIRTY.

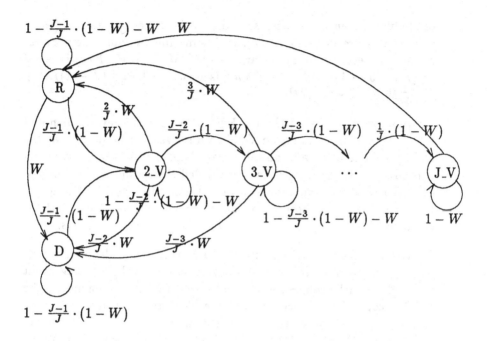

D : Dirty copy
R : Reserved copy
$k\_V$ : $k$ processors own a valid copy

Figure 2: Markov chain for the Write-Once coherence protocol

We denote the state of a block in the system by R, D, $2\_V$, ..., $J\_V$, where R and D mean that the block is owned by one cache and is a RESERVED and DIRTY copy, respectively; $k\_V$ means that there are VALID copies of the block in $k$ caches. The discrete Markov chain for the Write-Once coherence protocol is shown in Figure 2. This discrete Markov diagram is very similar to the one shown in Figure 1 with the following differences. The state $1\_RW$ in Figure 1 is split into two states, R and D; at the end of each Write burst, the next state is D if a miss occurs; otherwise, the next state is R.

### 3.2.2 Coherence Analysis

Three possible cache coherence events can occur:

1. **Miss:** This event is very similar to the $M$ event in the Basic cache coherence protocol except that the block is supplied by a remote cache rather than memory if the remote cache has a DIRTY copy

of the block. Hence, some misses cause cache-to-cache transfers (these miss events are denoted $M\_cc$), and some misses cause memory-to-cache transfers (these misses are denoted $M\_mc$.) $P(M\_cc)$ is equal to $[P_D \cdot (J-1)/J]/ls$; $P(M\_mc)$ is equal to $[(P_R \cdot (J-1)/J) + \sum_{j=2}^{J-1} P_{j\_V} \cdot (J-j)/J]/ls$;

2. **Transition from VALID to RESERVED**: this event, denoted $CS\_V\_R$ (Change State from Valid to Reserved), either occurs at the end of a Write burst and no miss event happened in the burst or occurs in a transition from R to R, provided the second access burst is executed by a different processor and starts with a Read. The modified *word* is written through to shared memory. Thus, $P(CS\_V\_R)$ is equal to $[W \cdot (1-f) \cdot P_R \cdot (J-1)/J + \sum_{j=2}^{J} W \cdot P_{j\_V} \cdot j/J]/ls$.

3. **Transition from DIRTY to VALID**: this event, denoted $CS\_D$ (Change State of a DIRTY copy), is very similar to the $CS\_RW$ event in the Basic cache coherence protocol except that the cache having the DIRTY copy of the block supplies the block to the requesting cache and also updates shared memory at the same time. $P(CS\_D)$ is equal to $[P_D \cdot (1-W) \cdot (J-1)/J + P_D \cdot W \cdot (1-f) \cdot (J-1)/J]/ls$. When the time to update shared memory is longer than the time of a cache-to-cache transfer, an extra penalty must be added to the miss penalty for the $CS\_D$ event. On the other hand, in systems where the latency of updating shared memory is less than that of the cache-to-cache transfer, no extra penalty is needed to account for memory update, since at the end of the $M$ event the shared memory has already been updated.

In addition to the $t_{mc}$ and $t_{inv}$ defined previously, we define two new terms, $t_{word}$ and $t_{cc}$, which are the times to write a word to shared memory and to transfer a block between two caches, respectively. Hence, $\lambda_{M\_mc}$ is equal to $t_{mc}$. $\lambda_{M\_cc}$ is equal to $t_{cc}$. $\lambda_{CS\_V\_R}$ which is equal to $\max(t_{word}, t_{inv})$, $\lambda_{CS\_D}$ is equal to $t_{diff}$ where $t_{diff} = (t_{mc} - t_{cc})$, if $t_{mc} > t_{cc}$, or $t_{diff} = 0$, otherwise.

## 3.3 The Synapse Coherence Protocol

In the Synapse protocol [10], there is a single-bit tag with each cache block in shared memory, indicating whether shared memory is to respond to a miss on that block. If a remote cache has a modified copy of the block, the bit will inhibit shared memory from supplying the block. Hence, this bit can prevent a possible race condition when the remote cache does not respond quickly enough to inhibit shared memory.

A cache block may be in one of the three states: INVALID, VALID (as RO in the Basic protocol), and DIRTY (as RW in the Basic protocol).

### 3.3.1 Protocol Description

The Synapse coherence protocol works in steady state as follows:

1. *Read hit*: The access may be processed locally without delay.

2. *Read miss*: If a remote cache has a DIRTY copy of the block, the modified block must first be written back to shared memory; the tag bit of the block in shared memory is set; the remote cache invalidates its local copy and sends a busy acknowledge signal to the requesting cache. When the requesting cache receives this busy signal, it must send an additional read miss request in order to get the copy of the block from shared memory. In all other cases the block is directly supplied by the shared memory. The state of the loaded block is always set to VALID.

3. *Write hit*: If the block is in state DIRTY in local cache, the Write can be processed locally without delay. If the local copy of the block is in state VALID, the procedure is as follows: shared memory has to transfer the ownership along with the copy to the requesting cache and each cache with a copy of the block observes this bus transaction and invalidates its copy of the block at the same time.

4. *Write miss*: If a remote cache has a DIRTY copy of the block, the remote cache transfers the ownership along with the block copy to the requester. If all copies of the block in the system are VALID, shared memory supplies the copy to the requesting cache and each cache which has a VALID block copy invalidates its copy at the same time. The tag bit in shared memory is reset.

We can denote the states of a block in the system by $D$, $1\_V$, $2\_V,\ldots, J\_V$, where $D$ is the state in which the block is owned by one cache and is a DIRTY copy; $k\_V$ means that there are VALID copies of the block in $k$ caches. If we observe state transitions at the end of each access burst, then the discrete Markov chain of the Synapse coherence protocol can be drawn and is shown in Figure 3. This discrete Markov diagram is very similar to the one shown in Figure 1 except that one more state, $1\_V$, is introduced.

118

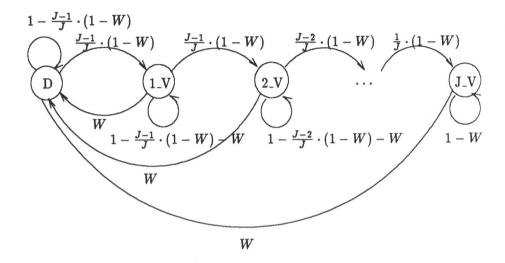

D : Dirty copy

i_V : i processors own the valid copy

Figure 3: Markov chain for the Synapse coherence protocol

### 3.3.2 Coherence Analysis

Three possible cache coherence events can occur:

1. **Miss:** There are two types of miss events (as in the Write-Once protocol); these events are denoted $M\_cc$ and $M\_mc$ for the cases of cache-to-cache and memory-to-cache transfers respectively. A miss causes a cache-to-cache transfer when a remote cache has a DIRTY copy of the block and the access burst is a Write burst. Therefore, $P(M\_cc)$ is equal to $[W \cdot P_D \cdot (J-1)/J]/ls$; $P(M\_mc)$ is equal to $[((1-W) \cdot P_D \cdot (J-1)/J) + \sum_{j=1}^{J-1} P_j \cdot (J-j)/J]/ls$;

2. **Transition from VALID to DIRTY on hit:** this event, denoted $IN\_V\_h$ (INvalidation of Valid Copy(ies) on hit), either occurs at the end of a Write burst and no miss event happened in the burst or occurs in a transition from D to D, provided the second access burst is executed by a different processor and starts with a Read. This event includes a block transfer from shared memory to the requesting cache. Thus, $P(IN\_V\_h)$ is equal to $[W \cdot (1-f) \cdot P(D) \cdot (J-1)/J + \sum_{j=1}^{J} W \cdot P_{j\_V} \cdot j/J]/ls$;

3. **Transition from DIRTY to VALID**: this event, denoted $CS\_D$, is the same as the $CS\_RW$ event in the Basic cache coherence protocol. $P(CS\_D)$ is equal to $[P_D \cdot (1 - W) \cdot (J - 1)/J + P_D \cdot W \cdot (1 - f) \cdot (J - 1)/J]/ls$.

The penalty of each event is thus as follows: $\lambda_{M\_cc}$ is equal to $t_{cc}$; $\lambda_{M\_mc}$ is equal to $t_{mc}$; $\lambda_{IN\_V\_h}$ is equal to $t_{mc}$; and $\lambda_{CS\_D}$ is equal to $t_{mc}$.

## 3.4 The Illinois Coherence Protocol

In the Illinois protocol [14], a block in a cache can be in one of four states: INVALID, EXCL-UNMOD (Exclusive-Unmodified; no other cache has this block; data in block is consistent with shared memory), SHARED-UNMOD (Shared-Unmodified; as RO in the Basic protocol) and EXCL-MOD (Exclusive-Modified; as RW in the Basic protocol).

### 3.4.1 Protocol Description

The scheme works in steady state as follows:

1. *Read hit*: The access may be processed locally without delay.

2. *Read miss*: If a remote cache has an EXCL-MOD copy of the block, the remote cache sends the copy to the requesting cache and updates shared memory at the same time. Otherwise, any one cache supplies the copy to the requester. Both caches set their copy to SHARED-UNMOD.

3. *Write hit*: If the local copy of the block is in state EXCL-MOD, it can be updated without delay. Otherwise, the Write cannot be processed until an invalidation signal is sent. The copy in the local cache is set to EXCL-MOD.

4. *Write miss*: A write miss request is broadcasted to all caches. Each cache with the copy of the block invalidates its copy. The block is always loaded from a remote cache and its state is set to EXCL-MOD.

We can denote the state of a block in the system by E, $2\_S, \ldots, J\_S$, where E means that the block is owned by one cache and is an EXCL-MOD copy; $k\_S$ means that there are SHARED-UNMOD copies of the block in $k$ caches. The discrete Markov chain of the Illinois coherence protocol is the same as the one shown in Figure 1 provided that the state names are changed.

### 3.4.2 Coherence Analysis

Three possible cache coherence events can occur:

1. **Miss:** This event is very similar to the $M$ event in the Basic cache coherence protocol except that the block is always supplied by a cache. $P(M)$ is equal to $[(P_E \cdot (J-1)/J) + \sum_{j=2}^{J-1} P_{j\_S} \cdot (J-j)/J]/ls$.

2. **Transition from SHARED-UNMOD to EXCL-MOD on hit:** This event, denoted $IN\_S\_h$ (INvalidation of SHARED-UNMOD Copy(ies) on hit), and the $IN\_V\_h$ event in the Synapse cache coherence protocol are very similar except that the coherence overhead of this event is to broadcast an invalidation signal. $P(IN\_S\_h)$ is equal to $[W \cdot (1-f) \cdot P_E \cdot (J-1)/J + \sum_{j=2}^{J} W \cdot P_{j\_S} \cdot j/J]/ls$.

3. **Transition from EXCL-MOD to SHARED-UNMOD:** This event, denoted $CS\_E$ (Change State of an EXCL-MOD copy), is the same as the $CS\_D$ event in the Write-Once cache coherence protocol. $P(CS\_E)$ is equal to $[P_E \cdot (1-W) \cdot (J-1)/J + P_E \cdot W \cdot (1-f) \cdot (J-1)/J]/ls$.

The penalty of each event is: $\lambda_M$ is equal to $t_{cc}$, $\lambda_{IN\_S\_h}$ is equal to $t_{inv}$, and $\lambda_{CS\_E}$ is equal to $t_{diff}$ where $t_{diff}=(t_{mc} - t_{cc})$, if $t_{mc} > t_{cc}$, or $t_{diff}=0$, otherwise.

## 3.5 The Berkeley Coherence Protocol

In the Berkeley protocol [12], a block in a cache can be in one of the following four states: INV (INValid; as INVALID in the Basic protocol), UNO (UNOwned; as RO in the Basic protocol), EXC (owned EXClusively; the block copy is unique, and therefore it can be updated locally without delay; the cache must respond to any request on the bus for a copy of the block; this state is equivalent to the RW in the Basic protocol), or NON (Owned NON-exclusively; the block copy is owned, but it cannot be modified without informing the other caches). At any time up to one NON copy and several UNO copies of a block can exist. In steady state, there is one and only one NON copy of a block in the system if there exist some UNO copies of the block; on the other hand, there is never a NON copy of the block in the system if there is an EXC copy of the block. The cache, which has a copy of the block in state NON or EXC, is called the owner of the block. If a block is not owned by any cache, shared memory is the owner; in a system with infinite caches, in which replacements never occur, the memory cannot be an owner in steady state.

### 3.5.1  Protocol Description

The Berkeley protocol works as follows in steady state, for the case of infinite caches.

1. *Read hit:* The access is processed locally without delay.

2. *Read miss:* The block is always loaded from another cache and its local state is set to UNO.

3. *Write hit:* If the local copy of the block is in state EXC, the Write is processed without delay. Otherwise, all copies must be invalidated before the Write can be processed; the cache sets its copy to state NON.

4. *Write miss:* The block always comes from another cache and each cache with the copy of the block invalidates its copy. The requesting cache sets its copy to state EXC.

We can denote the state of a block in the system by E, $2\_N, \ldots, J\_N$, where E means that the block is owned by one cache and is an EXC copy; $k\_N$ means that there are one NON and $(k-1)$ UNO copies of the block in $k$ caches. Provided the state names are changed, the Markov chain is the same as the one shown in Figure 1.

### 3.5.2  Coherence Analysis

In this scheme, two possible cache coherence events can occur:

1. **Miss:** The fraction of misses in this protocol is given by the same expression as in the Illinois protocol, that is, $P(M) = [(P_E \cdot (J - 1)/J) + \sum_{j=2}^{J-1} P_{j\_N} \cdot (J - j)/J]/ls$.

2. **Transition from UNO to NON on hit:** The fraction of references causing this event $IN\_U\_h$ (INvalidation of UNO Copy(ies) on hit), is given by the same expression as for the event $IN\_S\_h$ in the Illinois protocol, that is, $P(IN\_U\_h) = [W \cdot (1 - f) \cdot P_E \cdot (J - 1)/J + \sum_{j=2}^{J} W \cdot P_{j\_N} \cdot j/J]/ls$

The penalty of each event is: $\lambda_M = t_{cc}$, and $\lambda_{IN\_U\_h} = t_{inv}$.

Appendix A lists the formulas of miss ratio and total penalty for the five cache coherence protocols. Detailed derivation can be found in [16].

# 4 Multitasked S.O.R. Algorithm

The model has been applied to one particular multitasked algorithm, the S.O.R. (Successive Over Relaxation) iterative algorithm, to solve Laplace's equation $\nabla^2 x = 0$ on a rectangular domain of $R^2$. The S.O.R. algorithm is an iterative, compute-intensive algorithm. The infinite cache condition is met when the data cache of each processor is large enough to contain all the grid elements accessed by the processor. In this case, steady-state is reached after the first iteration. This important algorithm is therefore a good benchmark to apply the model. The details of the algorithm can be found in [8]. and many other sources.

In this algorithm, we have identified eight sets of shared writable blocks [8]. The values of the parameters for each set is given in Table 1 for a grid size of 128 × 128.

Table 1: Values of parameters for the eight different sets of S-blocks in the case of the S.O.R. iterative algorithm with a grid size of 128 × 128.

| Set | $q_s$ | $J$ | $W$ | $ls$ | $f$ |
|---|---|---|---|---|---|
| Type 1 | 0.03027 | 2.0000 | 0.2857 | 1.7143 | 0.0000 |
| Type 2 | 0.00041 | 2.0000 | 0.4000 | 2.0000 | 0.0000 |
| Type 3 | 0.01465 | 2.0000 | 0.1667 | 2.0000 | 0.0000 |
| Type 4 | 0.00037 | 2.0000 | 0.2222 | 2.0000 | 0.0000 |
| Type 5 | 0.00757 | 2.0000 | 0.2500 | 1.5000 | 0.0000 |
| Type 6 | 0.00012 | 2.0000 | 0.2500 | 1.5000 | 0.0000 |
| Type 7 | 0.00049 | 4.0000 | 0.2857 | 1.7143 | 0.0000 |
| Type 8 | 0.00012 | 4.0000 | 0.2500 | 1.5000 | 0.0000 |

The access burst model was also applied to four other algorithms in [7].

# 5 Discussion

In the computation of the total penalty, we examine two different systems. In system 1, the cache-to-cache transfer time is taken as eight time units: one time unit for bus arbitration, one time unit for address transfer, four time units for a block access and transfer, and two time units for acknowledgement. The memory-to-cache transfer time is taken as ten time units because an access to the memory takes six time units. The time to write a word to shared memory is seven time units: one time unit for bus arbitration, one time unit for address transfer, three time units for a word transfer and memory access, and two time units for acknowledgement. An invalidation signal only takes two time units: one for bus arbitration and one for signal broadcasting. The difference between system 1 and system 2 is the cache-to-cache transfer time. In system 2, the time to retrieve a block in a remote cache is eight time units so that the total cache-to-cache transfer time is twelve time units. Therefore, in system 1, a cache-to-cache transfer takes less time than a memory-to-cache transfer, while it is the opposite in system 2.

In the following, we will express all penalties in units of the penalty of transferring a single word between a cache and the shared memory, that is, $\lambda_{word} = 1$. If the penalty to read a word from memory is the same as the penalty to write a word to memory, then we can estimate the performance improvement due to the caching of shared writable data as $1 - \lambda_{total}$. In particular if $\lambda_{total} > 1$, then caching shared writable data is not productive. The penalties of different coherence events in system 1 are $t_{mc} = 10/7$, $t_{cc} = 8/7$, $t_{word} = 1$ and $t_{inv} = 2/7$; in system 2, they are $t_{mc} = 10/7$, $t_{cc} = 12/7$, $t_{word} = 1$ and $t_{inv} = 2/7$.

From Table 1, we can calculate the total penalty, $\lambda_{total}$, for the S.O.R. iterative algorithm for the five different protocols; the results are compared to the results of trace-driven simulations for the five protocols in Table 2 and Table 3.[3] The difference between model predictions and simulations is never more than 10%.

Figures 4 and 5 display the product (penalty $\times l_s$) as a function of $W$ and $J$ when $f=1$, and Figures 6 and 7 show the product (penalty $\times l_s$) as a function of $W$ and $J$ when $f=0$ (two extreme cases) for system 1. From these four figures, the Berkeley coherence protocol always shows the best performance. The Illinois coherence protocol always has less total penalty than the Write-once coherence protocol. The Basic or the Synapse coherence protocols always exhibit the worst performance. Our examples show that, under the access burst model with $f=1$, with $J$ less than 10 and $W=0.25$, the Synapse coherence protocol shows the worst performance; however, when $J$ is larger than 10 and $W=0.25$, the Basic coherence protocol has the worst penalty for shared data accesses; when $f=0$, the total penalty of the Synapse protocol is always higher than that of the Basic protocol. These conclusions are similar to Archibald and Baer's, in [2].

The above conclusion may vary for different values of the penalties, which

---

[3]Trace-driven simulation has a drawback that the same trace is re-used to evaluate all coherence protocols, while in reality the reference pattern might be different for each coherence scheme because of the timing differences. We neglected this possible effect in the trace-driven simulations.

Table 2: Comparison between the total penalties of the model and of the simulation

(system 1: $t_{mc} = \frac{10}{7}$, $t_{cc} = \frac{8}{7}$, $t_{word} = \frac{7}{7}$, $t_{inv} = \frac{2}{7}$)

| Protocol | Model Prediction | Simulation Result | Difference (%) |
|----------|------------------|-------------------|----------------|
| Basic | 0.01953 | 0.02047 | 4.59% |
| Write-Once | 0.01510 | 0.01583 | 4.61% |
| Synapse | 0.02996 | 0.03058 | 2.03% |
| Illinois | 0.01068 | 0.01119 | 4.56% |
| Berkeley | 0.00891 | 0.00934 | 4.62% |

Table 3: Comparison between the total penalties of the model and of the simulation

(system 2: $t_{mc} = \frac{10}{7}$, $t_{cc} = \frac{12}{7}$, $t_{word} = \frac{7}{7}$, $t_{inv} = \frac{2}{7}$)

| Protocol | Model Prediction | Simulation Result | Difference (%) |
|----------|------------------|-------------------|----------------|
| Basic | 0.01953 | 0.02047 | 4.59% |
| Write-Once | 0.01582 | 0.01729 | 8.50% |
| Synapse | 0.03088 | 0.03429 | 9.94% |
| Illinois | 0.01248 | 0.01309 | 4.66% |
| Berkeley | 0.01248 | 0.01309 | 4.66% |

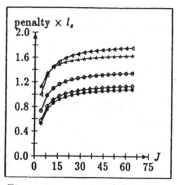

Figure 4: penalty $\times\ l_s$ for the access burst model ($W$=0.25, $f$=1, $t_{cc} = 8/7$)

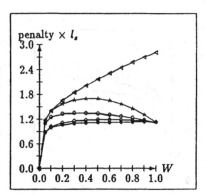

Figure 5: penalty $\times\ l_s$ for the access burst model ($J$=16, $f$=1, $t_{cc} = 8/7$)

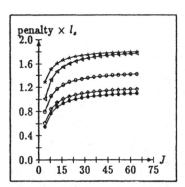

Figure 6: penalty $\times\ l_s$ for the access burst model ($W$=0.25, $f$=0, $t_{cc} = 8/7$)

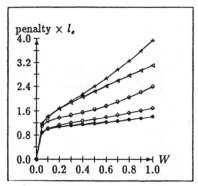

Figure 7: penalty $\times\ l_s$ for the access burst model ($J$=16, $f$=0, $t_{cc} = 8/7$)

◁ : Basic    ○ : Write-Once    ⋆ : Synapse    ◇ : Illinois    ● : Berkeley

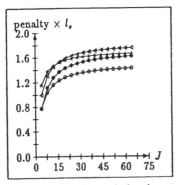

Figure 8: penalty × $l_s$ for the access burst model ($W$=0.25, $f$=1, $t_{cc} = 12/7$)

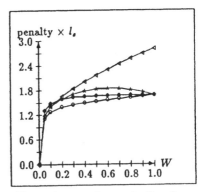

Figure 9: penalty × $l_s$ for the access burst model ($J$=16, $f$=1, $t_{cc} = 12/7$)

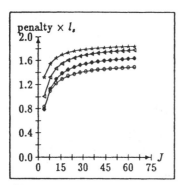

Figure 10: penalty × $l_s$ for the access burst model ($W$=0.25, $f$=0, $t_{cc} = 12/7$)

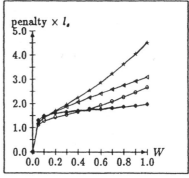

Figure 11: penalty × $l_s$ for the access burst model ($J$=16, $f$=0, $t_{cc} = 12/7$)

◁ : Basic    ○ : Write-Once    ⋆ : Synapse    ◇ : Illinois    ● : Berkeley

in turn depend on the architecture of the system. For system 2, Figures 8 and 9 display the product (penalty $\times$ $l_s$) as a function of $W$ and $J$ when $f=1$, and Figures 10 and 11 show the product (penalty $\times$ $l_s$) as a function of $W$ and $J$ when $f=0$. From these four figures, the Berkeley coherence protocol always has the same penalty as the Illinois coherence protocol since there is no extra time needed to update shared memory when the $CS\_E$ event occurs. The Write-once coherence protocol has the least penalty in most cases except that in the case of $W=0.25$, $f=0$ and $J \leq 4$ and in the case of $J=16$, $f=0$ and $W \geq 0.5$, the Illinois and the Berkeley coherence protocols show the best performance. The average penalty of the Illinois and the Berkeley coherence protocols is less than the average penalty of the Basic and the Synapse coherence protocols except in the case of $J=16$ and $W$ is less than 0.15. When work load model $f$ is equal to zero, the Synapse coherence protocol always shows the worst performance; however, when $f$ is equal to one, the Basic coherence protocol incurs more penalty than the Synapse coherence protocol in the case where $W=0.25$ and $J$ is greater than 16 and in the case where $J=16$ and $W$ is larger than 0.1.

The coherence protocols can be ranked in terms of increasing penalty (or decreasing efficiency). Overall, for system 1, the order is: the Berkeley, the Illinois, the Write-once, the Synapse and the Basic coherence protocols. Overall, for system 2, the order is: the Write-once, the Berkeley, the Illinois, the Synapse and the Basic coherence protocols. Therefore, while the Write-once coherence protocol is an *average* coherence protocol for system 1, it becomes the best coherence protocol for system 2 because the cache-to-cache transfer time has minor effect on the Write-once coherence protocol. Hence, the choice of a coherence protocol is greatly affected by the system architecture and parameters. The model proposed in this paper can be used for rapid evaluations of various protocols for a given system.

# References

[1] A. Agarwal, R. Simoni, J. Hennessy, and M. Horowitz. An evaluation of directory schemes for cache coherence. In *Proceedings of 15th Annual International Symposium on Computer Architecture*, pages 280–289, June 1988.

[2] J. Archibald and J.L. Baer. Cache-coherence protocols: Evaluation using a multiprocessor simulation model. *ACM Transactions on Computer Systems*, 4(4):273–298, November 1986.

[3] D.P. Bertsekas and J.N. Tsitsiklis. *Parallel and Distributed Computation*. Prentice-Hall, 1989.

[4] IBM Corporation. Special issue on IBM 3081. *IBM Journal of RES. and Devel.*, 26(1):2–19, January 1982.

[5] M. Dubois. Effect of invalidations on the hit ratio of cache-based multiprocessors. In *Proceedings of the 1987 International Conference on Parallel Processing*, pages 255–257, August 1987.

[6] M. Dubois and F.A. Briggs. Effects of cache coherency in multiprocessors. *IEEE Transactions on Computers*, C-31(11):1083–1099, November 1982.

[7] M. Dubois and J.C. Wang. Shared data contention in a cache coherence protocol. In *Proceedings of the 1988 International Conference on Parallel Processing*, pages 146–155, August 1988.

[8] M. Dubois and J.C. Wang. Analytical modeling of data sharing in cache based multiprocessors. Technical Report CENG 89-18, Computer Engineering Division, Electrical Engineering - Systems Department, University of Southern California, August 1989.

[9] S.J. Eggers and R.H. Katz. A characterization of sharing in parallel programs and its application to coherency protocol evaluation. In *Proceedings of 15th Annual International Symposium on Computer Architecture*, pages 373–382, June 1988.

[10] S.J. Frank. Tightly coupled multiprocessor system speeds memory-access times. *Electronics*, 57(1):164–169, January 1984.

[11] J.R. Goodman. Using cache memory to reduce processor-memory traffic. In *Proceedings of 10th Annual International Symposium on Computer Architecture*, pages 124–131, June 1983.

[12] R.H. Katz, S.J. Eggers, D.A. Wood., C.L. Perkins and R.G. Sheldon. Implementing a cache consistency protocol. In *Proceedings of 12th Annual International Symposium on Computer Architecture*, pages 276–283, June 1985.

[13] E. McCreight. The dragon computer system: An early overview. In *NATO Advanced Study Institute on Microarchitecture of VLSI Computers*, July 1984.

[14] M.S. Papamarcos and J.H. Patel. A low-overhead coherence solution for multiprocessors with private cache memories. In *Proceedings of 11th Annual International Symposium on Computer Architecture*, pages 348–354, June 1984.

[15] C.P. Thacker, L.C. Stewart, and E.H. Satterthwaite, Jr. Firefly: A multiprocessor workstation. *IEEE Transactions on Computers*, C-37(8):909–920, August 1988.

[16] J.C. Wang and M. Dubois. A performance comparison of cache coherence protocols based on the access burst model. *to appear in the Journal of the Computer Systems Science and Engineering*.

[17] J.C. Wang and M. Dubois. A performance comparison of cache coherence protocols based on the access burst model. In *Proceedings of the Second Annual Parallel Processing Symposium*, pages 73–87, April 1988.

[18] A.W. Wilson Jr. Hierarchical cache/bus architecture for shared memory multiprocessors. In *Proceedings of 14th Annual International Symposium on Computer Architecture*, pages 244–252, June 1987.

[19] Q. Yang, L.N. Bhuyan, and B.C. Liu. Analysis and comparison of cache coherence protocols for a packet-switched multiprocessor. *IEEE Transactions on Computers*, 38(8):1143–1153, Aughst 1989.

## Appendix A: Total Penalty for the Five Protocols

Basic

$$\lambda_{total} = \frac{1}{ls} \cdot \left\{ \frac{J \cdot (J-1) \cdot W \cdot (1+W)}{(1+(J-1) \cdot W) \cdot (J-1+W)} \cdot t_{mc} + \frac{(J-1) \cdot W \cdot (1-W \cdot f)}{J-1+W} \cdot t_{inv} \right\}.$$

Write-once

$$\lambda_{total} = \frac{1}{ls} \cdot \left\{ \frac{(J-1) \cdot W^2 \cdot (J^2 + 2JW - 2J - 2W + 2)}{(J-1+W)^2 \cdot (1+(J-1)W)} \cdot t_{cc} + \frac{(J-1) \cdot W \cdot (1-W) \cdot (J^2 + 2JW - 2J - 3W + 1)}{(J-1+W)^2 \cdot (1+(J-1)W)} \cdot t_{mc} \right.$$

$$+ \left[ \frac{(J-1)\cdot W \cdot (1-W^2)}{(J-1+W)\cdot(1+(J-1)W)} + \frac{(J-1)\cdot W^2 \cdot (1-f)}{J-1+W} \right] \cdot t_1$$

$$+ \frac{(J-1)\cdot W^2 \cdot (1-fW)\cdot (J^2+2JW-2J-2W+2)}{(J-1+W)^2 \cdot (1+(J-1)W)} \cdot t_2 \Bigg\},$$

where $t_1 = \max(t_{word}, t_{inv})$ and $t_2 = (t_{mc} - t_{cc})$, if $t_{mc} > t_{cc}$, or $t_2 = 0$, otherwise.

Synapse

$$\lambda_{total} = \frac{1}{ls} \left\{ \frac{(J-1)\cdot W^2}{J-1+W} \cdot t_{cc} + \frac{(J-1)\cdot W \cdot (JW-2W+J+2)}{(J-1+W)\cdot(1+(J-1)W)} \cdot t_{mc} \right. $$
$$\left. - \frac{2\cdot(J-1)\cdot W^2 \cdot f}{J-1+W} \cdot t_{mc} \right\}.$$

Illinois

$$\lambda_{total} = \frac{1}{ls} \cdot \left\{ \frac{(J-1)\cdot W}{1+(J-1)\cdot W} \cdot t_{cc} + \frac{(J-1)\cdot W \cdot (1-W\cdot f)}{J-1+W} \cdot t_2 \right.$$
$$+ \left[ \frac{(J-1)\cdot W \cdot (1-W^2)}{(J-1+W)\cdot(1+(J-1)W)} \right.$$
$$\left. \left. + \frac{(J-1)\cdot W^2 \cdot (1-f)}{J-1+W} \right] \cdot t_{inv} \right\},$$

where $t_2 = (t_{mc} - t_{cc})$, if $t_{mc} > t_{cc}$, or $t_2 = 0$, otherwise.

Berkeley

$$\lambda_{total} = \frac{1}{ls} \cdot \left\{ \frac{(J-1)\cdot W}{1+(J-1)W} \cdot t_{cc} + \frac{(J-1)\cdot W \cdot (1-W^2)}{(J-1+W)\cdot(1+(J-1)W)} \cdot t_{inv} \right.$$
$$\left. + \frac{(J-1)\cdot W^2 \cdot (1-f)}{J-1+W} \cdot t_{inv} \right\}.$$

# Performance of Parallel Loops using Alternative Cache Consistency Protocols on a Non-Bus Multiprocessor

**Russell M. Clapp**       **Trevor N. Mudge**
*Advanced Computer Architecture Laboratory*
*Department of Electrical Engineering and Computer Science*
*The University of Michigan*
*Ann Arbor, Michigan 48109-2122*

and

**James E. Smith**
*Cray Research, Inc.*
*900 Lowater Road*
*Chippewa Falls, Wisconsin 54729*

*Abstract*

*In this paper we present the results of a preliminary study of the performance of parallel loops on a non-bus shared-memory multiprocessor. Parallel loops are defined to be "do" or "for" loops whose iterations are independent and can therefore be executed in parallel. These are potentially the greatest source of parallelism in a program and, therefore, it is important to demonstrate that this potential can be realized before exploring other sources of parallelism. The sources of inefficiency that can limit the parallelism are the mechanism for maintaining cache consistency and the algorithm that schedules the loops across the processors. As part of our study we examined the impact on parallel performance of two software and two hardware cache consistency techniques as well as three scheduling policies.*

## INTRODUCTION

Parallel processing is an increasingly important technique used to speedup the execution of compute-intensive scientific codes. In this paper we consider the use of shared-memory multiprocessors in which the individual processors cooperate to speedup the execution of a single program. In order to avoid re-writing the large base of scientific codes written in sequential languages, methods have been developed to parallelize these programs. One of the most elementary of these methods is to simply execute multiple iterations of "do" loops or "for" loops in parallel. We will refer to these loops as "parallel loops".

Parallel loops can be detected through data dependency analysis performed at compile-time [6, 7]. However, several languages and language extensions have been proposed that contain **doall** and **doacross** style loops, which allow the programmer to explicitly state the parts of the loop that may be executed in parallel [8, 9, 10, 11].

A **doall** loop is one in which each iteration may be executed in any order and in parallel, i.e., there are no data dependencies between iterations. In a **doacross** loop, one or more data dependencies exist between iterations which imposes an order of execution. In this paper we limit our experiments to parallel loops that conform explicitly or implicitly to the **doall** semantics. They represent potentially the greatest source of parallelism in a program, therefore, as a first step, it is important to demonstrate that these loops can be executed in parallel with a high degree of efficiency before exploring other sources of parallelism.

To avoid performance degradation in a shared-memory multiprocessor due to memory congestion it is necessary to include a cache or local memory with each processor and provide a high-bandwidth connection to main memory. Furthermore, techniques must be employed (either in hardware or software) to maintain data consistency across the caches and main memory. Many hardware solutions to the cache consistency problem have been studied, but most are snooping protocols, best suited to shared-bus multiprocessors. Considerably less attention has been given to protocols for non-bus systems as well as software techniques for maintaining consistency.

In this paper, we examine the impact of two software and hardware cache consistency techniques in a non-bus multiprocessor on the performance of parallel loops. We also examine the impact of three scheduling policies for the microtasks that result from parallelizing the loops. We perform our experiments using a high performance register-transfer level simulator of the Astronautics ZS series of multiprocessors. The simulator interprets code from executable binaries. These binaries are created using compilers and an assembler for an existing uniprocessor version of the ZS series, the ZS-1. The sequential code is compiled and then hand parallelized by adding basic run-time system and synchronization code at the assembly language level. The run-time extensions include support for the three scheduling policies, as well as software consistency actions when necessary. Synchronization is performed using a special set of shared "semaphore" registers, which keeps the synchronization traffic separate from the cache and prevent it from skewing the results of the consistency overhead measurements. The use of a simulator for our experiments provides us with the flexibility to alter the consistency hardware, basic cache parameters, and the number of processors.

There have been a number of recent studies of multiprocessor cache performance reported in [1, 2, 3, 4, 5]. The first three of these studies focused on bus-based multiprocessors using snooping protocols for cache consistency. The other two examined the performance of hardware directory schemes and software schemes for cache consistency. The experiments in these two studies were for a "generic" RISC-based multiprocessor and relied on real multiprocessor traces from a collection of application programs. These traces were obtained from a four processor CISC-based multiprocessor and included operating system activity.

The distinguishing characteristics of our study are: 1) the target is an actual design for a multiprocessor system that is an extension of an existing uniprocessor computer, 2) the performance measurements are made by using an interpreter driven register-transfer level simulator, 3) the simulator inputs are real executable binaries of microtasking parallel programs that are constructed using existing compiler/assembler tools, and 4) there is no operating system code included in the measurements, nor is there any need to use the cache or main memory for synchronization purposes. While this approach produces results that are particular to this system and the parallel programs simulated, the results do provide a clear view of events that occur in a microtasking environment on a real multiprocessor system. In particular, the study exposes the difficulties and potential pitfalls in pursuing fine-grained parallelism on a non-bus multiprocessor.

In the remainder of this paper, we provide some background on the issues surrounding this problem area, describe our experimental testbed, and discuss the results of our experiments while offering some conclusions. The next section provides background on the run-time support necessary for parallel loops, directory schemes for hardware supported cache consistency, and software schemes for cache consistency. The following section describes our experimental testbed, including the ZS multiprocessor simulator, the construction of parallel programs for simulation, the implementation of the run-time support code, and the implementation of both software and hardware schemes for cache consistency. In the last two sections we present the results of our experiments and conclude with a discussion of those results.

# BACKGROUND

## Microtasking Run-Time Support

The run-time system that supports program parallelism is the vital component of the parallel processing system because it sets limits on the system's performance. A straightforward run-time system is sufficient to support loop parallelism. Its simplicity is derived from the restricted form of parallelism provided by loops. Since the multiple iterations of the loop execute with the same local environment (that of the enclosing subprogram), there is no need to set up separate data or stack areas. Further, there is no communication between loop iterations, therefore groups of one or more loop iterations can be scheduled as one *microtask* for an available processor without concern for dependencies between the microtasks. We also restrict parallel loops from being nested, to avoid complicating the microtask run-time support. By eliminating nested parallel loops, the implementation is simplified without a severe reduction in parallelism. Restructuring compilers may coalesce loops to increase parallelism and provide a larger grain size. The grain size must be large enough to mask the run-time support overhead, but not too large that it leads to load imbalance among the processors. Loop restructuring techniques are described in [12]. A complete description of loop types and their properties can be found in [13].

The run-time support for microtasking relies on the *self-scheduling* paradigm [14, 13, 15]. In this paradigm, the multiple processors executing a program access a shared run-queue to obtain units of work, loop iterates in this case. The work in the queue is represented by a record that indicates the address of the code as well as the number of times it is to be executed. In the simple case, the run-queue may only hold one such record at a time, providing for a very simple and efficient implementation. The processors used by the program are dedicated, and may access the shared run-queue without entering the operating system. This allows low overhead scheduling, which in turn provides an opportunity to exploit fine-grained parallelism. These microtasks follow *run-to-completion* semantics which enable the run-time system to schedule them only once before they complete.

In a microtasking system, a program runs serially on a processor until a loop is entered. It then performs a synchronization operation to allow other processors to begin accessing the run-queue. The queue is read and modified so that each processor obtains an increment of the work to be done. The processors continue to schedule more work for themselves until there is none left. When the microtasks finish, they usually synchronize at the point immediately following the loop. However, in some cases, the serial portion of the code following the loop may execute in parallel with some of the parallel microtasks. Any other available processor may also reload the run-queue at this point with data that represents the next loop to be executed in parallel. Data dependencies between the loop, the serial code, and any following loops determine how much overlap is possible.

There are several variants of self-scheduling that are possible. When work is obtained from the queue, a microtask of one or more loop iterations may be selected. The number chosen is referred to as the *chunk* size [13]. It is also possible to vary the chunk size dynamically as multiple processors are obtaining work. One such possibility is *guided self-scheduling* [15]. Another possibility is to compute an "optimal" chunk size based on the number of iterations and the number of processors available. These strategies all attempt to optimize the trade-off between load balancing and overhead. In our experiments, we compare the performance of self-scheduling with a fixed chunk size of 1 (which we simply call "self-scheduling"), guided self-scheduling, and optimal chunk size scheduling. The details of our implementations of these approaches are given in the EXPERIMENTAL TESTBED section below.

## Cache Consistency

With the emergence of bus-based shared-memory multiprocessors in recent years, the topic of cache consistency has received considerable attention. The bulk of this attention has been focused on *snooping* cache consistency protocols, which are ideal for bus-based systems. However, these schemes are not well suited to systems which use a non-bus style of interconnect between processors, their caches, and memory because they require the ability to broadcast addresses to each cache and main memory. In fact, several multiprocessors which do not use a bus interconnect do not support cache consistency in hardware (e.g., the Astronautics ZS series, the IBM RP3, and the Evans & Sutherland ES-1). Non-bus multiprocessor systems with caches or "transparent" local memories must rely on alternative cache consistency techniques.

We can categorize software mechanisms for cache consistency into three general types that rely on: 1) non-cacheable data; 2) bypass, write through, and/or flush of cache blocks; or 3) cached write buffers with merging. The first type is the classical technique where shared data is made non-cacheable, typically on a page boundary. The second type requires that the compiler utilize information about data dependencies and alignment of words in cache blocks to bypass the cache on a fetch if necessary, and to write through or flush blocks to main memory when needed. Several implementations to this approach have been proposed [16, 17]. The third type allocates cache blocks for result data areas, and then merges these blocks together at the conclusion of the parallel loop or section to form the final result in main memory. It has been implemented on an existing distributed memory multiprocessor using pages as the write buffer size [18]. In our experiments, we have tested this approach using the minimum number of cache blocks required to represent the entire result area of one parallel loop as the write buffer size.

Directory schemes for cache consistency typically keep information regarding cache block location and modification status in a central location. An early scheme proposed by Censier and Feautrier [19] keeps a directory entry for each potential cache block in memory. The entry contains bits to indicate which caches, if any, possess the block and whether or not the main memory version is up-to-date. Thus, for an $N$ processor system each entry would have at least $N + 1$ bits. A modification to this scheme is to restrict blocks to at most one cache and then replace the bits with an index value to indicate the cache where the block resides. In both cases, the directory information is used on cache misses or non-private hits to retrieve the up-to-date cache block and, if necessary, invalidate or update other copies and update the tags and directory according to the specifics of the protocol. A survey of several central directory based schemes can be found in [4].

## Synchronization

A synchronization instruction is usually based on an indivisible read-modify-write operation on either a main memory word or special memory hardware. Examples include test-and-set [20], fetch-and-op [21], and compare-and-swap [20]. The advantages of using main memory are generality and scalability. The disadvantages are slowness and added complexity to deal with the interaction between hardware cache consistency and synchronization [22]. Alternatively, special memories or shared registers may be provided for fast synchronization. Their disadvantages are that they are limited in number and they do not readily scale to large numbers of processors [23, 24, 25].

The parallel programs used for our experiments make use of the ZS's shared "semaphore" registers for synchronization. The ZS provides 32 sets of semaphore registers, each set consisting of 32 registers, each 32 bits long. Several fetch-and-op instructions are provided that operate on the semaphore registers. Instructions are also provided for the first 8 registers in each group that enable processors to block until the value of a particular register becomes either positive or negative. Together with the ability to read and write these registers, these instructions make the semaphore registers ideal for holding addresses, implementing barriers, and computing indices for a microtasking run-time system.

# EXPERIMENTAL TESTBED

## ZS Multiprocessor Simulator

The Astronautics ZS series of computers are based on a proprietary 64-bit processor directed at numeric applications. The processor is heavily pipelined and is capable of issuing two instructions per clock period. Memory accessing and floating point are decoupled by using distinct instruction issuing streams for each. Memory accesses are also buffered using processor queues for integer and floating point loads and stores. These features permit dynamic scheduling between addressing and floating point functions, and successfully hides memory latencies in many cases [26]. This type of architecture is referred to as Decoupled Access/Execute (DAE) [27].

The ZS-1, a uniprocessor, was completed (both hardware and software) and has been operational for some time. The hardware is constructed to support up to 16 processor systems, but multiprocessing software is incomplete. ZS-series multiprocessors use a shared set of registers for low-overhead interprocess communications. The multiprocessing hardware has been checked out and has been used for small test cases. Simulations reported in this paper use accurate timings based on the actual ZS multiprocessor hardware.

The interconnection network in the ZS multiprocessor system is essentially a crossbar network. The data path is four words (256 bits) wide, and is optimized for 16 word (one cache line) transfers. To support references to non-cacheable data, smaller transfers, down to one byte, can be accommodated, but the timing for smaller transfers is the same as for a full 16 word transfer.

The multiprocessor simulator is a register transfer-level simulator and program interpreter. Based on the instruction and address information supplied by the interpreter, the busy times of the functional units, load and store queues, cache, main memory, registers, pipelines, etc. are modeled. These devices are advanced each clock period in accordance with any dependencies that are present. A file of system parameters is also used by the simulator to define cycle time requirements for the functional units, memory access, and the queues. Additional parameters include cache line size and data associativity, functional unit requirements for each instruction, and the processor clock speed. Except where otherwise noted below, the simulations we ran used system parameter values consistent with the ZS-1 hardware. In the uniprocessor case, we found the simulator timing results to be within 5% of actual running time on the ZS-1. The discrepancy is due to the lack of address translation faults in the simulator. In order to avoid different versions of a "warm cache" between the different hardware configurations tested, the data cache for each processor is flushed before execution of the timed loop. The cold cache approach did not alter the results greatly, and provided each test case with identical starting positions.

## Parallel Program Construction

Parallel programs were constructed for our experiments from two different versions of a matrix multiply program written in (sequential) FORTRAN. The part that we parallelized and tested were the triply nested do loops that are the kernel of the multiply. These nested do loops can be thought of as triply nested doall loops, since there are no data dependencies between the iterations of the loops. The source code we used for our tests and the assembler code generated by the compiler are discussed in the RESULTS section below.

The programs were compiled on the ZS-1, and then disassembled. At the assembly source level, we added instructions to implement the self-scheduling run-time support. Each processor executes the same code, so the run-time support code is responsible for synchronizing these multiple threads of execution and assuring that each processor executes a unique subset of the total work to be done. The run-time support code added to both parallel programs was written to be independent of the number of processors used to execute it. This code only assumes that a count of the number of available processors is provided in one of the semaphore registers.

We parallelized our test programs by allocating microtasks that executed some subset of the iterations of the outermost doall loop. As stated above, we tested three different dynamic scheduling policies, all based on the concept of processor self-scheduling. The first, which we refer to as chunk scheduling, computes an "optimal" chunk size by dividing the number of iterations for the outermost doall loop by the number of processors available. If the numbers do not divide evenly, an extra "chunk" of the leftover iterations is also created. The second scheme, which we simply call self-scheduling, creates one microtask for each iteration of the outermost doall loop. The third technique, called guided-self scheduling, allocates a number of iterations equal to $\lceil \frac{R_i}{p} \rceil$ where $R_i$ is the number of iterations remaining to be scheduled at step $i$ and $p$ is the number of processors [13, 15].

For chunk scheduling, one processor computes the chunk size and places this result, the starting address, and the maximum iteration value in separate semaphore registers. At the starting address, just before the loop bodies, the beginning iteration value for a microtask is converted (using the chunk size and the iteration limit) into beginning and ending values to be used for the loops (e.g., multiplied by word size to make a proper array index). After reading the semaphore registers and before loop execution, another semaphore register is decremented. When this counter reaches zero, it indicates that the semaphore registers can be reloaded with values pertaining to the next parallel loop for execution. While the code to compute the chunk size and load the semaphore registers is executing, all other idle processors are waiting to enter the scheduling code. When the semaphore register holding the total number of iterations to be executed is written and becomes greater than zero, the waiting processors begin executing a fetch&decrement operation on the register to acquire a unique index for that microtask.

The self-scheduling code is similar but less complex. There is no need to compute a chunk size since the chunk size is always equal to one. Also, there is no need to compute an ending value, since the outermost loop is executed only once. This simplifies the code of the loop body by eliminating the test at the end of the outermost loop that normally would determine whether or not the last iteration for that microtask had been executed.

The code for guided self-scheduling is a little more complex. As part of the process of acquiring a unique index for each microtask, several computations must be made to get the proper chunk size as well as the starting and ending values for the iteration range. Because the global number of iterations remaining is the basis for these computations, they must be performed in mutual exclusion until this global value can be updated. This effectively creates a critical section of several assembly language instructions to perform a self-scheduling operation. In addition to holding addresses and key index values, the semaphore registers are also used to implement a binary semaphore that ensures mutual exclusion for the scheduling operation. While the chunk scheduling approach also requires a chunk calculation, it is performed only once before any microtasks begin. For guided self-scheduling, a chunk calculation must be performed at each scheduling point, thus increasing the scheduling code critical section from one fetch&decrement instruction to a lock acquisition and several integer arithmetic instructions.

## Implementing Cache Consistency

In our experiments, we evaluated two software and two hardware consistency schemes. The software schemes consisted of 1) making result data non-cacheable, and 2) using local memory management instructions to merge multiple copies of the result data. The ZS provides mechanisms to make pages of virtual memory non-cacheable as well as several instructions for allocating and flushing cache blocks. The hardware schemes we evaluated are two variants of a central directory based approach to cache consistency. In order to evaluate the hardware schemes accurately, the ZS simulator was modified to incorporate them. These consistency techniques are described in more detail below.

**Software Consistency**   While the first software cache consistency scheme is straight-forward, the second warrants some further explanation. This second consistency technique utilized the "allocate block" and "flush block" instructions to manage a local copy of the result data in each cache. Each processor allocated enough blocks to hold the entire result array at a temporary virtual address distinct from that used by the other processors and distinct from the result area. As a side effect of the allocate block instruction, each word in each block is initialized to a value of zero. Each processor then proceeds with its share of the parallel loop iterations, performing one or more scheduling operations depending on the self-scheduling technique used. After all iterations have been scheduled, the first processor to complete its work proceeds by flushing its entire result area to main memory at a virtual address reserved for the result using multiple flush block instructions. Each successive processor to complete its iterations then, in mutual exclusion with other processors, reads each 64 bit word from the result area, performs an "OR" operation between that word and the corresponding word stored at its temporary location, and places the result at the result area's virtual address. After each word is read and updated, the cached result area is flushed to main memory.

An alternative approach to software consistency would be to flush blocks as they are written in the body of the loop. Techniques for this style of consistency have been proposed in the literature [16]. However, due to the fact that loop iterations are allocated dynamically with our run-time support, and that the compiler produced code accesses words in blocks in a non-sequential fashion, we would have to completely rewrite the generated code as well as restrict iteration allocation in order to ensure consistent results. This problem would be simplified if individual words could be flushed instead of blocks, or if the word size and cache block size were the same. However, reducing the cache block size to such a small value would eliminate the positive effects of spatial locality obtained with a multiword block. A policy of prefetching one word blocks may compensate for this problem [28], but this requires sophisticated compilers and architectural modifications and is beyond the scope of our study.

Several properties of the codes we simulated enabled us to use the temporary result area approach to consistency. The most important property is that while any number of processors may need to access the same logical block, no two processors require access to the same word within a given block. This creates a situation where each cache contains a temporary result area with words that contain either zero or a final result, and, no two caches contain a final result in the same logical word. This enables the OR instruction to be used to merge the temporary result areas. This approach to data consistency has been used in various forms in other systems (e.g., the Myrias computer [18]).

If the temporary result areas are too large to remain in the cache along with the other referenced data for the duration of the loop iteration executions, each processor must allocate its temporary result area at a different virtual address. If block replacement in the cache then effects the result area, its values will not be corrupted by collision with other processor's temporary results. This approach may require that a large virtual memory space be available to the parallel program.

**Hardware Consistency**   The hardware cache consistency schemes we evaluated are based on the central directory approach proposed in [19]. While this approach is similar to the one originally proposed by Tang [29], it requires fewer cache tags and a smaller central directory. A survey of directory based cache consistency techniques can be found in [4].

The hardware consistency scheme implemented requires a central directory with an entry for each block. This entry contains several bits that indicate which caches contain the block and whether or not the main memory copy is up-to-date. In one scheme, originally proposed in [19], each directory entry contains one bit for each cache in the system to indicate the block's presence in that cache. There is also one bit for each entry that indicates whether main memory is up-to-date with a cached block. If it is not, this bit is set, and the block may reside in only one cache. This consistency scheme does not require any additional cache tags than those already provided by the hardware. These include a valid bit, a dirty bit, and least recently used bits.

A write miss makes a block dirty and consequently exclusive to that cache. The directory must be consulted to invalidate any other cached entries. A write hit must also consult the directory and propagate invalidations if the the block is not already dirty (and thus private). The modified bit in the directory must also be set when a write to a block is performed. Read hits and dirty write hits may proceed without accessing the directory. A read miss requires a directory update for that cache's presence bit for that block. Read and write misses must also supply the up-to-date value of the block to the requesting cache. If the modified bit is set in the directory on a cache miss, main memory must read the block from the cache containing the up-to-date value and clear the associated dirty bit before supplying the data to the requesting cache.

A variation of this scheme proposed in [4] was also tested. Instead of providing a presence bit for each cache in each directory entry, only enough bits are provided to encode an index to one cache in the system. This scheme provides exclusive access for each cached block, and requires an invalidation whenever a processor accesses a block that is cached elsewhere in the system.

As mentioned above, our experiments for evaluating hardware cache consistency techniques required some modifications to the simulator, effectively changing the architecture of the ZS. We also made several simplifying assumptions to avoid a detailed redesign of the hardware. The first assumption is that no race conditions exist between checking local cache tags and accessing the central directory. The simulator updates the cache tags, the directory, and performs invalidations at the point of the cache miss. The processor in this case then idles the required number of cycles to simulate the time taken to perform these updates. Any subsequent accesses by other processors always see the most up-to-date cache tags and directory values. Because individual words are not shared in our test programs, subsequent block accesses by other processors need not wait for previous ones to complete before updating cache tags and directory values. The first processor will cache the block and load the referenced word into the load queue, but the block will no longer be valid.

Although cache tags and directory entries are updated instantaneously, processors must wait additional cycles before accesses are complete if the requested memory bank is busy or the block to be accessed is dirty in another cache. We assume that the directory is interleaved across the memory banks so that the block requested resides in the same memory bank as its directory entry. This provides mutual exclusion for directory entries, since only one processor may access a given memory bank at any one time. We also assume that the directory can be updated, any necessary invalidations can be sent, and main memory can be read all in the time it takes to perform a main memory access. If the requested memory block is dirty in another cache, we assume that memory can be updated and the value supplied in one additional main memory access time. Since the requesting processor has control of the main memory bank when the modified bit is checked, we do not queue the request to write the up-to-date cache block back to main memory and update the directory.

The simulator provides interlocks and memory bank arbitration so that banks are accessed in mutual exclusion. Bank conflicts will add delays to the completion of requests, and these times are effectively added to the base memory access times we assume for directory accesses. While our assumptions about race conditions, the ability to send invalidations, the ability to read up-to-date blocks in other caches, and the ability to add a directory to the memory system most certainly simplify our experiments, we believe that these tests do reflect the additional delays brought about by cache misses due to invalidations and memory accesses to modified blocks.

# RESULTS

## Source Code

The programs we used in our experiments are two versions of a double precision floating point matrix multiply. The basis for these programs is kernel 21 of the Livermore FORTRAN Kernels [30]. We produced two versions of generated code for this kernel by interchanging the order of the do loops. In order to encourage the compiler to unroll inner loops and to make parallelization of the program easier, we produced the first version of the code by making the innermost do loop into the outermost do loop. This resulted in the following FORTRAN code:

```
      dimension PX(25,101), CX(25,101), VY(101,25)

      do 15 j = 1, n
      do 15 k = 1, 25
      do 15 i = 1, 25
         PX(i,j) = PX(i,j) + VY(i,k) * CX(k,j)
   15 continue
```

This version produced the fastest code in the sequential case for several reasons. In addition to enabling the compiler to unroll the innermost loop, the indexing patterns in this case produced a unit stride in each of the three arrays. With the large (128 byte) cache line size, this version warmed the cache quickly and produced a minimum of cache misses. Because the innermost loop accesses a different element of the result matrix on each iteration, the compiler did not accumulate partial results in registers. This did not degrade performance, however, as the low number of cache misses combined with the ZS's dual instruction issue capability enabled the average number of cycles per instruction to approach 0.6.

Although the version of the code shown above is the fastest in the uniprocessor case, its heavy use of memory caused it some performance problems when running on multiple processors with consistent caches. For this reason, we tested another version of the matrix multiply kernel. The alternate version was produced by interchanging the "k" and "i" do loops in the program shown above. We chose this restructuring to keep the variable length do loop as the outermost one. This allows a parallelization strategy that creates n microtasks of a fixed granularity, the same technique as used in the previous version. With this strategy, each microtask computes the final result for one column of the PX array. This helps keep different microtasks from accessing values of the PX array that lie within the same cache line.

The indexing pattern of this second version produced unit strides for the PX and CX arrays, but not the VY array. This caused three additional cache misses for the entire multiply in the sequential case. Also, because the innermost loop in this case computes a final result for one element of the PX array, the intermediate results are accumulated in registers before being written to memory. As part of the execution of the "j" loop, some registers are used to hold values of the CX array, reducing the number of memory references in the inner loops. However, all available floating point registers are not used, and some values of the CX array are copied to the local stack instead. Although this version of the code produced only 3 additional cache

|  | ZS-1 | | Private | | Shared | |
|---|---|---|---|---|---|---|
| Program | Time | Eff. | Time | Eff. | Time | Eff. |
| V. 1, n=25 | 2745 | 1.00 | 2745 | 1.00 | 2762 | 0.99 |
| V. 1, n=50 | 5272 | 1.00 | 5272 | 1.00 | 5305 | 0.99 |
| V. 2, n=25 | 3645 | 1.00 | 3645 | 1.00 | 3670 | 0.99 |
| V. 2, n=50 | 7261 | 1.00 | 7261 | 1.00 | 7311 | 0.99 |

Table 1: Sequential code performance for different hardware configurations.

misses, it ran quite a bit slower than the previous version, averaging slightly less than 1 cycle per instruction. This slowdown is caused by the increase in instructions executed to copy the CX array as well as a reduction in execution overlap due to registers being busy during the multiplies and adds of the innermost loop.

## Basic Performance

Table 1 shows the running time (in microseconds) and the efficiency of the first two sequential versions of the code for **n=25** and **n=50** on the different hardware configurations tested. The efficiency of sequential code on the ZS-1 is defined to be 1. The private column refers to the hardware cache consistency scheme where there is an index in the central directory that indicates which cache (if any) has a copy of a block. The shared column refers to the hardware consistency scheme where the directory contains an entry for each block that has a presence bit for each cache. The times for the ZS-1 and private cache consistency configurations are identical, because the cache consistency actions have no effect when only once processor and cache is in use. The times are slightly greater for the shared cache consistency configuration. This reflects the overhead necessary for a directory access on a write hit when the cache block is not already dirty. This situation occurs when data is read (and cached as non-dirty) before it is written. The extra overhead required in this case, however, is minimal.

Table 2 shows the performance for the sequential and parallel versions of the code running on the ZS-1 configuration. The original program is the version generated by the compiler for the uniprocessor. The chunk, self, and guided columns refer to the parallelized codes running on the uniprocessor without any instructions to implement software cache consistency. The running times for the parallel versions of the code are less than the original code in many cases. Although the parallel codes have additional instructions for scheduling and synchronization, their effect is more than offset by the elimination of instructions in the inner loops that is brought about by the parallelization. The eliminated instructions include calculation, comparison, and branch instructions for loop bounds as well as some "nop" instructions that were used to force the proper alignment. Certainly, the run-time support code added to parallelize the program does not significantly degrade performance when the code is run on a single processor.

Figures 1 and 2 show the speedups of the parallel programs for both versions of the code when **n=50** and the codes are simulated for the unmodified ZS hardware. Figure 2 shows the speedups when calculated using the sequential times for both versions of the program. This is done to show both the speedup of this particular

|  | Original | | Chunk | | Self | | Guided | |
|---|---|---|---|---|---|---|---|---|
| Program | Time | Eff. | Time | Eff. | Time | Eff. | Time | Eff. |
| V. 1, n=25 | 2745 | 1.00 | 2641 | 1.04 | 2630 | 1.04 | 2587 | 1.06 |
| V. 1, n=50 | 5272 | 1.00 | 5216 | 1.01 | 5202 | 1.01 | 5108 | 1.03 |
| V. 2, n=25 | 3645 | 1.00 | 3657 | 1.00 | 3720 | 0.98 | 3655 | 1.00 |
| V. 2, n=50 | 7261 | 1.00 | 7274 | 1.00 | 7411 | 0.98 | 7272 | 1.00 |

Table 2: Sequential and parallel code performance the ZS-1.

code and to demonstrate the performance of the second version when it is compared to the "best sequential algorithm". The results are similar for both codes when n=25, but the speedups are about 15% less for 8, 12, and 16 processors. Also, for n=25, the three scheduling algorithms perform almost identically except in the case of 16 processors, where guided self-scheduling is about 11% slower and chunk scheduling is about 3% slower than self-scheduling.

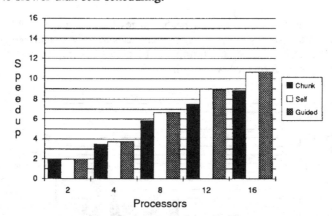

Figure 1: Speedups for n=50, first program version, assumed consistency.

The results in Figs. 1 and 2 represent an upper bound on parallel performance because software or hardware cache consistency has been omitted. The only slow-down in the code due to memory references are due to bank conflicts when multiple processors attempt to access main memory after a cache miss. Based on the small amount of scheduling overhead observed in the single processor results shown above and on the instruction counts for each processor, we can conclude that load balancing is the major limiting factor in the speedup of these programs.

## Software Consistency

Perhaps one of the most interesting results was observed when cache consistency was enforced by making result data non-cacheable. Because the first version of the code does not place temporary results in registers, the speedups of the code in this case is never greater than 1. The second version of the code, however, writes to the result array much less frequently, and the speedups for n=50 when compared to both versions' sequential running times are shown in Fig. 3. These

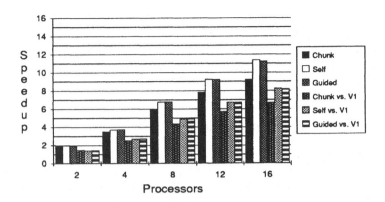

Figure 2: Speedups for n=50, second program version, assumed consistency.

results demonstrate that while non-cacheable pages may be a reasonable technique for maintaining consistency in some cases, such cases must be detectable at compile-time so that the appropriate restructuring can be done. If compile-time detection is not possible, poor performance will result.

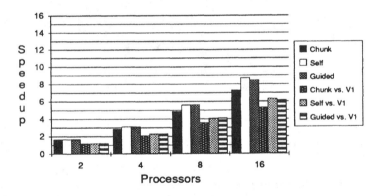

Figure 3: Speedups for n=50, second program version, non-cacheable result.

The performance of the codes implementing cache consistency with temporary result areas and cache management instructions was poor overall. For the first version of the program, the speedup never exceeded 1, and for the second version, it never exceeded 2.4. Although our algorithm for this consistency technique updated the final result area one processor at a time, we computed results based on the assumption that the merging of temporary result areas can be done pairwise in parallel using $\log_2 P$ steps where $P$ is the number of processors. We computed the time needed for one reduction step by taking the differences between successive finishing times for all processors in our original version. We took an average of these differences (which were almost constant) and multiplied it by the number of steps required, $\log_2 P$. (We performed this calculation for values of $P$ equal to 4, 8, and 16). This merging time was then added to the time taken by the processor that finished first in our simulations. This "base" time was only slightly greater than the times for assumed consistency shown above. This calculation of the merging time is optimistic, though, since is does not consider the extra synchronization required to implement this algorithm.

The calculated results for both versions of the source program using each of the scheduling algorithms were nearly identical, indicating that the software consistency actions dominated the running times. The speedup calculated versus the sequential running time of the first version of the source code was never greater than 2.5, while the speedup calculated versus the sequential running time of the second version of the source code was never greater than 3.5. The results did show an increase in speedup as more processors were employed, whereas the original code that updated the final result area one processor at a time showed its best performance at 2.4 with only 4 processors.

## Hardware Consistency

For the hardware consistency tests, the simulator was modified as described in the EXPERIMENTAL TESTBED section above. Since cache consistency was enforced in hardware, there was no need for the programs to use any special cache management or data alignment instructions. The programs used for these tests were identical to those used in the assumed consistency tests shown in Figs. 1 and 2.

The performance of the private hardware scheme for cache consistency was similar to that of the calculated results for software consistency. For the first version of the program, the performance of hardware consistency was worse for fewer number of processors, and better for greater numbers of processors. For the second version of the source code, the private hardware consistency technique always performed worse than the software results, with maximum speedups being less than 2.7 and 2.0 when compared to both versions of the sequential code.

While there was not much variation depending on scheduling algorithms or the value of n for the second version of the source code, the first version showed much more variability. Figure 4 shows the results for the first version of the program with n=50. The results for n=25 show similar trends but smaller speedups, with the exception of chunk scheduling for 2 processors, which performs as well as guided self-scheduling.

It is interesting to note here the difference in performance of the various scheduling algorithms. In the other tests where consistency is assumed or main memory traffic is otherwise reduced, self-scheduling has a slight performance edge for larger numbers of processor because of its improved dynamic load balancing. However, in Fig. 4 we see that chunk scheduling and guided self-scheduling perform better in these experiments. Because they allocate chunks of iterations greater than 1, multiple adjacent iterations are allocated for each schedule. This provides additional spatial locality on each processor which reduces cache misses. This result is more visible for the first version of the program, where memory is accessed frequently.

The other interesting result in Fig. 4 is the performance of chunk scheduling for 16 processors. It is slower than the same program running on 12 processors, because of the chunk calculation algorithm. It computes an optimal chunk size of 1,

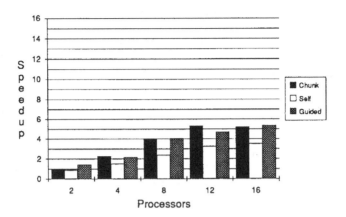

Figure 4: Speedups for n=50, first program version, private hardware consistency.

because that is the result of 25 **div** 16. However, for 12 processors, the chunk size is 2, with 1 extra chunk of size 1 required to finish the loop. The program requires 25 microtasks to run on 16 processors, and the scheduling introduces the locality problem observed with self scheduling. For 12 processors, only 13 microtasks are created, and the first 12 execute 2 adjacent iterations each.

The major problem with the private hardware consistency technique is the slow-down caused by the prevention of sharing of read-only data. This is especially evident for the second version of the source code, where each of the microtasks access the elements of one of the operands in the same order in a non-unit stride fashion. Since an access to any block must invalidate any other copies of that block, there are many more cache misses using this consistency technique.

The performance of the shared hardware consistency scheme was better than any of the other techniques, and approached the performance of assumed consistency for the second version of the source program. The shared hardware consistency mechanism allows any cache block to reside in more than one cache. As long as the block is not modified, no consistency actions are required. This approach avoids the difficulties encountered by the private scheme with read-only data.

Tables 3 and 4 show the running times for both versions of the program using shared hardware consistency. While the execution times for the first version of the source code are faster than those for private hardware consistency, they do show the same trends for the different scheduling algorithms. Because the second version of the program references memory much less often, the speedup of this code for for larger numbers of processors is greater. The performance of the second version of the program using 16 processors and shared hardware consistency is competitive with the first version of the program using assumed consistency. This version also shows more even performance between the different scheduling algorithms, again because memory is accessed less often. Figures 5 and 6 show the speedups for both versions of the program when n=50.

| | Version 1 Times | | | Version 2 Times | | |
|---|---|---|---|---|---|---|
| P | Chunk | Self | Guided | Chunk | Self | Guided |
| 1 | 2656 | 2646 | 2603 | 3683 | 3745 | 3681 |
| 2 | 1420 | 3105 | 1387 | 1941 | 1977 | 1934 |
| 4 | 800 | 1697 | 909 | 1068 | 1080 | 1062 |
| 8 | 493 | 1032 | 628 | 639 | 634 | 627 |
| 12 | 394 | 744 | 637 | 498 | 490 | 489 |
| 16 | 740 | 742 | 632 | 377 | 364 | 405 |

Table 3: Parallel code running times for n=25 with shared hardware consistency.

| | Version 1 Times | | | Version 2 Times | | |
|---|---|---|---|---|---|---|
| P | Chunk | Self | Guided | Chunk | Self | Guided |
| 1 | 5247 | 5235 | 5141 | 7324 | 7460 | 7322 |
| 2 | 2660 | 6193 | 2638 | 3686 | 3780 | 3716 |
| 4 | 1526 | 3294 | 1685 | 2090 | 1983 | 1964 |
| 8 | 910 | 1968 | 959 | 1219 | 1090 | 1082 |
| 12 | 705 | 1353 | 794 | 941 | 793 | 798 |
| 16 | 606 | 1120 | 732 | 812 | 653 | 651 |

Table 4: Parallel code running times for n=50 with shared hardware consistency.

## Scheduling Algorithms

Our experiments did not suggest that any of the three scheduling algorithms tested was clearly the best. The results for assumed consistency suggest that self-scheduling and guided self-scheduling perform about the same, with chunk scheduling running slower. Self-scheduling provides the most speedup for 16 processors, while guided self-scheduling runs faster on fewer processors. Since self-scheduling allocates only 1 iteration for each schedule, it provides the best dynamic load balancing. However, guided self scheduling can come close in load balancing, since smaller chunks are allocated during later schedules. Also, since chunk scheduling and guided-self scheduling allocate more iterations per schedule on average, they have fewer scheduling points at run-time. For this reason, these approaches may incur less scheduling overhead than self-scheduling, even though their scheduling code requires more instructions to compute chunk size and loop bounds.

For the other tests, the performance of the scheduling algorithms depended on the amount of memory accesses in the code. For the first version of the source program, where the number of memory accesses is great, the performance of chunk scheduling was best, with guided self-scheduling being next. As mentioned earlier, this is due to the spatial locality in memory referencing that occurs when adjacent iterations are executed on the same processor. For the second version of the program, where memory accesses are much fewer in number, the pattern described above for assumed consistency was observed, with self-scheduling providing the most speedup in most cases.

These results suggest that different scheduling techniques be used for depending

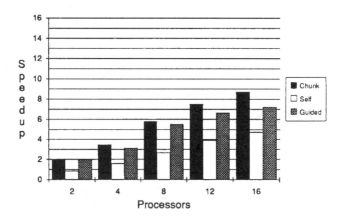

Figure 5: Speedups for n=50, first program version, shared hardware consistency.

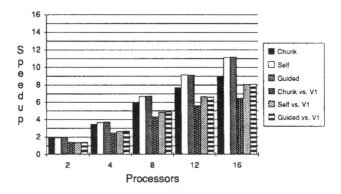

Figure 6: Speedups for n=50, second program version, shared hardware consistency.

on the characteristics of the code inside the parallel loop. However, having seen that the code that accesses memory the least is the most likely to achieve the highest speedup, it seems that compilers should optimize in favor of this type of code, and use self-scheduling because it is easiest. More experiments using larger grain sizes and different source codes are needed before any firm conclusions can be made regarding the scheduling algorithm used.

## CONCLUSIONS AND FUTURE WORK

While our investigation studied several aspects of the performance of parallel loops on a non-bus multiprocessor, it should not be assumed that the results observed in our tests will be repeated on other multiprocessors or with different parallel programs. This work is preliminary and much remains to be done before definite conclusions can be stated. We can, however, reach the following preliminary conclusions based on our experiments.

Our results show shared hardware consistency to be the best technique for maintaining cache consistency. It outperformed the other techniques we tested, including private hardware consistency. This differs with the conclusions offered in [4], where it is conjectured that the performance of shared and private hardware consistency is roughly equal. This may be attributable to the different types of parallelism present in the test programs. We found that a fine-grained parallel program is more likely to shared data than those parallelized at the program level. Also, our tests accounted for the effects of sharing cache blocks even when individual words are not shared. This level of sharing caused too many invalidations in the private hardware consistency case.

The software schemes we tested did not fare well at all, with the possible exception of non-cacheable data for the second version of the source program. The overhead of temporary result areas for consistency seems to be too great for microtasking. Experiments using programs with much higher granularities should be run. However, as the size of the result area grows, so does the overhead in merging these areas. As for non-cacheable data, the performance is directly dependent on the number of references to this data. In some cases, the effect can be devastating. If this technique were to be used seriously in a real machine, hardware techniques to speedup these accesses without blocking the cache should be employed.

While the shared hardware consistency approach performed the best in our tests, there are other tradeoffs to consider when choosing a cache consistency technique. The major disadvantage of this hardware technique is the size of the central directory required. Since a presence bit is required for each cache in the system, the size of the directory is proportional to the number of caches in the system as well as the size of main memory. This situation can prevent the use of this technique in systems with a large number of processors.

There are also problems and tradeoffs to consider when using software schemes for consistency. While the techniques we tested did not perform well, it is possible that techniques using cache management instructions embedded within the parallel loop bodies may perform better. However, these techniques require sophisticated compilers, as well as protection from interrupts or context switching by the operating system. The compiler has to manage the mapping between memory words and cache blocks, to ensure that implicit block sharing does not introduce inconsistency. If the software also assumes the presence of, or absence of, cache blocks based on prefetching or cache management instructions, the operating system must prevent context switching and microtask migration from violating these assumptions. For these reasons, we believe that software consistency schemes are best suited for single user compute-intensive parallel processing systems.

Finally, we can state some basic conclusions about our experience with parallel processing at the microtasking level. First, different optimization strategies must be employed by the compiler depending on the number of processors targeted and the cache consistency technique used. As we have seen in the results listed above, a version of a program that runs slower on a single processor may run faster on multiple processors. Also, optimizing for fewer memory references reduces cache consistency overhead and allows a different scheduling algorithm to be used.

Run-time support overhead for microtasking is not significant, but load balancing and overhead for cache consistency are problems. The single processor results demonstrated that run-time support overhead for parallelism was not expensive. This is probably due, at least in part, to the low overhead synchronization provided by the semaphore registers. The results for multiple processors and assumed consistency demonstrated that load balancing was a limiting factor in speedup for larger numbers of processors. Also, we saw from the results of tests that included cache consistency techniques that the performance of assumed consistency could never be matched. With the exception of shared hardware consistency, this overhead was a major factor in the slowdown of the parallel program.

More parallelism of varying grains is needed. This conclusion follows directly from the previous point. Mechanisms to create more microtasks that are ready to run at any given time should help the load balancing problem. Although this may require more overhead in run-time support code, the tradeoff may well be worth it, since this overhead is quite low with the current technique. Our results also show a maximum efficiency less than 75% with 16 processors. If the source program has a significant fraction of sequential code between parallel loops, overall program efficiency will be quite low. Language extensions or alternate loop restructuring techniques are needed to exploit more parallelism and raise this efficiency level.

In order to confirm all of our conclusions and provide more detailed results, more experiments need to be conducted. We are currently studying the speedup potential of different doacross loops, where cross iteration data dependencies exist that require additional synchronization. We are also developing some language extensions and their run-time support code to provide more parallelism of varying grain sizes. In addition to these new approaches, we also plan to test more loops and complete programs to study the speedup potential of parallel loops with very large iteration counts as well as the effects of sequential sections in complete programs.

**Acknowledgments**   This work is supported in part by the Astronautics Corporation of America and by NSF grant MIP-8802771.

# References

[1] J. Archibald and J. L. Baer, "Cache coherence protocols: Evaluation using a multiprocessor simulation model," *ACM Trans. Computer Systems*, vol. 4, no. 4, pp. 273–298, Nov. 1986.

[2] S. J. Eggers and R. H. Katz, "The effect of sharing on the cache and bus performance of parallel programs," in *Proc. 3rd Int. Conf. Architectural Support for Programming Languages and Operating Systems (ASPLOS III)*, pp. 257–270, Apr. 1989.

[3] S. J. Eggers and R. H. Katz, "Evaluating the performance of four snooping cache coherency protocols," in *Proc. 16th Int. Symp. Computer Architecture*, pp. 2–15, June 1989.

[4] A. Agarwal, R. Simoni, J. Hennessy, and M. Horowitz, "An evaluation of directory schemes for cache coherence," in *Proc. 15th Int. Symp. Computer Architecture*, pp. 280–289, June 1988.

[5] S. Owicki and A. Agarwal, "Evaluating the performance of software cache coherence," in *Proc. 3rd Int. Conf. Architectural Support for Programming Languages and Operating Systems (ASPLOS III)*, pp. 230–242, Apr. 1989.

[6] D. Kuck, Y. Muraoka, and S. Chen, "On the number of operations simultaneously executable in FORTRAN-like programs and their resulting speedup," *IEEE Trans. Computers*, vol. C-21, no. 12, , Dec. 1972.

[7] R. Allen and K. Kennedy, "PFC: A program to convert FORTRAN to parallel form," Tech. Rep. MASC-TR 82-6, Dept. of Mathematical Sciences, Rice University, March 1982.

[8] M. D. Guzzi, D. A. Padua, J. P. Hoeflinger, and D. H. Lawrie, "Cedar FORTRAN and other vector and parallel FORTRAN dialects," in *Proc. Supercomputing '88*, pp. 114–121, Nov. 1988.

[9] B. Leasure et al., "PCF FORTRAN: Language definition," Tech. Rep. Version 1, The Parallel Computing Forum, Aug. 1988.

[10] A. J. Musciano and T. L. Sterling, "Efficient dynamic scheduling of medium-grained tasks for general purpose parallel processing," in *Proc. 1988 Int. Conf. Parallel Processing*, pp. 166–175, Aug. 1988.

[11] A. Norton and W. L. Chang, "Self-scheduling in the runtime environment," Technical Report RC 12572 (#56256), IBM T. J. Watson Research Center, Yorktown Heights, NY, Feb. 1987.

[12] M. Wolfe, "Multiprocessor synchronization for concurrent loops," *IEEE Software*, pp. 34–42, Jan. 1988.

[13] C. D. Polychronopoulos, *Parallel Programming and Compilers*, Kluwer Academic Publishers, Norwell, MA, 1988.

[14] B. J. Smith, "Architecture and applications of the HEP multiprocessor computer system," in *Real Time Processing IV, Proc. of SPIE*, pp. 241–248, 1981.

[15] C. D. Polychronopoulos and D. J. Kuck, "Guided self-scheduling: A practical scheduling scheme for parallel supercomputers," *IEEE Trans. Computers*, vol. C-36, no. 12, pp. 1425–1439, Dec. 1987.

[16] H. Cheong and A. V. Veidenbaum, "A cache coherence scheme with fast selective invalidation," in *Proc. 15th Int. Symp. Computer Architecture*, pp. 299–307, June 1988.

[17] R. Cryton, S. Karlovsky, and K. P. McAuliffe, "Automatic management of programmable caches," in *Proc. 1986 Int. Conf. Parallel Processing*, pp. 229–238, Aug. 1986.

[18] M. Beltrameti, K. Bobey, and J. R. Zorbas, "The control mechanism for the myrias parallel computer system," *ACM Computer Architecture News*, Aug. 1988.

[19] L. M. Censier and P. Feautrier, "A new solution to coherence," *IEEE Trans. Computers*, vol. C-27, no. 12, pp. 1112–1118, Dec. 1978.

[20] K. Hwang and F. A. Briggs, *Computer Architecture and Parallel Processing*, McGraw-Hill, New York, New York, 1984.

[21] A. Gottlieb et al., "The NYU Ultracomputer—Designing a MIMD, shared memory parallel machine," *IEEE Trans. Computers*, vol. C-32, pp. 175–189, Feb. 1983.

[22] M. Dubois, C. Scheurich, and F. A. Briggs, "Synchronization, coherence, and event ordering in multiprocessors," *IEEE Computer*, pp. 9–21, Feb. 1988.

[23] Cray Research Inc., *Cray X-MP Mainframe Reference Manual*, Minneapolis, MN, 1982.

[24] Astronautics Corporation of America, *ZS Central Processor – Architecture Reference Manual*, Madison, WI, 1988.

[25] B. Beck, B. Kasten, and S. Thakkar, "VLSI assist for a multiprocessor," in *Proc. 2nd Int. Conf. Architectural Support for Programming Languages and Operating Systems (ASPLOS II)*, pp. 10–20, Oct. 1987.

[26] J. E. Smith, "Dynamic instruction scheduling and the Astronautics ZS-1," *IEEE Computer*, vol. 22, no. 7, pp. 21–35, July 1989.

[27] J. E. Smith, "Decoupled access/execute computer architectures," *ACM Trans. Computer Systems*, vol. 2, no. 4, pp. 289–308, Nov. 1984.

[28] R. L. Lee, P.-C. Yew, and D. H. Lawrie, "Data prefetching in shared memory multiprocessors," in *Proc. 1987 Int. Conf. Parallel Processing*, pp. 28–31, Aug. 1987.

[29] C. K. Tang, "Cache system design in the tightly coupled multiprocessor system," in *AFIPS Proc. National Computer Conf.*, vol. 45, pp. 749–753, 1976.

[30] F. H. McMahon, "The livermore FORTRAN kernels: A computer test of the numerical performance range," Tech. Rep. UCRL-53745, Lawrence Livermore National Laboratory, Livermore, Calif. 94550, Dec. 1986.

# Predicting the Performance of Shared Multiprocessor Caches

Hendrik A. Goosen and David R. Cheriton
*Computer Science Department*
Stanford University

### Abstract

We investigate the performance of shared caches in a shared-memory multiprocessor executing parallel programs, and formulate simple models for estimating the load placed on the bus by such a shared cache. We analyze three parallel program traces to quantify the amount of sharing that takes place during program execution. These results indicate that shared caches can substantially reduce the load placed on a bus by a large number of processors.

Keywords: shared-memory multiprocessors, shared cache, data reference characteristics.

## 1 INTRODUCTION

There is considerable interest in the design of scalable shared memory multiprocessors. The problem of building such machines is largely that of building a memory system that is fast enough to supply the multiple processors with the data they need to execute programs and communicate with each other.

Modern microprocessors require a multi-level cache design to approach peak performance [8], and some processors already have large instruction and data caches on-chip (e.g., 12 Kbytes in the Intel i860). In such a multilevel cache hierarchy, the majority of the traffic (90% to 99% in uniprocessors with large cache blocks [9]) is absorbed by the first-level cache, which means that the higher level caches are idle most of the time.

In a multiprocessor system, the utilization of a higher-level cache can be increased by sharing it among several processors. Sharing a cache between several processors executing the same parallel program can also improve the hit ratio of the shared cache, and so increase the scalability and performance of the machine.

A bus is an attractive option for connecting multiple processors to a shared memory since it is cheap, reliable, and has low latency. Unfortunately, because of electrical constraints and limited bandwidth, only a small number of processors can be connected to a bus. This problem can be solved by a tree-structured memory system consisting of a hierarchy of shared busses and caches. In such a scheme, only a small number of processors are connected to each bus.

Several such machines have been proposed and are under construction, e.g., the Encore Gigamax [13], and the VMP-MC [3]. The VMP-MC architecture exploits shared caches to increase the scalability of the machine. Preliminary results indicate that substantial reductions are possible in the shared memory bandwidth required per processor when the machine is executing parallel applications. This enables more processors to be used in the system, and therefore increases the potential performance of the machine.

In the rest of this paper we describe simple models for estimating the load placed on the bus by a shared cache. We also present the results of an analysis of parallel program traces, which provide an indication of the potential benefit that can be gained from using shared caches.

## 2  A MODEL

The $n$ processors in the system are divided into $m$ *groups*, where each group of $p = n/m$ processors shares a cache. This is shown in Figure 1. We shall refer to subsystems which are closer to the source of the references than the shared cache is as *upstream*, and anything closer to memory as *downstream*. The nodes labeled $P_1, P_2, \ldots, P_n$ are the processors, the nodes $S_1, S_2, \ldots, S_m$ are the shared caches, and the node labeled *Bus* is the downstream bus. The shared caches $S_i$ are the same size, irrespective of the number of PEs sharing the cache. In the special case where there is no sharing ($m = n, p = 1$), the private caches are denoted by $\hat{S}_1, \hat{S}_2, \ldots, \hat{S}_n$.

The amount of data that has to be transferred from the downstream memory system into a PE or cache will be called the *load* placed by the PE or cache on the downstream bus. The load placed on the bus by $S_i$ is denoted by $l_i$. The load is measured in number of block transfers per second.[1] We use $\hat{l}_i$ to represent the load of $\hat{S}_i$.

---

[1] In this model we consider only the data transfers. In reality there are also other

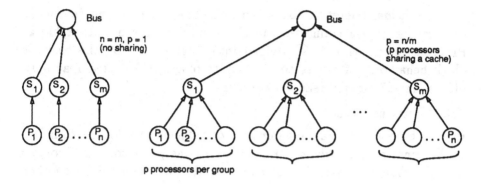

Figure 1: Sharing structure.

The main purpose of a shared cache is to reduce the load that is placed on the downstream system. A reduction in the per-processor load means we can connect more processors to the bus without saturating it. Provided that the latency does not increase too much, the result is that the performance of the system increases (for programs which can use the extra processor cycles).

In this study, the performance of a shared cache configuration is measured by the ratio $R$ between the load placed on the downstream bus by the shared caches, and the load placed on the downstream bus if caches are private:

$$R = \frac{\sum_{i=1}^{m} l_i}{\sum_{j=1}^{n} \hat{l}_j} = \frac{L}{\hat{L}}.$$

$L$ is the total load placed on the downstream bus by the $m$ shared caches, while $\hat{L}$ is the total load placed on the bus by the $n$ caches when the caches are private. If $R = 1$ for a given system, it means that it performs the same as a system with private caches. If $R < 1$, the system performs better than a system with private caches.

A parallel program is considered to execute in a single address space, with multiple lightweight processes (threads). Two processes share a block simply by referring to it with the same virtual address. The programming paradigm we consider here uses a number of processes executing identical code on different items of shared data [5]. Data items are obtained from one or more queues. Barrier synchronization is used to separate different phases in the computation.

---

bus transactions, e.g., invalidation signals, but most of the bus bandwidth is consumed by the block transfers.

We consider references to a given cache block of data, and determine the amount of bus traffic that results from a reference to that block. Program references can be divided into three groups on the basis of block behavior: references to (1) private blocks, (2) shared read-only blocks, and (3) shared read/write blocks.

## 2.1   Private Data

Private blocks interfere with our goal of reducing the downstream bus traffic, since a block which is referenced by one processor, and brought into the shared cache, will not subsequently be referenced by another processor. Although these references form a substantial fraction of the data references (60% to 70%) in the parallel programs we examined, most of these references hit in the caches, and do not cause any bus traffic.

Most of the code in a parallel program is shared by all the processors, so there are few instruction fetches from private code. Private data is dominated by references to the stack and dynamic temporary variables.

Finally, the shared caches are large and block replacement is rare. Private blocks tend to stay in the cache for a long time, which means that reference to private blocks is largely a cold-start phenomenon. Therefore we do not further consider private data.

## 2.2   Shared Read-only Data

The *degree of sharing* $(k)$ of a shared block is defined as the number of different processors that access the block during program execution. For shared read-only blocks, the reduction of traffic depends on $k$.

Although $R$ depends on the exact sequence of references made by each processor, we can estimate the value of $R$ under a set of reasonable assumptions. We assume infinite caches, and that blocks are never replaced once they are in a cache. If a block is shared by $k$ processors, then there are $\binom{n}{k}$ ways to assign the block to $n$ processors. Each of these combinations $c$, where $1 \leq c \leq \binom{n}{k}$, places a load $L_c$ on the downstream bus. The total load $C$ on the downstream bus is found by summing the products of $P\{c\}$ (the probability of $c$) and $L_c$. We assume that each combination $c$ is equally likely, so that $P\{c\} = 1/\binom{n}{k}$:

$$C = \sum_{c=1}^{\binom{n}{k}} L_c P\{c\} = \frac{1}{\binom{n}{k}} \sum_{c=1}^{\binom{n}{k}} L_c. \qquad (1)$$

The load $L_c$ can be calculated by noticing that one block transfer is required into every shared cache which contains at least one processor

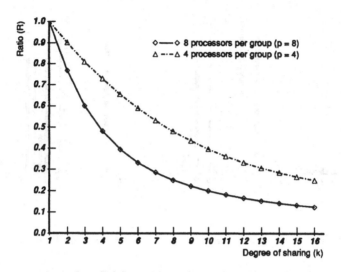

Figure 2: Ratio $R$ for $p = 4$ and $p = 8$ configurations, $n = 16$.

referencing that block. If there are no processors referencing the block in a particular shared cache, no block transfer is required into that cache.

Figure 2 shows $R$ for two different configurations of a 16 processor system, calculated using equation 1. In the first configuration, the system consists of four groups of four processors each ($m = p = 4$), and in the second it consists of two groups of eight processors each ($m = 2, p = 8$). If $k = n$, then $R = 1/p$, which means the downstream traffic out of a shared cache is independent of the number of processors sharing the cache.

To get an idea of the performance improvement one can expect from real programs, we measured $k$ for all the read-only shared data in the three programs (*mp3d*, *dcsim*, and *locusroute*) described in Appendix A. The histograms in Figure 3 show the number of reads to all read-only blocks for each value of $k$.

From these histograms we can calculate an average value for $k$ to use in estimating $R$. For *mp3d*, $k = 14$, for *locusroute* $k = 4.5$, and for *dcsim* $k = 8.5$. These values were obtained by weighting each value of $k$ according to the number of references it received. $R$ can be read off the graph in Figure 2.

With finite caches, replacement interference becomes a factor. If the shared cache is the same size as the private cache, it is likely that the

158

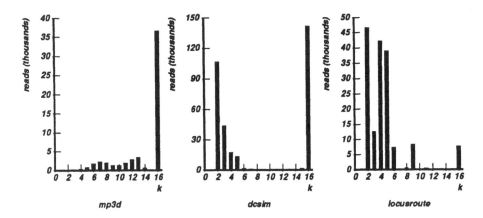

Figure 3: Number of references to shared read-only data (block size 4 bytes).

interference in the shared cache will be higher than that in the private cache, simply because the combined working sets of the PEs connected to the shared cache will be larger than the working set of the single PE connected to the private cache. However, with very large caches this is a small effect, since replacement is very rare in large caches. In addition, it is always possible to increase the size of the shared cache to the point where the interference will be comparable to that of the private case.

## 2.3 Read/write Shared Data

The behavior of read/write shared blocks is more complex, since consistency has to be maintained between all the caches. The details of this behavior depends on the cache coherence protocol that is used. As a reference point, this discussion is carried out in terms of the ownership protocol used in the VMP multiprocessor [4].

The VMP ownership protocol works as follows: a cache block can be in one of two states, shared or private. In shared mode, only read access is allowed. If a processor wants to write to a block, the block has to be in private mode. In shared mode, a block can be present in more than one cache at a time, while in private mode it may only be in one cache at a time. When a block is read in private mode, all copies of the block in other caches have to be invalidated. The protocol also allows a shared block to be converted to a private block, but we will not consider that case here.

The parameter $k$ is not useful for predicting the performance of a shared cache on read/write shared data, since these blocks typically do not stay in a cache for very long, but are invalidated whenever another processor wants to write to that block. To take this into consideration, we propose the *readership* metric ($d$):

**Readership:** the average number of different processors (excluding the owner of the block) which read a block between the start of one write run and the start of the next write run[2] on the block. The readership measures the extent of read-sharing of read/write shared blocks. If the readership of a block is high, a shared cache can reduce the traffic on the downstream bus as we discussed earlier for read-only shared blocks.

We investigate the behavior for two simple systems of $n$ processors. Assume that $k = n$, and consider the ratio $R$ for two extreme cases: $d = n - 1$ and $d = 0$. Again, we assume infinite caches with uniformly distributed references from all processors which share a block.

1. If $d = n - 1$, all processors are expected to read the block before somebody writes it. $\hat{L} = n$, since there are $n - 1$ transfers of the block when everybody reads it, followed by 1 transfer when it is written back, for every write. In the case where $p$ processors share a cache, there will be $m$ transfers for every write, using the same arguments as for read-only shared blocks. Therefore, $R = m/n = 1/p$.

2. When $d = 0$, all references to the shared block are writes (this serves to show the other extreme of behavior). The probability that any $P_i$ will read the block is $1/n$. $\hat{L} = 2(n - 1)/n$, since if $P_i$ has a block in private mode, the next write will be from $P_i$ with probability $1/n$ and cost 0, or it will be from one of the other processors with probability $(n - 1)/n$ and cost 2 block transfers (one for the write-back, one for the read). $L = 2(m - 1)/m$, since if $P_i$ has the block in private mode, it will also be in the shared cache $S_j$, where $j = \lfloor i/p \rfloor + 1$, and the next processor to read the block will be in the same group with probability $1/m = p/n$ and cost 0, or in another group with probability $(m - 1)/m$ and cost 2

---

[2]A write run [5] is defined as a sequence of write references to a shared block by a single processor, uninterrupted by any accesses by other processors.

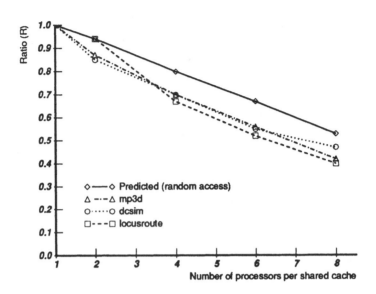

Figure 4: Measured and predicted values of $R$ for random read/write access.

block transfers. Therefore,

$$R = L/\hat{L} = \frac{n(m-1)}{m(n-1)}. \tag{2}$$

Figure 4 shows the value of $R$ plotted using equation 2, as $p$ changes from 1 to 8. Also shown in this figure is $R$ measured for three different programs, *dcsim*, *mp3d*, and *locusroute*. These results are from [3], and were obtained using trace-driven simulation. The programs were designed to run on a conventional multiprocessor, and no attempt was made to exploit locality in the data structures. The data reference patterns are random, and the results are close to those predicted by equation 2.

The preceding discussion assumed a uniform distribution of references from processors sharing a block. However, in the case of read/write shared data, there is the potential to achieve very small values of $R$ by appropriately structuring the algorithm and data structures. For example, if we can ensure that all processors in one group will write to the block before a processor from another group writes to it, $R$ will improve to $m/n = 1/p$, the same as for shared read/only data. We can do even better than this if we write programs so that read/write data is parti-

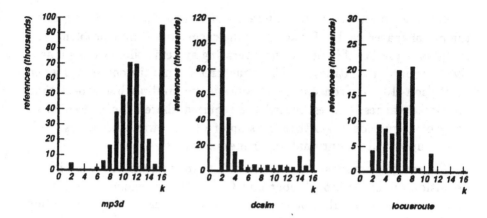

Figure 5: Number of references to shared read/write data (block size 4 bytes).

tioned so that only one group accesses a partition most of the time. In this case, $R$ can approach 0.

This is of course predicated on the degree of sharing that actually exists in parallel programs: if it turns out that $k$ is small, it will not help very much to organize data for maximum sharing. To get an idea of the values of $k$ that one can expect in real programs, we collected the same type of histograms for read/write shared data that we earlier showed for read-only data.

Calculating average values from these histograms (using the same method as for read-only blocks) yield $k = 12$ for mp3d, $k = 7$ for dcsim, and $k = 6$ for locusroute. These values suggest that it may indeed be possible to achieve significant improvements in $R$ by proper data placement and the best assignment of processes to processors. This is especially important since our simulations indicate that read/write shared data accounts for most of the traffic in a shared-memory multiprocessor executing parallel programs.

We are developing a measure of this group locality, so that we can evaluate how successful our efforts at program restructuring are. Such a metric must be a good predictor of shared cache performance, and must also be computationally feasible.

## 3  RELATED WORK

Multi-level bus structures were first proposed in the Cm* [10] architecture. Several commercial machines have used shared caches [7, 2], although their motivations are different from ours. Yeh [15, 14] suggested the use of shared caches for avoiding the cache consistency problem, and recognized the benefits of sharing operating system code. A comprehensive overview of multi-level cache structures for multiprocessors is given by Wilson [13]. He concentrated more on the multiple bus aspect than on shared caches, and estimated the required shared cache sizes as an order of magnitude larger than the sum of all the lower level caches. This is not supported by our analysis or measurements.

Eggers [5, 6] proposes the notion of a write run, which we use in our definition of readership. Weber and Gupta [11] provided distributions of the number of invalidations per write, so the readership distribution can be calculated from their data. Agarwal and Gupta [1] defined and measured clings and pings for shared data, and also provided some initial data on write invalidation distributions for small numbers of processors.

## 4 SUMMARY AND CONCLUSIONS

We presented simple models that can be used to arrive at rough estimates of the expected performance of a shared cache under various circumstances. These models show that a shared cache can reduce the load placed by multiple processors on a global bus. We presented initial results of a study of parallel program traces, and gave values for the degree of block sharing for these programs. This showed that, in the traces we examined, both read-only and read-write shared data were shared by a significant fraction of the processors in the system. This paper describes work in progress, and we are currently developing better models of group locality. Specific efforts include: measuring the effect of data restructuring and processor assignments on group locality, comparing different group locality metrics in terms of computational cost and quality, and measuring the effect of block size on locality.

## 5 ACKNOWLEDGMENTS

The Defense Advanced Research Projects Agency partly sponsored this work under Contract N00014-88-K-0619. Hendrik Goosen is supported by an IBM graduate fellowship. We are grateful to Wolf Weber and Anoop Gupta for providing the traces used in this study. Thanks are also due to Ed Sznyter, Kieran Harty and John Hennessy for comments on earlier drafts of this paper.

# Appendix A   Program Traces

The traces used in these studies were all multiprocessor traces of 16-processor machines, obtained by running a multiprocessor simulator using the VAX T-bit mechanism to step the processes through their references in round-robin fashion. The traces do not include operating system references. Each trace consists of more than 7 million references, of which about half are data references. For a more detailed description of the programs see [11].

locusroute:   This is a global router for VLSI standard cells. Each processor removes a wire from the task queue and selects the best route for that wire. The cost data structure on which the routing is based is shared by all the processors, and updates to this global structure is made without locking.

mp3d:   This is a three-dimensional particle simulator for rarefied flow. Particle properties are stored in separate arrays. During each time step, the particles are moved one at a time. One lock protects an index into the global particle array. Because of the poor data layout, this program will not perform well on a cache-based multiprocessor.

dcsim:   This is a distributed logic simulator which does not rely on a global time during simulation. The trace does not include references to locks.

# References

[1] A. Agarwal and A. Gupta. Memory reference characteristics of multiprocessor applications under MACH. In *Proc. SIGMETRICS*, 1988.

[2] Alliant. FX/Series product summary. Technical report, Alliant Computer Systems Corporation, June 1985.

[3] D.R. Cheriton, H.A. Goosen, and P.D. Boyle. Multi-level shared caching techniques for scalability in VMP-MC. In *Proc. 16th Int. Symp. on Computer Architecture*, pages 16–24, May 1989.

[4] D.R. Cheriton, G. Slavenburg, and P. Boyle. Software-controlled caches in the VMP multiprocessor. In *Proc. 13th Int. Conf. on Computer Architecture*, pages 366–374, June 1986.

[5] S.J. Eggers and R.H. Katz. Sharing in parallel programs. In *Proc. 15th Int. Symp. of Computer Architecture*, pages 373–382, June 1988.

[6] S.J. Eggers and R.H. Katz. The effect of sharing on the cache and bus performance of parallel programs. In *Proc. ASPLOS-III*, pages 2–15, April 1989.

[7] A. Hattori, A Koshino, and S. Kamimoto. Three-level hierarchical storage system for FACOM M-380/382. In *AFIP*, pages 253–262. AFIP, June 1982.

[8] S. Przybylski, M. Horowitz, and J.L. Hennessy. Performance trade-offs in cache design. In *Proc. 15th Int. Symp. on Computer Architecture*, pages 290–298, May 1988.

[9] A.J. Smith. Cache Evaluation and the Impact of Workload Choice. In *Proc. 12th Int. Symp. on Computer Architecture*, pages 64–73, June 1985.

[10] R.J. Swan, S.H. Fuller, and D.P. Siewiorek. Cm*: a modular multi-microprocessor. In *AFIPS Conf. Proc.*, volume 46. National Comp. Conf., 1977.

[11] W.D. Weber and A. Gupta. Analysis of cache invalidation patterns in multiprocessors. In *Proc. ASPLOS-III*, pages 243–256, April 1989.

[12] W.D. Weber and A. Gupta. Exploring the benefits of multiple hardware contexts in a multiprocessor architeture: Preliminary results. In *Proc. 16th Int. Symp. on Computer Architecture*, pages 273–280, May 1989.

[13] Andrew W. Wilson, Jr. Hierarchical cache/bus architecture for shared memory multiprocessors. In *Proc. 14th Int. Conf. on Computer Architecture*, pages 244–253, June 1987.

[14] P.C.C. Yeh. *Shared cache organization for multiple-stream computer systems*. PhD thesis, Univ. Illinois, 1982. Coordinated Science Lab., Rep. R-904.

[15] P.C.C. Yeh, J.H. Patel, and E.S. Davidson. Shared cache for multiple-stream computer systems. *IEEE TC*, C-32(1):38–47, January 1983.

# THE CACHE COHERENCE PROTOCOL OF THE DATA DIFFUSION MACHINE

Erik Hagersten and Seif Haridi
Swedish Institute of Computer Science
Box 1263
S-164 28 Kista, Sweden
hag@sics.se, seif@sics.se

David H.D. Warren
Dep. of Computer Science
University of Bristol
Bristol BS 8 1 TR, U.K.
warren@compsci.bristol.ac.uk

**Abstract** *The Data Diffusion Machine (DDM) is a scalable shared address space multiprocessor in which the location of a datum in the machine is completely decoupled from its address. In particular, there is no distinguished home location where a datum must normally reside. Instead data migrates automatically to where it is needed, reducing access times and traffic.*

*The hardware organisation consists of a hierarchy of buses and data controllers linking an arbitrary number of processors each having a large set-associative memory. Each data controller has a set-associative directory containing status bits for data under its control. The controller supports remote data access by "snooping" on the buses above it and below it. The data access protocol it uses provides for the automatic migration, duplication and replacement of data while maintaining data coherency.*

*The machine is scalable in that there may be any number of levels in the hierarchy. Only a few levels are necessary in practice for a very large number of processors. Most memory requests are satisfied locally. Requests requiring remote access cause only a limited amount of traffic over a limited part of the machine, and are satisfied within a small time that is logarithmic to the number of processors. Although designed particularly to provide good support for the parallel execution of logic programs, the architecture is very general in that it does not assume any particular processor, language or class of application.*
Keywords:Multiprocessor, hierarchical architecture, hierarchical buses, multilevel cache, shared memory, split transaction bus, cache coherence.

---

[1] A different version of this paper is to appear in the Proceedings of the Parallel Architectures and Languages Europe Conference, PABLE, 1989.

# 1   INTRODUCTION

Message-passing machines and shared-memory machines are the two main classes of parallel (MIMD) computer, and are generally considered to be quite distinct. Message-passing machines typically have many processors with large private memories, linked together by a communications network. Shared-memory machines typically have only a limited number of processors with small private memories or caches, connected by a common bus to a large, physically shared, memory. Message passing machines usually require software to view memory access and communication with other processors as quite separate mechanisms. Software often simulates a form of shared address space, by translating references to remote objects into appropriate messages. Shared-memory machines, on the other hand, usually support shared address space directly, thereby allowing software to achieve communication implicitly through memory access, but require some locking mechanisms to support this. Message-passing machines are generally **scalable** to arbitrary numbers of processors, whereas in shared-memory machines the shared bus and memory is a bottleneck, placing a limit on the number of processors that can be attached. However, message-passing machines place a much heavier burden on software to partition the computation effectively, and so the scalability of the hardware is only useful insofar as the software can keep communication to a minimum.

The DDM is like a message-passing machine in that memory is distributed and the machine is scalable to an arbitrary number of processors. The DDM is like a shared-physical-memory machine in that it supports a shared address space and processors are connected via buses. The key idea behind the DDM, which distinguishes it from both message-passing machines and shared memory machines, is that the location of a data item in the machine is completely decoupled from its address.

The design of the DDM is based on the following considerations. Where a piece of data resides is not really relevant to the software. Ideally, the physical location of data should be transparent to the software. All the software needs is some means of identifying each data item, which is just the address. Rather than have software control the physical placement of data, this should be taken care of automatically by hardware. Thus addresses should be mapped into physical location in a totally flexible manner. The mapping should be dynamic, allowing data to migrate to where it is most needed. It may be desirable to have multiple copies of a particular data item, but they will all share the same address. To summarize, from a software point of view there will be of a number of processes sharing data that is arranged logically in a single shared address space; from a hardware point of view, processes will be mapped into processors and addresses into physical locations in such a way that most of a processor's memory accesses can be satisfied by its local memory. In other words, the data structure that the software sees will distribute itself automatically over the machine in such a way as to reduce data access times and minimize data traffic.

The DDM was motivated by our work on logic programming execution models and represents our ideas on how these models can best be supported by hardware. The design, however, is very general in that it does not assume any particular kind of processor, language or application. We feel this is very

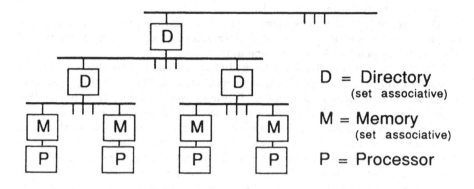

Figure 1: The Data Diffusion Machine

important if the machine is to gain practical acceptance, and is an important factor in the commercial success of machines such as the Sequent. It should be noted that software designed for conventional shared-memory machines can run without change on a DDM.

The remainder of the paper is organized as follows. In the first section we describe the main feature of the hardware organization. The next section is an introduction to the protocol. Next is a discussion over the need for and implementation of replacement, followed by some remarks of the hardware requirements of the machine. Next we analyze performance characteristics of the machine, and compares it with other architectures. We conclude the paper by bringing up various other issues and a summary of the main novel features of the design. At the end of the paper protocol tables defining the protocols used is to be found.

# 2   OVERVIEW OF THE ARCHITECTURE

The machine is hierarchical (see fig. 1). At the tips of the hierarchy are processors each with a large local memory (possibly accessed via a conventional cache). The memory contains an image of some part of the global shared address space. The memory is set-associative, and is organized like a (very large) cache, but it should be emphasized that this is the sole form of main memory in the machine. The memory is connected via a memory controller to a local bus. The local bus connects a cluster of similar configurations of processor, cache, memory and controller. The local bus may itself be connected via a controller to a higher bus, and so on up the hierarchy. The higher level controllers each have access to a directory of status information, and are termed directory controllers. The directory is set-associative, and has space for status bits for all the data items in the memories below.

Data are stored in blocks, items. The item size is fairly small, possibly a couple of words, and is to be decided after extensive simulation. Memory and directories views a block as being one unit.

The function of a controller is to mediate between the bus above it and the subsystem below it. Its behavior is a generalization of the "snooping" caches in single-bus shared memory processors. It allows memory requests to be handled as locally as possible, but where a request cannot be handled locally, it is responsible for transmitting that request upward or downward to enable it to be satisfied. The controller has access to a directory which tells it which part of the shared address space is mapped into the memory of the subsystem below it, and whether any of those addresses are also mapped into memory outside the subsystem. Thus for any address, the controller can answer the questions "Is this item below me?" and "Does this item occur elsewhere (not below me)?".

The controller prevents unnecessary communication from entering and leaving its subsystem. A memory request will not be transmitted outside a subsystem if (1) it is a read of a local item or (2) it is a write to an unshared local item. In particular, this means that if a processor tries to read an item in its local memory or write an unshared item in its local memory, no external communication is required. Normally, this will cover the vast majority of memory references. A memory request will not be transmitted into a subsystem unless (1) the item resides in the subsystem and (2) the subsystem is selected (only if the item resides in more than one subsystem).

If a subsystem tries to read a nonlocal item, a read request will be propagated as far as is necessary to retrieve a copy of the item, and the item will be marked as shared where necessary. If a subsystem tries to write a shared item, a request will be propagated to erase all other copies of the item, and the item will then be marked as unshared.

If a memory becomes full, data items that are shared elsewhere can be discarded; the machine will select items which are least recently used; if there is no such item, an exclusive item that is least recently used will be moved elsewhere. This is another means by which data tend to reside only where it is being actively used.

The following points should be noted. The data that a processor creates itself will automatically reside in its own memory and will not be copied anywhere else unless another processor requires it. A processor is likely to spend most of its time accessing such data. A processor is not obliged to repeatedly access an item from a remote memory, if the data is initially remote. Instead, remote data tends to migrate to where it is being actively used, and is not tied to some fixed "home" location.

# 3 INTRODUCTION TO THE DDM PROTO-COLS

A multicache system introduces the cache coherence problem. A item can reside in many caches. On writes, the consistency of the system has to be kept, i.e., at any time a item can only have one value. Single-bus systems use snooping protocols where all caches snoop all transactions on the common bus to maintain consistency. We have developed a hierarchical snooping protocol, where caches (our memories) and directories only snoop the bus above them, i.e., only a small portion of the transactions in the system. Transactions are received from below in parallel with the snooping.

Each item has a state associated with it. The protocol specifies a new state and a transaction to perform based on the current state and the transaction received. The protocol is specified by four state-transition tables at the end of the paper: memory below, memory above, directory below and directory above.

## 3.1 The Ideal Model

The examples below show the state changes and transitions for **one** address. We will walk through a couple of examples.

There are three stable states in the DDM:

**I** Invalid. The subsystem does not contain the item.

**E** Exclusive. This subsystem and no other contains the item.

**S** Shared. This subsystem and possibly other subsystems contain the item.

Transient states will be introduced when needed.

Figure 2 shows a picture of an initial, two-level system with the item residing in the second of the ten processors, P2. Thus, P2 and all directories directly above it each have the item in state E. Everywhere else the item is in state I (nonexistent).

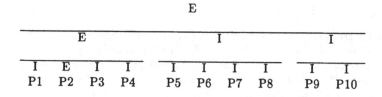

Figure 2: The initial system

The examples assume an ideal system; i.e., memories never get full, buses are never busy, all transactions take the same time, all buses work synchronously and independently of each other, and no buffers are used. State transitions and bus transactions are indexed to indicate in which order they take place.

## 3.2 Local Read on One Bus

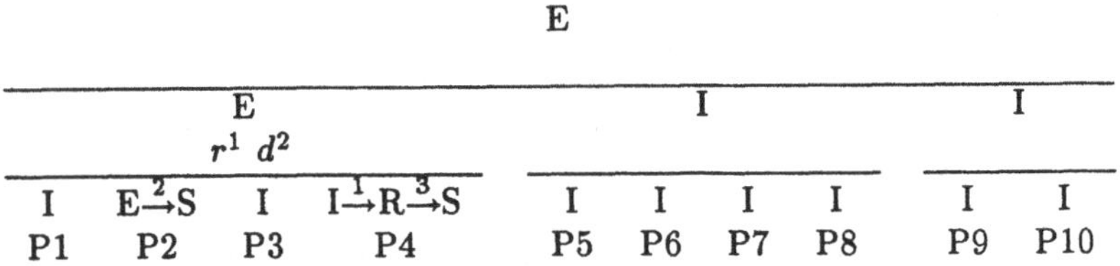

E

```
              E                        I                I
           r¹ d²
  ─────────────────────────   ───────────────   ──────────
   I   E-²→S   I   I-¹→R-³→S     I   I   I   I     I    I
   P1   P2    P3     P4          P5  P6  P7  P8    P9  P10
```

[1] A read by processor 4 to the I item generates a *read* (r). P4 changes its state to R.

[2] The memory with a copy of the item responds with a *data* (d) and changes its state to S.

[3] The requesting memory receives the *data* and puts it in state S.

NOTE: The directory above the bus in the example did not interact in the action described, since the action was local to its subsystem. The directory had the item in state E and anticipated a response from somewhere in its subsystem. No unnecessary bus traffic was generated outside the subsystem.

Figure 3: Local read on one bus

Processors read item in state S or E locally without involving the protocol. In the figure 3, however, P4 tries to read an item in state I. The memory controller generates a *read* transaction on the bus above and temporarily changes the state to R. The need for this state is explained later.

## 3.3 Nonlocal Read

The *read* and *data* transactions in figure 3 are two separate transactions. The bus is released between the two transactions, while *data* is being prepared. The R state is used to remember which memory asked for the item. Nonlocal reads involve several buses. Here it is even more important not to lock all those buses for the whole read operation. Let's introduce two transient states.

**R** Reading. This subsystem has sent a *read* request and is waiting for *data* to arrive.

**A** Answering. This subsystem has promised to answer a *read* request.

State R marks the path of the *read* request on its way up, and state A marks the path on its way down. The *data* uses these states to find its way back to the requesting memory. In figure 4 we start with the final state of figure 3. Now P6 tries to read the item.

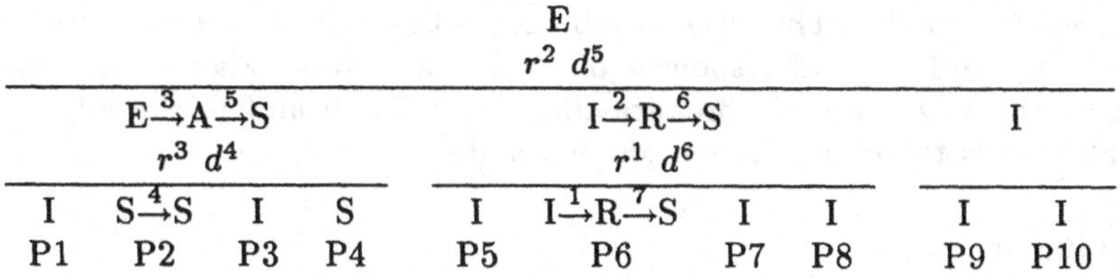

$$E$$
$$r^2\ d^5$$

| $E \xrightarrow{3} A \xrightarrow{5} S$ | $I \xrightarrow{2} R \xrightarrow{6} S$ | $I$ |
|---|---|---|
| $r^3\ d^4$ | $r^1\ d^6$ | |

| I | $S \xrightarrow{4} S$ | I | S | I | $I \xrightarrow{1} R \xrightarrow{7} S$ | I | I | I | I |
|---|---|---|---|---|---|---|---|---|---|
| P1 | P2 | P3 | P4 | P5 | P6 | P7 | P8 | P9 | P10 |

[1] A read by P6 to an I item generates a *read* and changes the state to R.

[2] The directory detects a nonlocal action and repeats the *read* upwards, changing its state to R.

[3] A directory with state E answers the request by changing its state to A, sending *read* below.

[4] One of the memories, P2, is selected to service the *read*. It stays in S and sends *data* .

[5] The directory in state A has promised to answer. It send *data* above and changes its state to S.

[6] The directory in state R is waiting for the *data*. It changes state to S and sends the *data* below.

[7] The memory in state R is waiting for the *data*. It receives the *data* and changes state to S .

NOTE 1: Many subsystems on a bus may have an item in state S. Letting all of them reply with the *data* would produce unnecessary bus transactions; instead, one is selected in phase 4.

NOTE 2: After phase 3, the return path for data is marked with As and Rs.

Figure 4: Nonlocal read

## 3.4  Combining Reads

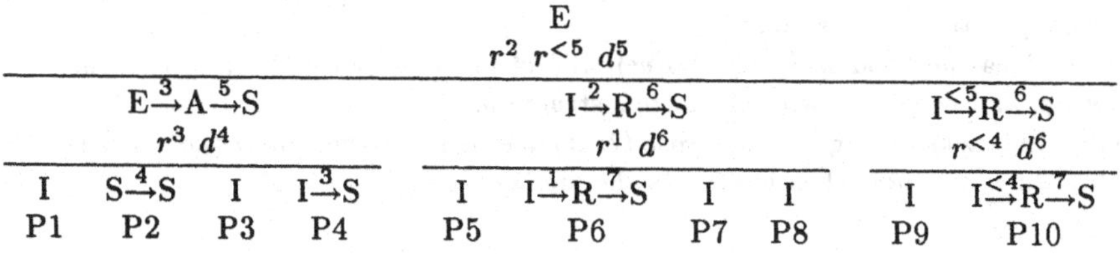

$$E$$
$$r^2\ r^{<5}\ d^5$$

| $E \xrightarrow{3} A \xrightarrow{5} S$ | $I \xrightarrow{2} R \xrightarrow{6} S$ | $I \xrightarrow{<5} R \xrightarrow{6} S$ |
|---|---|---|
| $r^3\ d^4$ | $r^1\ d^6$ | $r^{<4}\ d^6$ |

| I | $S \xrightarrow{4} S$ | I | $I \xrightarrow{3} S$ | I | $I \xrightarrow{1} R \xrightarrow{7} S$ | I | I | I | $I \xrightarrow{<4} R \xrightarrow{7} S$ |
|---|---|---|---|---|---|---|---|---|---|
| P1 | P2 | P3 | P4 | P5 | P6 | P7 | P8 | P9 | P10 |

[<4] P10 also reads before phase 4.

[<5] A second *read request* will appear on the top bus generating no extra action.

[6,7] The *data* originally intended for P6 will also be received by P10.

Figure 5: Combining read, broadcasting

It is common that many processors try to read the same item; i.e., "the hot spot phenomenon" [8]. The DDM combines read requests to the same item on their way up and on read responses on their way down. Figure 5 shows combining on the way down, or "broadcasting." It differs from figure 4 only in that P10 also reads the item between phase 1 and 4.

## 3.5 Writing

While the main goal of reading is finding and delivering an item, writing involves worrying about the consistency. Processors are only allowed to write to an item in state E. If the item is in state S, all other copies are erased before writing is allowed. A subsystems waiting for all other copies to be erased use a new transient state.

**W** Waiting. This subsystem is waiting to become exclusive.

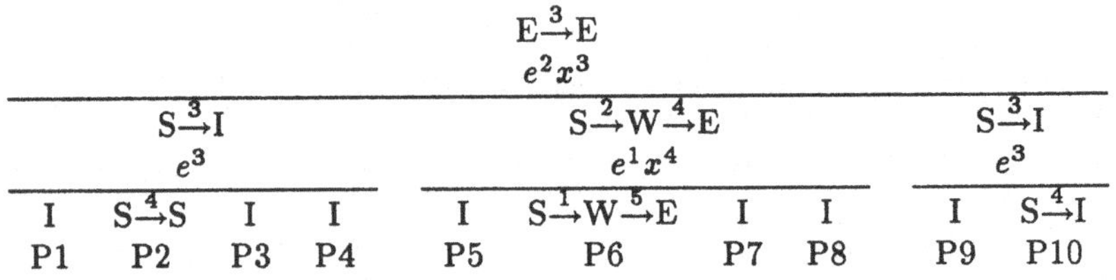

$$E \xrightarrow{3} E$$
$$e^2 x^3$$

| $S \xrightarrow{3} I$ $e^3$ | | | | $S \xrightarrow{2} W \xrightarrow{4} E$ $e^1 x^4$ | | | | $S \xrightarrow{3} I$ $e^3$ | |
|---|---|---|---|---|---|---|---|---|---|
| I | $S \xrightarrow{4} S$ | I | I | I | $S \xrightarrow{1} W \xrightarrow{5} E$ | I | I | I | $S \xrightarrow{4} I$ |
| P1 | P2 | P3 | P4 | P5 | P6 | P7 | P8 | P9 | P10 |

[1] P6 tries to write to the shared item generates an *erase* (e) and changes state to W.

[2] The directory detects a non local *erase*, changes its state to W and retransmits *erase* above.

[3] Directories in state S detecting receiving an erase from above, change state to I and repeat the *erase* below. The top directory detects a local erase in its subsystem and replies with an *exclusive* (x) below.

[4] The directory in state W receiving a *exclusive* from above knows that it has the only valid copy. It changes to state E and repeats the *exclusive* below. P2 and P10 also gets their copies erased .

[5] P6 receives the good news (*exclusive*), and changes its state to E, carries out the write, and continues with the next instruction.

NOTE: The acknowledge of the *erase* (*exclusive*) is sent when the *erase* reaches the top directory, not when it reaches the memories.

Figure 6: Nonlocal write

Trying to write to an item in state I (write miss) results in a read followed by a write.

Figure 6 starts with the final state of figure 5, P6 writes to a shared item.

## 3.6 Write race

Race conditions, like two memories trying to write the same item, are solved by the bus arbitration of a real system. Unlike the ideal system in our examples, a real bus arbitrates between the subsystems connected to it. One is selected to carry out the next transaction. The first *erase* to be selected by a bus will cancel any other erases to the same item and wins the write race. The losing memory will generate a new write automatically.

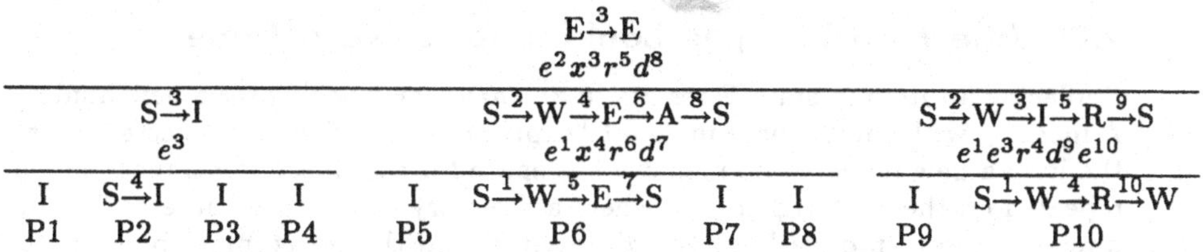

$$E\xrightarrow{3}E$$
$$e^2x^3r^5d^8$$

| $S\xrightarrow{3}I$ | | | | $S\xrightarrow{2}W\xrightarrow{4}E\xrightarrow{6}A\xrightarrow{8}S$ | | | | $S\xrightarrow{2}W\xrightarrow{3}I\xrightarrow{5}R\xrightarrow{9}S$ | |
|:---:|:---:|:---:|:---:|:---:|:---:|:---:|:---:|:---:|:---:|
| $e^3$ | | | | $e^1x^4r^6d^7$ | | | | $e^1e^3r^4d^9e^{10}$ | |
| I | $S\xrightarrow{4}I$ | I | I | I | $S\xrightarrow{1}W\xrightarrow{5}E\xrightarrow{7}S$ | I | I | I | $S\xrightarrow{1}W\xrightarrow{4}R\xrightarrow{10}W$ |
| P1 | P2 | P3 | P4 | P5 | P6 | P7 | P8 | P9 | P10 |

[1-2] Similar to figure6, both *erases* work their way up towards the top bus.

[3] The *erase* originating in P6 is the winner and is carried on the top bus. All other directories change their states to I and retransmit the *erase* below.

[4] P10 receives the bad news (*erase*). Instead of just invalidating it starts a read transaction.

[5] P6 becomes the exclusive owner of the item and carries out the write.

[7] The *read* from P10 reaches P6, which changes state to S and sends *data* containing the new value.

[10] The *data* reaches P10 which changes state to W and once more sends an erase. We wish it better luck this time.

Figure 7: Write Race

Figure 7 is identical with figure 6, except that both P6 and P10 try to write at the same time.

# 4 REPLACEMENT IN MEMORY

When a write-miss or a read-miss occurs, a new item will eventually be read into the memory. If the set where the new item is to be stored is full, an old item is chosen to leave its space for the new item; this is called replacement. There are two types of replacement transactions, depending on the state of the item being replaced: moving out and inject.

## 4.1 Moving Out

If the item selected for replacement is in state S, the replacement is made with a moving-out operation. Moving an item out is more complicated than just throwing away the shared copy. One has to make sure that all copies in the system are not thrown away at the same time. The job is to find another copy of the item.

The replacing memory initiates the *out* by sending an *out* transaction on the bus. The space of the item can now be reclaimed. If the *out* "sees" a subsystem underneath it in either of states S,R,W, or A, it terminates. If not, the directory above will transfer the *out* transaction to the next higher bus and change its state to I, since its subsystem no longer contains the item. The *out* will propagate all the way to the top bus if needed.

## 4.2  Inject - a Refugee Looking for a New Home

Replacing an item in state E results in an *inject*, or "looking for a new home". A memory with empty space in its set "expresses interest" and, if selected, gives the item a new home. If no memory has space for the *inject*, the transaction is repeated on the next higher bus, where a directory can "express interest". The directory can't "promise" anything, however, and the *inject* might be rejected lower in the system. A counter that follows the *inject* tells how many times an *inject* has been rejected. After the counter has passed a limit, the *inject* will not be given any more tries, and will be sent to the backup storage. A memory that would "like" to send an item directly to the backup storage can do so with an *inject* counter initiated above the limit. The limit of the system might be changed at runtime, according to the system load. The behavior of the *inject* results in a scalable memory, i.e., a single processor running sequential code can use the all the memory in the system.

## 4.3  Is a Shared Item Always Shared?

An item in state S might actually be either shared or exclusive. The reason for this might simply be that there used to be two copies of the item, but the other one was moved out of its subsystem. This situation is perfectly safe, even if it involves some unnecessary work on the next write. However, it is possible for a directory to detect when one of its clients should be changed from S to E and to change its state. If the item is in state E in the directory and only one subsystem says "got it" to an *out* transaction, the state of the subsystem should be changed to E. It is however unclear whether this will save any work or not.

If the last copy of an item marked with state S is replaced, this will cause an *out* that fails to find another copy in the system. However, when the *out* eventually reaches a directory in state E, it is converted into an *inject*. The *out* carries the data value, which will rarely be used, just to make this conversion possible.

The last two items moving out at the same time is just a special case of the above.

## 4.4  Having Promised to Answer When the Data Is on its Way Out

A subsystem in state A has "promised" to answer a *read*. Before the *read* reaches the item in the memory, however, the memory has started a replacement, and an *inject* or *out* message now appears on the bus below. This is perfectly fine, since these transactions carry the data value of the item, and the directory can send *data* on the bus above to keep its promise. One has to be careful if it is an *inject* transaction that was accepted by a subsystem on the bus below. The subsystem "believes" that it has the only copy of the item, so the directory can't make use of the data value for answering a read request. Instead, a new read request is sent below.

# 5    REPLACEMENT IN DIRECTORY

The memory size (size here meaning number of entries) of the directories increases higher up in the hierarchy. However, in order to guarantee space in a directory for all item in its subsystem, it is not enough to just increase the size of its set-associative memory. The memory should also be N ways, where N is the product of the number of memories in its subsystem and their number of ways. In big systems N would be in the range of hundreds. Even if implementable, such memories would be expensive and slow. We have chosen to use directories with smaller sets, called imperfect directories, and to give them the ability to perform replacement.

## 5.1    The Need for Replacement

The reason for a replacement is a *read* from below to an item in state I, where I is an interpretation of "doesn't exist." A directory with an item in state I receiving a *read* from below is supposed to change its state to R and repeat the *read* on the bus above. However, if the set where the new item is supposed to be is full, an old item has to be chosen and thrown out of the subsystem before the *read* can be carried out.

## 5.2    Replacement Algorithm

During replacement, the directory has to deal with two different items. The *read* item is called the new item, and the item being replaced is called the old item. The directory starts the replacement with a *leave* transaction of the old item below. One of its subsystems is selected to carry out the *leave*. It sends a *leave* below, and it changes state to the transient state:

L Leaving. This item is about to leave the subsystem.

All the other subsystems erase their copies of the item. When the *leave* finally reaches one memory, the memory changes its state to I and replies with an *up*. The *up* that contains the data value of the item is transferred up through all directories in state L, changing their states to I. When the *up* finally reaches a directory not in state L, it either generates an *out* or an *inject* transaction, depending on the state of the directory. The *read* of the new item has to be repeated while there is space in the directory. The naive way of achieving this is to send an *erase* of the new item immediately after the *leave* of the old item on the bus below the replacing directory. The *erase* will eventually reach the memory initiating the *read*, which will repeat the *read*. Hopefully, there will be enough space this time.

A HW optimization of the above is a small fully associative memory in the directory that stores the item about to leave. This immediately makes space for the new item that carries on with its *read*. The naive *erase* of the new item is needed only if this memory is full. Such memory can be small and still have an impact on performance.

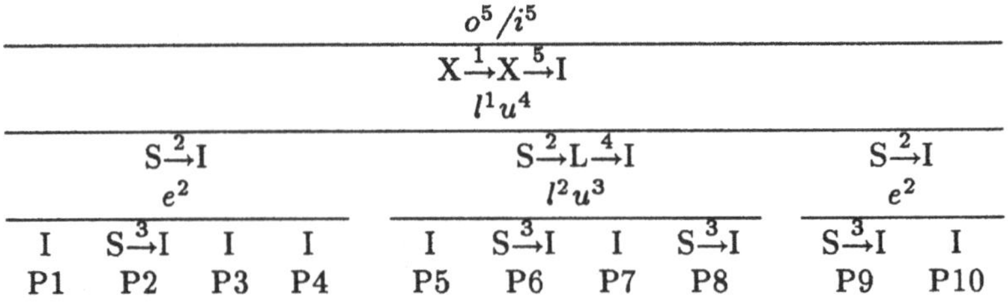

$$o^5/i^5$$
$$X \xrightarrow{1} X \xrightarrow{5} I$$
$$l^1 u^4$$

| $S \xrightarrow{2} I$ | | $S \xrightarrow{2} L \xrightarrow{4} I$ | | | | $S \xrightarrow{2} I$ | |
|---|---|---|---|---|---|---|---|
| $e^2$ | | $l^2 u^3$ | | | | $e^2$ | |
| I | $S\xrightarrow{3}I$ | I | I | I | $S\xrightarrow{3}I$ | I | $S\xrightarrow{3}I$ | $S\xrightarrow{3}I$ | I |
| P1 | P2 | P3 | P4 | P5 | P6 | P7 | P8 | P9 | P10 |

[1] The directory starts the replacement by sending *leave*. It keeps its state.

[2] The subsystem in the middle is selected to carry on the *leave*. The others merely *erase* their copies.

[3] P6 is selected to carry on the *leave*. It responde by sending *up*. All processors change their states to I.

[4] The *up* reaches the directory in state L, which changes to I and repeats the *up* above.

[5] The replacement is completed. The top directory changes state to I and sends an *out* or *inject* above depending on its state.

Figure 8: Replacing initiated of the top directory

Figure 8 illustrates the above, let's assume our picture of the DDM is a subsystem in a bigger machine. A *read* of another item has forced our top directory to replace the item we are looking at. The state of our item in the top directory does not matter and is marked with X.

# 6   HARDWARE REQUIREMENTS

So far we have presented an ideal picture of the machine. This chapter will put the DDM into the scope of the real world.

## 6.1   DDM Bus

The transactions thus far presented have assumed a bus functionality that cannot be found in existing buses.

- The DDM bus carries split transactions, i.e., a request and its response are two separate transactions.

- Each transaction is tagged with a transaction identifier.

- Each subsystem can say "got it" (a := yes). The answers are ORed together to one signal saying "at least somebody got it" ($a \geq 1$), or "nobody got it" (a=0).

- Some transactions, like *read* require the bus to select one of the subsystems servicing the requests.

- Each bus also has an "emergency brake," used to halt the bus in some cases of full buffers.

- Bus arbitration also differs from normal requirements: it should keep the buffers limited. The next bus master is chosen according to the following priorities:

  1. The subsystem selected in the last transaction.

  2. Directory above.

  3. Round robin between the rest of the subsystems.

The DDM bus can be implemented as a superset of an existing bus, which would save us the work of electrical definitions and give support with tailor-made components targeted for that bus.

## 6.2  Buffers

Since only one subsystem can send at a time, buffers are needed to avoid dead-locks. Buffers also supply a "rubber band" effect, allowing the subsystems a more even execution. Each subsystem has an output buffer above (OA). Directories also have an input buffer below (IB) and an output buffer below (OB) as shown in figure 9. In some transactions on the bus, killing operations should be performed by the OA buffers below, erasing transactions with a lower priority targeted for the same item. Killing transactions are in priority order: *erase, out, leave*. Bus arbitration limits the OA buffers to a depth of three.

## 6.3  Flow Control

Since buffer sizes are limited, part of the machine must eventually be halted, using the bus emergency brake, while full buffers are being emptied.

- IB is full either because OA is full or because the directory controller is too busy to empty IB. The directory pulls the emergency brake below. Note that a subsystem being frequently selected to service transactions is more likely to be given a higher priority in bus arbitration.

- OB is full. Directory pulls emergency brake above. Note that this is not very likely since the directory above become bus master every second time in the worst case.

- OA never needs to halt the system because of bus arbitration.

In case of IB and OB buffers both being full, both the buses above and below are halted. This is a deadlock situation. A response transaction (erase, data, or exclusive) is chosen from the OB buffer to be carried out on the bus below freeing up space in the OB and releasing the bus above. These transactions are safe to carry out, since they will not generate any additional traffic.

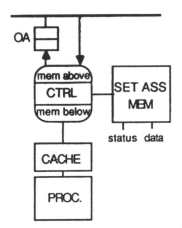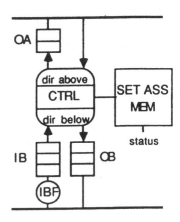

Figure 9: The architecture of the memory and directory

## 6.4 Top Directory

The number of entries in a directory is greater higher up in the hierarchy. The directory at the very top needs to have one entry for each item in the whole system. Since all item in a top directory are in state E anyhow, the directory and its memory can be replaced by a simple state machine outlined at the end of the paper.

## 6.5 Broadening Higher Buses

The system described so far has two obvious bottlenecks:

- The size of the directories grows the higher up one gets in the hierarchy. The biggest directories will be found right underneath the top bus. A practical limit to how big these directories can be made limits the size of the system.

- Although most memory accesses will tend to be localized within the machine, the higher level buses may nevertheless demand a higher bandwidth not to become a bottleneck. Snooping in the big directories will make the top bus slower rather than faster.

These two problems both have the same solution: broadening of higher buses. It is possible to split a big directory into two directories of half the size. The directories deal with different halves of the address space (even and odd). The number of buses above is also doubled, each bus dealing with its own address space. This more than doubles the bus bandwidth, since it also brings down the size of the snooping directories. Repeated splits will effectively make a bus as wide as possible, and directories as small as needed. The splitting can be used at any level.

Another way of taking the load off the higher buses is to have a smaller branch factor at the top of the hierarchy than lower down [7]. This solution, however, makes the big directories even bigger.

## 6.6 Input Below Filter

Not all transactions on a bus need to reach the directory state machine above. A simple filter can eliminate some transactions without using the state in the directory. The input below filter is outline at the end of the paper.

## 6.7 Size and Overhead of Memories and Directories

An important question is whether it is feasible to store in the higher directories the exact status of all the words below, or whether the higher directories should maintain only lower resolution information based on blocks of words. It appears to be feasible to store exact information. Assuming that memories and directories are 4-way set associative, address space is 1 Gitems, and that each level-1 memory contains 1 M words, each memory or directory at a given level contains the following:

Level 1: 1 M items with 3-bit status, 12-bit key, data value
Level 2: 16 M items with 3-bit status, 8-bit key,
Level 3: 256 M items with 3-bit status, 4-bit key.
Top : No directory needed.

where the keys are the high-order address bits that must be stored to support set-associativity. Thus in a 3-level machine, the overhead per item of storing the extra status information and address keys in both memory and the higher directories is $3+12+3+8+3+4 = 33$ bits. With items as small as one word, we are still only doubling the memory requirement in order to provide the DDM's complete flexibility of address to physical location mapping. This seems a tolerable price to pay.

## 6.8 Disks

A data diffusion machine may have one or more disks attached to it. Disks behave as secondary memory subsystems which can hold overflow data. The disks may be distributed all over the system. Each disk will be dedicated to hold some portion of the shared address space. A *read* reaching the top directory without being serviced will be converted into a *physical-read* finding its way to the disk responsible for that portion of the address space. In a similar way, an *inject* reaching the top directory will be converted to a *physical-write* updating the responsible disk. These conversions are to be found in the top directory state machine, but the *physical-read* and *physical-write* are not included in the protocols.

## 6.9 Reliability

The probability of faulty hardware increases with the size of a system, and reliability is important for systems of this size. Our plan is to focus on error detection rather than error recovery. Since data do not have home locations and can reside in any part of the system, a detected faulty subsystem can simply be disabled, and the execution rerun. Only a simple error detection and correction code should be used to catch glitch errors.

# 7 PERFORMANCE CHARACTERISTICS

The data that a processor creates itself will automatically reside in its own memory. As long as no other processor requests the data, the processor that created it can access it without causing any bus traffic. This is likely to cover the vast majority of data accesses. When a item is created by one processor and subsequently accessed by another, the item only needs to be copied once. There is no need to repeatedly access a remote item from its home location, as in most machines. If two nearby processors request the same remote item, one of the processors can obtain it from its neighbour without needing to fetch it twice from the remote location.

A remote read takes at most 4N-2 bus transactions on an N-level machine (2N-1 read requests to pass it up to the topmost bus and down to the data, and the same number of read responses to pass it in the opposite direction). For example, there would be at most 10 transactions on a 3-level machine. To make a item exclusive (in order to perform a write), an erase request goes up to the directory controller level where the item is exclusive; the directory controller acts as a lock and sends erased requests downward. Thus the item becomes exclusive after at most 2N transactions on an N-level machine (N erase requests up and N erased responses down). For example, there would be at most 6 transactions on a 3-level machine.

In general, the protocols have a combining effect on read requests going up, similar to that provided by the IBM RP3 multiprocessor [8], and a broadcast-data effect when read responses are going down, thus eliminating the "hot spot" phenomenon of the RP3. Thus, in a 3-level machine, if one processor has a item and the remaining processors request the same item, more or less simultaneously, all processors will get the item in no more than 10 bus transactions.

In general, remote data accesses only cause traffic within the subsystem concerned. For a read, only buses on the path between the source of the request and the source of the data are involved. For an erase, only buses on paths from the source of the write to copies of the data are involved.

The machine is scalable because theoretically there can be any number of levels in the hierarchy. Note that the data-access protocols are completely independent of the number of levels in the machine or the number of subsystems per bus. In practice there can be quite a few subsystems per bus (e.g., 16), so only a few levels are necessary to support a very large number of processors.

Preliminary simulations with traces from execution of parallel Prolog [6], show hit rates around 98.5 – 99 percent. The average remote-access delay (time from suspension of a processor until it is running again) in a two-level

DDM ranges between 40 and 70 processor cycles depending on the topology and on the load on the buses. The processor utilization (percentage of time the processor is not suspended) range between 70 and 50 percent.

# 8   BEHAVIOUR IN LOGIC PROGRAMS

An important characteristic of logic programs is that most data items are only written once and thereafter are read-only. Moreover, there is much data that is entirely read-only, including the usually very large volume of program code and the smaller but critically important emulator code (which is in many ways equivalent to microcode).

Shared memory machines such as the Sequent, with no significant local memory (apart from the relatively small caches), will, when executing Prolog, typically waste a large part of the shared bus bandwidth in repeatedly fetching program code and (worse still) emulator code. Ideally a processor should retain a local copy of the emulator and probably a significant part of the program code. Also it should be able to retain within local memory data that has become read-only and data that is not currently being shared with other processors. The data diffusion machine has these characteristics.

# 9   LOCKING

Some operations, depending on the nature of the processor, need to be performed atomically. For example if the processor provides a test-and-set instruction this will lead to a read-modify transaction being performed by the memory controller. A read-modify behaves like a write except that before the data item is overwritten the original value of the item is fed back to the processor. With such an implementation of read-modify, together with the general behavior of the machine, it is possible to perform spin-locking locally without generating any traffic, as shown below:

```
Lock(X):
  Start: Flag := Test&Set X;
         if Flag = 0 then Exit;
  Loop:  if X=1 then goto Loop
                   else goto Start;
  Exit:

Unlock(X):
          X := 0;
```

where **Flag** is a machine register and **Loop** causes local spinning until **X** is modified. Locking can also very well be built into the DDM protocol with the introduction of a couple of extra states for the memories. A similar locking scheme is presented in [1], where a separate lock directory is introduced in parallel with the cache directory. The cache is intended for a KL1 machine where lock conflicts are rare. Busy wait is used by the waiting processor.

A multiprocessor with thousands of processors, like the DDM, has to explore more fine grained parallelism. In such the support of synchronization between processes will be of higher importance. The behavior of I-structure memory [2], used for synchronization in dataflow, can be achieved with a slight change of our protocol. A locked item can be marked "waited on" in the producer's memory, and marked R in the consumer's (consumers') memory.

# 10  CONCLUSION

The data diffusion machine is a scalable, shared-address-space multiprocessor where the location of a item in the machine is completely decoupled from its address. In particular, there is no distinguished home location where a item must normally reside. Instead, data migrates automatically to where it is needed, reducing access times and traffic.

The machine is scalable in that there may be any number of levels in the hierarchy. Only a few levels are necessary in practice for a very large number of processors. Most memory requests are satisfied locally. Requests requiring remote access generally cause only a limited amount of traffic over a limited part of the machine and are satisfied within a small time that is logarithmic to the number of processors. Although designed particularly to provide good support for the parallel execution of logic programs, the architecture is very general in that it does not assume any particular processor, language, or class of application.

In future work, we plan to refine the design of the machine to a lower level and to carry out detailed simulations to verify its behavior both in general and particularly on the SRI and Andorra execution models. We will extend the machine to support several lightweight processes per processor, allowing us to "hide" access delays with fast process switches.

# 11   RELATED WORK

The hardware organisation of the DDM was partly influenced by a proposal of Hermenegildo [5] to provide an address-escaping mechanism in clustered shared-memory architecture (essentially a hybrid between a shared memory machine and a message-passing machine). The DDM has many similarities to Wilson's proposal [10] for a hierarchical shared-memory architecture, and certain similarities to the Wisconsin Multicube [3]. However, all of these machines, unlike the DDM, depend on physically shared memory providing a "home" location for data. The Wisconsin Multicube can also be contrasted with the DDM in that certain requests need to be broadcast througout the entire machine.

# 12   ACKNOWLEDGEMENTS

DDM is part of the Esprit project 2741 "PEPMA". We thank the many colleagues involved in or associated with the project.

# 13   LIST OF STATES

**I** Invalid. The subsystem does not contain the item.

**E** Exclusive. This subsystem and no other contains the item.

**S** Shared. This subsystem and possibly other subsystems contain the item.

**R** Reading. This subsystem is waiting for a data value.

**A** Answering. This subsystem has promised to reply to a read request.

**W** Waiting. This subsystem is waiting to become exclusive.

**L** Leaving. This subsystem is about to get rid of this item.

# 14   DDM BUS

The DDM bus provides the following functionality:

**Init**: initiation of a transaction carrying the transaction code and the address of an item.

**Data**: carrying the data part of an item.

**Ctr**: carrying the counter value of a transaction.

**Answer**: the listening subsystems can answer yes. During this phase it will be determined if none or at least one answered yes.

**Select**: one of the subsystems answering yes is selected.

# 15   LIST OF TRANSACTION

Bus functionality of each transaction is listed in the parentethes:

**r, read** (init, answer, select). There is a request somewhere in the system to read this item

**e, erase** (init). Erase all your copies of this item.

**d, data** (init, data). A (possibly) shared copy of the item.

**i, inject** (init, data, ctr, answer, select). The one and only copy of an item is looking for a subsystem to move into.

**o, out** (init, data, answer). An item on its way out of the subsystem. It will stop when another copy of the item is found.

**x, exclusive** (init). Now there is only one copy of the item in the system.

**l, leave** (init, answer, select). This item should leave the subsystem.

**u, up** (init, data). Item about to leave the subsystem. It can only move up.

**pr, physical-read** (init). A read request on its way to a disk.

**pw, physical-write** (init,data). The last copy of an item on its way to a disk.

# 16 THE PROTOCOL TABLES

The tables define the DDM protocol. They describe how a controller responds to the different transactions according to the state in which the data item is when the transaction arrives. Each state has its own column and each signal its own row. Actions have the format: guard$\rightarrow$NEWSTATE:transaction-to-send$_{Index}$, where index A means to the bus above and index B means to the bus below. An empty square means no action, the rest of the symbols are explained below.

$\emptyset$ This situation is impossible.

$\perp$ The processor may continue with its operation.

$a := yes$ The client is answering yes.

$a = 0\rightarrow$ No client answered yes.

$a \geq 1\rightarrow$ At least one client answered yes.

$selected\rightarrow$ The client is answering yes. No other client finished the transaction; the client was selected during the selection phase.

$X:y_{+1}$ The counter is incremented before the transaction y is sent.

$ctr > limit\rightarrow$ The counter has passed the limit.

| MEMORY PROTOCOL FOR TRANSACTIONS BELOW | | | | | |
|---|---|---|---|---|---|
| Trans-action | States | | | | |
| | I | E | S | R | W |
| read | $R{:}r_A{}^1$ | $\perp$ | $\perp$ | $\emptyset$ | $\emptyset$ |
| write | read;write | $\perp$ | $W{:}e_A$ | $\emptyset$ | $\emptyset$ |
| replace[2] | $\emptyset$ | $I{:}i_A$ | $I{:}o_A$ | $\emptyset$ | $\emptyset$ |

[1] Preceded by a replace if no empty space in corresponding set.

[2] The replace first chooses an item to be replaced.

| TOP DIRECTORY BELOW | | |
|---|---|---|
| Trans-action | $a = 0\rightarrow$ | $a \geq 1\rightarrow$ |
| r | $pr_B$ | |
| e | $x_B$ | $x_B$ |
| d | | |
| x | | |
| o | $i_B$ | |
| i | $pw_B$ | |
| l | $\emptyset$ | $\emptyset$ |
| u | $\emptyset$ | $\emptyset$ |

| INPUT BELOW FILTER | | |
|---|---|---|
| Trans-action | $a = 0\rightarrow$ | $a \geq 1\rightarrow$ |
| r | r | |
| e | e | e |
| d | d | d |
| x | | |
| o | o | o |
| i | i | i |
| l | l | l |
| u | u | u |

| Trans-action | States | | | | |
|---|---|---|---|---|---|
| | I | E | S | R | W |
| r | | $S{:}d_A$ | $selected{\rightarrow}S{:}d_A$ | $R{:}{-}$ | $W{:}{-}$ |
| e | | $\emptyset$ | $I{:}{-}$ | $R{:}r_A$ | $I{:}write$ |
| d | | $\emptyset$ | | $S{:}\perp$ | |
| x | | $\emptyset$ | $\emptyset$ | $R{:}r_A$ | $E{:}\perp$ |
| o | | $\emptyset$ | $a := yes$ | $a := yes$ $S^1{:}\perp$ | $a := yes$ |
| i | $selected{\rightarrow}^2 E{:}{-}$ | $\emptyset$ | $\emptyset$ | $a := yes$ $S^1{:}\perp$ | $\emptyset$ |
| l | | $I{:}u_A$ | $selected{\rightarrow}I{:}u_A$ $I{:}{-}$ | | $selected{\rightarrow}I{:}u_A;write$ |
| u | | | | $R{:}r_A$ | $I{:}write$ |

**MEMORY PROTOCOL FOR TRANSACTIONS ABOVE**

[1] Might actually be exclusive.

[2] If empty space in the corresponding set.

| Trans-action | States | | | | | | |
|---|---|---|---|---|---|---|---|
| | I | E | S | R | W | A | L |
| r | $R{:}r_A{}^1$ | | | | | | |
| e | | $E{:}x_B$ | $W{:}e_A$ | $\emptyset$ | $\emptyset$ | $W{:}e_A$ | |
| d | | | | $\emptyset$ | $\emptyset$ | $S{:}d_A$ | |
| o | | $a = 0{\rightarrow}E{:}i_B$ | $a = 0{\rightarrow}I{:}o_A$ | $\emptyset$ | $\emptyset$ | $a = 0{\rightarrow}I{:}o_A$ $a \geq 1{\rightarrow}S{:}d_A$ | |
| i² | $\emptyset$ | $a = 0{\rightarrow}I{:}i_{+1 A}$ | $\emptyset$ | $\emptyset$ | $\emptyset$ | $a = 0{\rightarrow}I{:}o_A$ $a \geq 1{\rightarrow}A{:}r_B$ | $a = 0{\rightarrow}I{:}u_A$ $a \geq 1{\rightarrow}L{:}l_B$ |
| u | | $I{:}i_A$ | $I{:}o_A$ | $\emptyset$ | $\emptyset$ | $I{:}o_A$ | $I{:}u_A$ |

**DIRECTORY PROTOCOL FOR TRANSACTIONS BELOW**

[1] If corresponding set is full, an item x is chosen to be replaced; then the following transactions are sent: $l(x)_B$; $e_B$.

[2] The transaction might be sent by the directory itself.

| DIRECTORY PROTOCOL FOR TRANSACTIONS ABOVE | | | | | | | |
|---|---|---|---|---|---|---|---|
| Trans-action | | | | States | | | |
| | I | E | S | R | W | A | L |
| r | | A:r$_B$ | selected→A:r$_B$ | | | | A:- | a := yes |
| e | | ∅ | I:e$_B$ | R:r$_A$ | I:e$_B$ | I:e$_B$ | I:e$_B$ |
| d | | ∅ | | S:d$_B$ | | S:- | |
| x | | ∅ | ∅ | R:r$_A$ | E:x$_B$ | ∅ | ∅ |
| o | | ∅ | a := yes | a := yes S:d$_B$ | a := yes | a := yes S:- | a := yes |
| i | ctr > limit→I:- selected→E:i$_B$ | ∅ | ∅ | a := yes S:d$_B$ | ∅ | ∅ | ∅ |
| l | | L:l$_B$ | selected→L:l$_B$ I:e$_B$ | | selected→L:l$_B$ | selected→L:l$_B$ I:e$_B$ | L:- |
| u | | ∅ | ∅ | R:r$_A$ | I:e$_B$ | ∅ | |

# References

[1] Masatoshi Sato Akira Matsumoto, Takayuki Nakagawa. Locally parallel cache design. TR 327, ICOT, 1988.

[2] Robert A Iannucci Arvind. Two fundamental issues in multiprocessing: the dataflow solution. MIT/LCS/TM 241, MIT, 1983.

[3] J.R. Goodman and P.J. Woest. The Wisconsin Multicube: a new large-scale cache-coherent multiprocessor. In *Proceedings of the 15th Annual International Symposium on Computer Architecture, Honolulu, Hawaii*, pages 442–431. IEEE, 1988.

[4] Seif Haridi and Per Brand. Andorra Prolog–an integration of Prolog and committed choice languages. In *International Conference on Fifth Generation Computer Systems 1988*. ICOT, 1988.

[5] M. Hermenegildo and P. McGehearty. Address escaping and reference classification in the design of a cached, multiple cluster, shared-memory architecture. PP-SRS-Technical Memo 12, MCC, 1987.

[6] Ewing Lusk, David H. D. Warren, Seif Haridi, et al. The Aurora or-parallel Prolog system. In *International Conference on Fifth Generation Computer Systems 1988*. ICOT, 1988.

[7] Gurindar S Sohi Mary K Venon, Rajeev Jog. Performance analysis of hierarchical cache-consistent multiprocessors. In *Conference Proceedings of International Seminar on Performance of Distributed and Parallel Systems*, pages 111 – 126, 1988.

[8] G.F. Pfister et al. The IBM Research Parallel Processor Prototype (RP3). In *Proceedings of the 1985 International Conference on Parallel Processing, Chigago*. IEEE, 1985.

[9] David H. D. Warren and Seif Haridi. Data Diffusion Machine–a scalable shared virtual memory multiprocessor. In *International Conference on Fifth Generation Computer Systems 1988*. ICOT, 1988.

[10] A. Wilson. Hierarchical cache/bus architecture for shared memory multi-processor. Technical report ETR 86-006, Encore Computer Corporation, 1986.

[11] Andrew W Wilson. *Organization and Statistical Simulation of Hierarchical Multiprocessors*. PhD thesis, CMU, 1985.

[12] Rong Yang. Programming in Andorra-I. Internal Report, Gigalips Project, August 1988.

# SCI
# (Scalable Coherent Interface)
# Cache Coherence

*David V. James*
*Apple Computer, MS 22Y*
*20525 Mariani Ave.*
*Cupertino, CA 95014*
*Phone: 408 974-1321*
*Fax: 408 974-6489*
*Email: dvj@apple.com*

## Abstract

*SCI — Scalable Coherent Interface — is the name of a local or extended computer "backplane" interface, being defined by an active IEEE Standard (P1596). The interconnect is scalable, meaning that up to 64K processor, memory, or I/O nodes can effectively interface to a shared SCI interconnect.*

*The (distributed) memory can be cached by the processor nodes, and the caches will be coherent. The cache coherence protocols, which are used to maintain coherence between locally-cached copies of memory, are directory based. For each sector in memory, a tag identifies the first processor in the sharing list. Distributed tags in the processor caches identify others in the sharing list.*

*We describe the sharing list structures and how they are updated. We discuss performance optimizations which are currently included in the protocol, as well as promising optimizations sill under investigation.*

**Keywords:** SCI, P1596, scalable coherent interconnect, distributed memory, caching, coherence, sharing lists

# 1 SCI OVERVIEW

## 1.1 Alternative Coherence Protocols

In present buses that support cache techniques, coherence is usually achieved by eavesdropping or snooping: all processors listen to the bus and invalidate or update their caches when memory is written into <1>. Alternative directory schemes have been considered <2>, but most of these schemes limit the number of processors in the sharing lists. Although performance simulations indicate that most sharing is among a few processors <3><4>, such hard limits would violate our charter to develop a truly *Scalable* Coherent Interface.

Our high-performance design goals (1Gbyte/sec per node), plus the fundamental laws of physics, forced us to migrate from bussed backplanes to a full-duplex point-to-point interface specification. We define one set of input signals and one set of output signals. Packets are sent to the interconnect through the *output* link, and packets are returned to the node on the *input* link. Control information (to control the flow-rate of demanding nodes) is transmitted in the otherwise idle symbols between packets.

SCI defines the interface between nodes and the external interconnect. Since we expect to see a wide variety of passive and active interconnect technologies, we consider them beyond the scope of the SCI standard. However, we would like to validate our protocols on several interconnect technologies, including (but not limited to) the two interconnect options illustrated below:

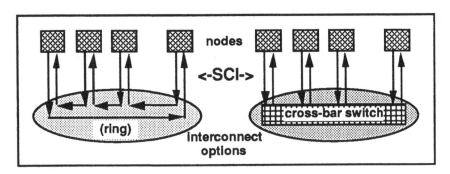

Figure 1: SCI - Abstract Interconnect Models

In most of our illustrations, the interconnect is illustrated as a non-specific ellipse, called the "blob". The distance between interfaces to the blob, or the bandwidth of SCI links, depends on the physical standard which is selected. We are specifying a high-speed 1Gbyte/sec 16-signal copper interface (for high-speed backplane upgrades), as well as a 1Gbit/sec 1-signal fiber interface (for high-speed cluster or peripheral connections).

In such an environment, we have abandoned the concept of broadcast transactions or eavesdropping third parties. The broadcast protocols are hard to implement on standard backplanes; accurate status summaries are hard to generate and fault detection is often compromised. Experienced switch designers have convinced us that broadcasts are hard ("nearly impossible") to route efficiently or reliably through active switches. With the large number of nodes on SCI (and therefore a high cumulative error rate), fault recovery is also a primary objective.

Therefore, coherence protocols are based on point-to-point transactions, initiated by a requester and completed by a responder. Most transactions consist of a request subaction followed by a response subaction. For example, the request subaction transfers the address to a memory controller and the response subaction returns data or caching status from the memory controller to the processor. These two transaction phases are illustrated below:

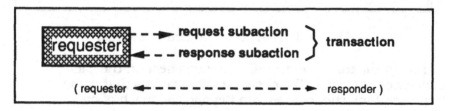

Figure 2: SCI - Transaction Components

Each subaction evokes the transmission of an additional echo packet. Since the echo is primarily used for flow-control purposes, we will not discuss echoes in the remainder of this article.

## 1.2 Requester Design Model

The design of any cache coherence protocol is based on processor and memory-controller design models. For the cache coherence protocols, we have assumed that the processor has an instruction buffer, a data-write buffer, and a cache, as illustrated below:

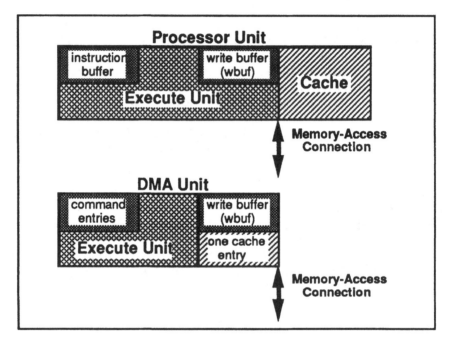

Figure 3: Instruction Execution Model

Although the instruction buffer has no effect on the cache coherence protocols, the design model clarifies that some prefetched instructions remain beyond the reach of cache coherence protocols.

The DMA adapter can be a full participant in cache coherence protocols. A minimum one-entry cache is sufficient, but additional cache entries can be used to improve the efficiency of DMA transfers.

We have included a write buffer in our processor design model, and illustrate how write buffers must be flushed to maintain strict sequential consistency <5>. The SCI protocols can efficiently support weakly-ordered data accesses as well, since data can be used while redundant shared copies are being purged.

### 1.3 Physical Addressing

For simplicity and interoperability, the SCI Coherence protocols assume that a physical address is sufficient to extract cache entries from a cache. From discussions with Faye Briggs <6>, we feel that this does not constrain the design of future processor architectures. Although primary caches will continue to be virtually indexed, we expect that large secondary caches will isolate the interconnect from the virtual addresses generated by the processor.

We have not, however, prohibited the use of processors with virtually-indexed caches. Between compatible processors, virtual index bits can be transferred in fields reserved for vendor-specific uses. If standard DMA devices are used, explicit cache flushes may be required (in a virtual cache environment) before and after DMA transfers, as is done on the HP-PA Precision architecture. Vendor-dependent DMA controllers, which supply both the physical address and the virtual index bits, can also be used.

## 2 Sharing-Lists

### 2.1 Sharing-List Structures

Since SCI by its nature can have no eavesdrop or broadcast capabilities, an alternative directory-based coherence protocol is used. Unlike central directories, our sharing lists are effectively unbounded in length. Our sharing lists are dynamically created, pruned, and destroyed, rather than being managed less frequently by software <7>.

In limited configurations, a central directory would be sufficient to implement coherence protocols. However, the central directory limits the configuration size, or a (less efficient or more complex) directory overflow protocol is required. SCI avoids these scaling limitations by distributing the directory among the sharing processors.

With the distributed directories, we also distribute the communication between sharing processors. We prefer this to concentrating the bandwidth at a heavily-shared memory controller.

Each coherently-cached sector is entered into a list of processors sharing the sector. Other sectors may be locally cached, and are not visible to the coherence protocols. For illustration purposes, both coherent and non-coherent sectors are illustrated below:

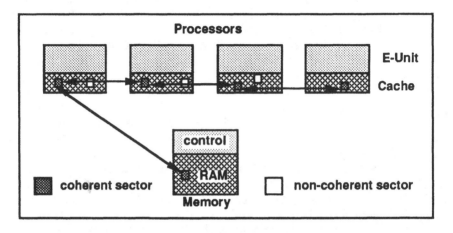

Figure 4: Distributed Cache Tags

We recognize that non-coherent copies may also be made coherent by higher level software, perhaps on a page-level basis. However, the details of such software coherence protocols are beyond the scope of the SCI standard.

For every sector address, the memory directory has additional tag bits. Part of these identify the first processor in the sharing list (called the head). Double links are maintained between other processors in the sharing list, with forward and backward pointers. The backward pointers support independent (and perhaps simultaneous) deletions of entries in the middle of the list.

## 2.2 Memory&Cache Tags

The memory tags include a two-bit memory state, **mstate**, and a 16-bit **forw_id** field. The forw_id field specifies the first node in the sharing list, in terms of the 16 most-significant bits of an SCI address. These tag bits are illustrated below:

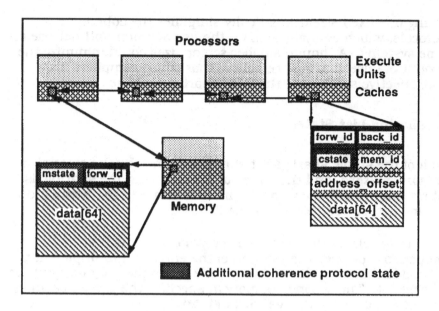

Figure 5: SCI Coherence Tags

Each cached entry contains the cache state, **cstate**, and two 16-bit forw_id fields. For entries in the middle of the list, **forw_id** and **back_id** point to the adjacent sharing-list entries.

The back_id and forw_id pointers are not currently used for entries at the head and tail of the list respectively. Instead, the head of the sharing list uses the **mem_id** portion of the physical memory address as a return pointer to the initial memory directory.

As shown above, we have assumed a fixed 64-byte cache sector size. We feel that the 64-byte size is near optimal for most systems, for the following reasons:

1.    Small Tag Overhead. The size of memory-directory and processor-entry tags are significantly less than the sector of data.

2.    Reasonable Efficiency. The 64-byte SCI transaction is relatively efficient; approximately 2/3 of the consumed bandwidth is used by for data transfers.

4.    Uniformity. The 64-byte size is shared by other bus standards (Futurebus+) and processor architecture (HP-PA), which have standardized their coherence check size.

Having one fixed size dramatically simplifies the coherence protocols, which compensates for the use of a non-optimal size on some systems. Although smaller sector sizes could minimize the amount of false sharing, we believe that smart compilers are a more effective solution to the false-sharing problem.

### 2.3 Sharing-List States

Each of the stable sharing-list states is defined by the state of the memory, **mstate**, and the states of the entries in the sharing list, **cstate**. In normal operation, memory is either in the **home** (no sharing list) or **cached** (a sharing list) states.

The sharing-list states have two components. The first component specifies the location of the entry in a multiple-entry sharing list (**head, mid, or tail**), or identifies the **only** entry in the sharing list. The second component specifies the entry's caching properties (**clean, dirty, valid, or stale**).

To simplify the sharing-list updates, the head is always responsible for administration of the list. This distributes the administrative overhead, rather than concentrating the function at the shared memory controller. As new sharing-list entries are added, the administrative load is passed to the new sharing-list head, further distributing the administrative load (at the heads) among more nodes in the system.

Since the head normally administers the return of dirty data to memory, it differentiates between the **clean** (same as memory) and **dirty** (possibly different than memory) states. The head also distinguishes between dirty copies which are shared and an exclusive (**excl**) copy which can be modified freely.

Other sharing-list entries distinguish between **valid** data copies (same as head copy) and **stale** data copies (possibly different than head copy). The stable and legal combinations of these entry states are illustrated below:

## Stable Sharing-List States

| mem | first | middle | last | Description |
|---|---|---|---|---|
| home | ---- | ---- | ---- | Uncached data |
| cached | only_clean | ---- | ---- | One clean |
| " | head_clean | ---- | tail_valid | Two clean |
| " | head_clean | mid_valid | tail_valid | More clean |
| cached | only_dirty | ---- | ---- | One dirty |
| " | head_dirty | ---- | tail_valid | Two dirty |
| " | head_dirty | mid_valid | tail_valid | More dirty |
| cached | head_excl | ----- | tail_stale | Writeable,stale |
| " | head_excl | mid_stale | tail_stale | Writeable,stales |

Figure 6: Stable Sharing-List States

The **stale** state is a performance optimization. We currently use the stale states to efficiently support the producer/consumer (one writer/one reader) data sharing model, and are considering the use the stale state option for barrier synchronization optimizations.

# 3 Sharing-List Updates

### 3.1 Sharing-List Creation

Initially, memory is in the home state and all caches are invalid. The sharing-list creation begins at the cache, where an entry is changed from the **invalid** to the **pending** state. Next, a read_cached transaction is generated, to obtain a coherently-cached copy. The read updates the memory-directory state (from **home** to **cached**), and the new entry state is changed accordingly (from **pending** to **only_clean**).

This sequence is illustrated below, using a dotted line (from requester to responder) to specify transactions and a solid line to specify sharing-list links:

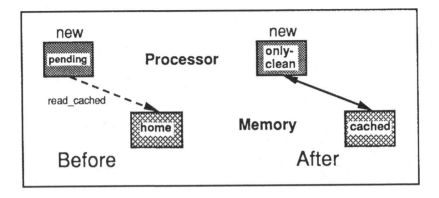

Figure 7: Sharing-List Creation

Although sharing lists are created in the **only_clean** state, an only_clean copy can be immediately converted into the only_dirty state, and generates no additional transactions.

Multiple requests can be simultaneously generated, but they are processed sequentially at the memory controller. After the first entry is processed, the others are added to the recently created sharing list, as described in the following section.

### 3.2 Sharing-List Additions

For subsequent accesses, the memory state is **cached** and the head of the sharing list has the (possibly dirty) data. A new requester tries to fetch the data from memory, but receives an indirect pointer in the returned status instead. The pointer is used to fetch the data from the old sharing-list head, as illustrated below:

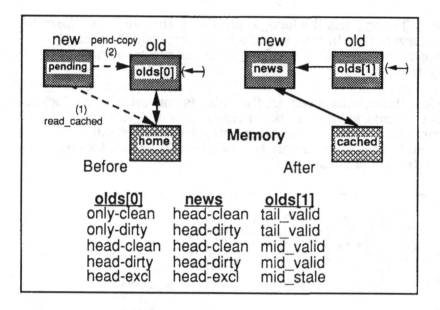

Figure 8: Sharing-List Additions

The states of the new and old sharing-list heads are a function of the old sharing-list head. Except for the one-entry sharing lists, the state of the new and old sharing-list heads is the same (the list ownership is transferred, but its caching state is unchanged). The state of mid and tail entries is unaffected by sharing-list additions.

We have not illustrated an old head in a pending state, which is in the processing of adding itself to the same sharing-list. In such cases, the transaction status returns the **pending** state from the next waiting-list entry. The transaction is re-sent until the pending status changes.

Note that the memory controller can always add an entry to the waiting list. Then, head-ownership is passed sequentially through the list. The addition of new sharing-list entries is thus performed in FIFO order, as defined by the arrival of coherent requests at the memory controller.

## 3.3 Sharing-List Deletions

Any sharing-list entry may delete itself from the list, e.g. when its cache entry is needed for other purposes. The sharing-list deletions involve the update of the back_id in the next (closer to the tail) entry, and the forw_id pointer in the previous (closer to memory) entry. In the case of a tail entry, only the second transaction, to update the forw_id in the previous entry, is required.

Before the deletions begins, the entry is converted into a locked state. A mid_valid entry is converted into mid_valid_lock (or simply **mid_vlock**); a tail_stale entry is converted into tail_stale_locked (or simply **tail_slock**). These sharing-list updates are illustrated below:

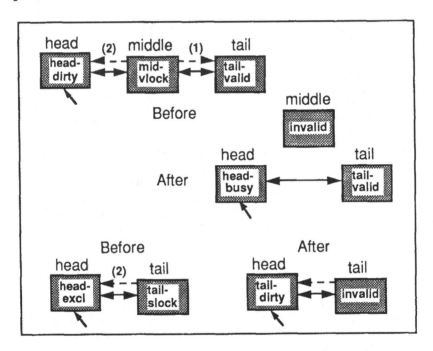

Figure 9: Entry Deletions

The lock inhibits deletions from previous sharing-list entries, while a downstream deletion is being performed. Locks are needed to maintain sharing-list integrity, when multiple entries are simultaneously deleted from the list.

Simultaneous deletions never generate deadlocks or starvation in the list-deletion process — the deletion of the next entry has precedence, and the tail-entry deletion always succeeds.

## 3.4 Sharing-List Purges

The head of the list has the authority to purge other entries from the list, to obtain an exclusive (and therefore modifiable) entry. Other mid and tail entries have no such rights — they must delete themselves from the list and re-enter as a new sharing-list head.

The purges are performed sequentially. The first transaction purges the second sharing-list entry, and returns its forw_id pointer. The forw_id pointer is used to purge the next (previously the third) sharing-list entry. The process continues until the tail entry is reached. The first two steps in this update process are illustrated below:

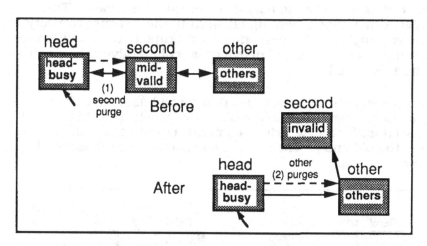

Figure 10: Head Purging Others

Simultaneous deletions may temporarily corrupt the **back_id** pointers in one or more of the sharing-list entries. Since the head-initiated purge uses only the **forw_id** pointers, the purges and deletions can be safely performed at the same time.

The **head-busy** state is similar to the **pending** state, in that new sharing-list additions are delayed while the purges are being performed.

### 3.5 Fault-Tolerant Updates

The cache coherence protocols are fault tolerant, in that dirty data is never lost when transactions are discarded. We are not concerned with mis-interpretation of data after undetected errors, since a 16-bit CRC guarantees that nearly all errors are detected.

We considered the use of redundant sharing-list pointers, so the list could be purged from both ends in the event of a failure. However, such schemes increase the overhead of the most frequent transactions (which are successful), and only protect against single transaction errors.

We selected a alternative software intensive approach. When an error is detected, the memory directory state is locked. This inhibits other sharing-list updates, until the software recovery process completes. Processors are interrupted, to flush the most-valid copy from cache and delete other coherently-cached entries at the effected address.

This recovery strategy assumes that a valid data copy always exists, and is never lost *in transit.* This constraint adds a third transaction, for a new writer to enter an existing sharing list and purge the old entry. These three transactions are illustrated below:

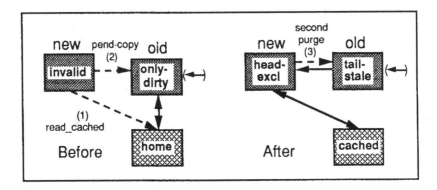

Figure 11: New Writer Prepend

The additional transaction is not required when a new reader enters an existing sharing list. Also, the apparent performance loss is offset by the producer/consumer optimization, which relies on the use of the **tail_stale** state.

# 4 Performance Enhancements

## 4.1 Enhancement Overview

We have developed several enhancements to the basic coherency protocols, to improve the performance of frequently occurring events. To simplify the low-cost implementations, which may not need these enhancements, we are structuring them as extensions, rather than changes, to the basic coherence protocols.

This also simplifies the verification efforts. Since the optimizations have not changed the base-level protocols, the verification is complete when the extensions and the base-level protocols are shown to be equivalent.

## 4.2 DMA Access

When a DMA read is performed, we assume the I/O adapter needs a coherent copy of data, but has no need to cache the copy for future uses. The data can be transferred from the current sharing-list head, without changing the state of the sharing list. This is illustrated below:

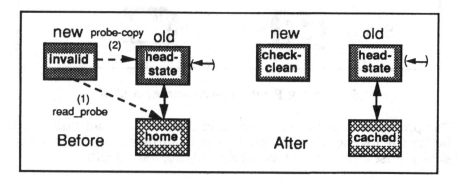

Figure 12: Optimistic DMA Reads

The optimistic read is not guaranteed to succeed. Between the first *read-from-memory* and the second *read-from-list* transactions, the sharing-list state may change. For example, this would occur if the data is being modified while the DMA transfers is being performed. When this unlikely event occurs, a slower (but always successful) cached-read is performed.

Most DMA writes can also be optimized, since all bytes in the sector are usually modified. When the DMA adapter writes a full sector to memory, it is returned a pointer to the old list, which must be purged (the DMA adapter need not become a new sharing-list head).

### 4.3 Producer/Consumer

We are able to simply optimize the frequent one-writer/one-reader (producer/consumer) form of data sharing. The (duplicate copy) invalidate by the writer (the head) and the (new data) fetch by the reader (the tail) can both be performed as direct cache-to-cache transfers, which are illustrated below:

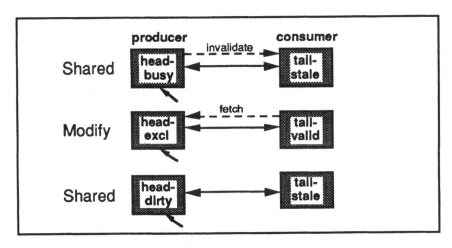

Figure 13: Producer-Consumer States

The producer changes from the head-dirty to the head-busy state before the invalidate is initiated. The head-busy state delays new sharing-list additions, to maintain sharing-list integrity.

A new sharing-list head could be starved if the producer/consumer transfers continued indefinitely. We define special states, to delete the consumer when a new sharing-list head is waiting.

Its harder to implement pairwise-sharing, since we have assumed that all data modifications are performed at the sharing-list head. However, we are considering options to support this option.

## 4.4 Combined Requests

We are very concerned with memory hot-spots, which are generated when multiple (and nearly simultaneous) processor accesses to shared data structures. Such hot spots not only degrade the performance of the requesting processor; they degrade the performance of other transactions which share portions of the congested connection path. Based on inputs from Gurindar Sohi <8> we have found ways to simply combine such requests within the switching elements.

Multiple requests to the same memory location are combined in an active switch, while the first request is being blocked. While the first request is blocked, additional requests are completed by adding them to a local wait queue. The switch element accepts the responsibility of processing the wait queue.

When the first request is unblocked, the addresses of the first and last entry in the wait queue are both sent to memory. The first address specifies the route for the response subaction (which returns memory status and data); the second address updates memory's sharing-list pointer (forw_id). The combining of memory-request transactions is illustrated below:

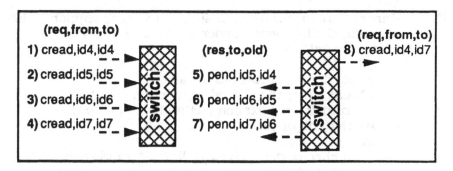

Figure 14: Request Combining

The memory-request combining is simpler than combining of uncached fetch_and_add transactions <9> — when fetch-and-adds are combined, all request must be held until the first memory response is returned.

# 5 Continuing Investigations

We have developed a set of cache coherence protocols, based on the use of tagged memory and distributed sharing lists. Although initially forced to such non-traditional protocols by our point-to-point interconnect constraints, we feel the protocols could be used on bus-based systems as well. The added costs of memory and processor tags is offset by the elimination of broadcast transactions (and the associated fast eavesdrop port on the cache).

We have initiated an effort to formally verify the correctness of the coherence protocols. We may expect some errors in the (apparently first) application of formal verification techniques to cache coherence. However, the combination of a simple basic protocol, extensive hardware simulations, and formal verification techniques should catch the errors in the initial definitions.

We are considering other performance-enhancement extensions, which have minimal impact on the basic coherence protocols. Since these proposals are highly preliminary, we have listed only the proposal summaries:

1)     Barrier Synchronization. If stale-list purges support write-through, the following barrier synchronization code is more efficient:

```
/* barrier synchronization call.
 * cnt_ptr is the shared completion counter
 * next is the next completion barrier value */
barrier(cnt_ptr,next) {
integer check;
    {{ check= (*cnt_ptr+= 1); }}      /* {{ indivisible }} */
    if (check==next) {
        make_only(cnt_ptr);           /* purge stales */
    else                              /* completion wait */
        while(stale_load(cnt_ptr)&&&count<next);}
```

2)     Fast Purging. The performance of sharing-list purges could be improved, if mid and tail entries delete themselves from the list (when so requested). We are considering two ways to save pointers for initiating such activity:

a)     Approximate-Tail Pointer. The head of the list saves a pointer to the tail, in its otherwise unused back_id location. The deletions (initiated from the tail-to-head) are initiated while the purges (initiated from the head-to-tail) are being performed.

b)     Approximate-Tree Pointers. Cache entries contain an additional pointer, which saves the value returned by the active switch (where requests were combined).

Approximate pointers are only used as performance hints, and could become invalid. The overhead of maintaining accurate pointers (when they are not used) would probably offset their performance advantage (when they are used).

3)     Fast Data Distribution  The memory request combining eliminates hot-spots, and reduces the number of processor-to-memory transactions. However, the migration of cached data to the new sharing-list heads is still linear in time. We are considering the use of approximate-tree pointers, to reduce the latency on such weakly-ordered reads.

## 6 Acknowledgments

The IEEE-P1596 Scalable Coherent Interface (SCI) was started as a study-group under the name of SuperBus, by Paul Sweazey. Dave Gustavson is now the chairman, and is responsible for the continuing development efforts. Others initially or currently involved with the Cache Coherence issues have included Marit Jensen, John Moussouris, Hans Wiggers, Ernst Kristiansen, Knut Alnes, Dave James, Stein Krogdahl, and Ellen Munthe-Kaas.

Recent contributions from Gurindar S. Sohi and Jim Goodman at the University of Wisconsin have simplified the basic proposals, and triggered many of our continuing investigations.

## Bibliography

1)     "IEEE-P896.1", Futurebus+ Working Group Drafts, 1989.

2)      Anant Agarwal, Richard Simoni, John Hennessy, and
        Mark Horowitz, "An Evaluation of Directory Schemes for
        Cache Coherence," *Proceedings of The 15th Annual
        International Symposium on Computer Architecture,*
        Honolulu, Hawaii, 1989.

3)      Susan J. Eggers and Randy H. Katz, "A Characterization of
        Sharing in Parallel Programs and its Application to
        Coherence Protocol Evaluation", *Proceedings of The 15th
        Annual International Symposium on Computer Architecture,*
        Honolulu, Hawaii, 1988.

4)      Wolf-Dietrich Weber and Anoop Gupta, "Analysis of Cache
        Invalidation Patterns in Microprocessors," *Proceedings of
        Architectural Support for Programming Languages and
        Operating Systems (ASPLOS III),* 1989, pp 243-256.

5)      M. Dubois, S. Scheurich and F. Briggs, "Memory Access
        Buffering in Microprocessors", *Proceedings Thirteenth
        International Symposium on Computer Architecture,* 14, 2
        (June 1986(, 434-442

6)      D. James and D. Gustavson, "SCI (P1596) Minutes",
        February, 1989.

7)      Tom Knight, "Proposed S-1 Coherence Lists", Viewgraphs
        from Lawrence Livermore presentation, ~1988

8)      Evening discussions between Dave James and Gurindar S.
        Sohi, Madison WI, 1989.

9)      G.F. Pfister, W.C. Brantley, D.A. George, S.L. Harvey, W.J.
        Kleinfelder, K.P. McAuliffe, E.A. Melton, A. Norton, and J.
        Weiss, "The IBM Research Parallel Processor Prototype
        (RP3): Introduction and Architecture" In *Proceedings ICPP,*
        pages 764-771, August 1985.

# Performance Evaluation of Wide Shared Bus Multiprocessors

*Andy Hopper, Alan Jones, Dimitris Lioupis*

Olivetti Research Ltd.
24A Trumpington Street
Cambridge CB2 1QA
England

## ABSTRACT

*We compare the simulated performance of a family of multiprocessor architectures based on a global shared memory. The processors are connected to the memory through caches that snoop one or more shared buses in a crossbar arrangement.*

*We have simulated a number of configurations in order to assess the relative performance of multiple versus wide bus machines, with varying amounts of prefetch. Four programs, with widely differing characteristics, were run on each configuration. The configurations that gave the best all-round results were multiple narrow buses with 4 words of prefetch.*

## INTRODUCTION

Multiprocessors are used today to provide better performance at lower cost. Many commercially available systems are based on a shared memory, shared bus architecture. These machines have a relatively straightforward implementation since they are an extension of the uniprocessor bus system. Their globally shared memory and consistency mechanisms give a programming model that is very similar to systems of cooperating processes on uniprocessors. Commercial systems such as the Encore [ROS85] and Sequent [SEQ84] claim significant speed-ups at very low cost.

A major limitation of shared bus multiprocessors is the bandwidth of the bus, which limits the number of processors that can be connected to the same memory, and thus the performance of the system. To solve this problem we can increase the speed of the bus [DEC88], which is not always easy because of technology limitations, or we can use more wires to connect to the memory. For a given technology, more wires provide more bandwidth, but it is not obvious which is the best way to connect the wires because of complications such as caches, code sharing and system complexity.

Wide buses are simpler to build but they provide only one path to memory. Multiple buses are more complex to implement but they reduce contention because of multiple paths to memory and more wires for control and addresses.

In this paper we study the effect of bus architecture on performance. Keeping the number of data wires constant, we found that multiple buses can provide better effective bandwidth to memory, and thus better performance. Multiple bus machines ran our sample programs from 0.9 to 3.5 times faster than wide bus machines.

The rest of the paper is organised as follows. In the next section we give a brief description of the proposed architecture and we compare it with existing designs. In section 3 we review the factors that may affect program performance to aid in understanding the results. Section 4 describes the simulator environment used to obtain the results included in section 5. We conclude with an overall analysis in section 6.

## ARCHITECTURAL DESCRIPTION

Conventional multiprocessors (such as SPUR [HIL86], Firefly [THA87], and others) are connected to the shared memory by a single bus as shown in figure 1 (a).

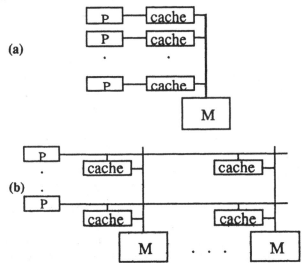

**Figure 1 : Shared bus multiprocessors**

To increase the bandwidth to memory, we use a multiple bus architecture. The resulting architecture shown in figure 1 (b), uses a grid of buses with a cache at each cross-point to connect to memory.

Each memory module contains a portion of the memory space and memory references are interleaved in cache block size intervals. If the cache block size is four words, then addresses 0 to 3 will reside in the first memory module, 4 to 7 in the second and so on. The caches implement the Berkeley protocol [KAT85] to maintain consistency on each memory bus by ownership and snooping. Because each portion of the address space (e.g. 0 to 3) is always mapped onto the same memory module, consistency can be maintained independently on each memory bus by the snooping mechanism in the corresponding caches.

The resulting architecture maintains the same programming model as conventional shared bus multiprocessors, whilst providing a higher bandwidth to memory. The number of memory buses is limited by the electrical load on the processor bus to about 4-8. We simulated up to 4 memory buses.

As we increase the number of memory buses, there is a linear increase in the number of cache chips, and in the number of buses. Many organisations, including Olivetti, are working on high density silicon-based interconnection technologies which could be used to implement such crossbar systems.

Recently many architectures have been proposed utilising both wide bus and multiple bus approaches. They all address the shared memory bottleneck problem by increasing the width of the data path to memory.

A multiprocessor with a 128 bit wide bus is under investigation by Olivetti. It is designed to accommodate up to 8 processors connected through a write back cache onto a pended bus. A processor issues a request, and releases the bus, then the corresponding memory module requests the bus when it has the reply ready. The bus operates at 20 MHz and can be extended by connecting two similar buses with a special interface. In our simulations we study a similar architecture which employs a write back cache, but with a different policy (Berkeley ownership). We use a master slave bus model which will behave differently to a pended model. Our multiple bus case however, shares the ability to have several transactions in progress at the same time, and these results may relate to the pended model.

The Wisconsin Multicube[GOO88], is a shared memory multiprocessor which uses a grid of buses to connect to memory. In this design there is a processor at each cross point resulting in a large number (up to 1024) of processors. We envisage a smaller number (up to 100) of processors connected to memory through caches at each cross point as shown in figure 1b. This simplifies the cache consistency mechanism which is a major problem in the Multicube. Consistency checks occur independently on the vertical memory buses, as in a conventional single bus multiprocessor.

Multiple buses are used on Aquarius as reported in [NGU88]. Processors are connected to memory buses through caches at each cross point. Aquarius is a multiprocessor designed for Prolog, which has a different model of execution to conventional languages, and imposes higher demands on the memory system. Due to the increased number of memory writes, separate buses are used to carry the invalidations to other caches. Its designers believe that multiple buses can provide enough bandwidth to meet these demands. We concentrate on the parallel execution of conventional languages and in particular programs written in C.

## FACTORS AFFECTING THE PERFORMANCE OF A PROGRAM

This section discusses some of the factors that can affect the performance of multiprocessor systems. The different running times of a program on various configurations may not be directly related to the cache/memory bandwidth. The cache/memory parameters can subtly alter important factors such as load balance, synchronisation, or the detailed access pattern of the program. The programs that we use were chosen to depend differently on such factors.

As a concrete example for this section, we shall assume that 128 wires are used to carry the data on the memory bus, organised as a single transfer unit in the wide bus case, and as four independent 32-bit word units in the multiple bus case. The processor to cache bus is assumed to operate with 32-bit quantities.

On a cache miss, the wide bus case is assumed to transfer four sequential words, aligned on a four-word boundary. If these four words are not all useful to the processor during their time in the cache, then some of the extra bandwidth provided by the bus width is being wasted. However, other studies show that a few words of prefetch generally improve the cache hit rate, and that this outweighs any wasted data fetches [DEC88].

When an algorithm is designed to operate on a number of processors, it is often difficult to avoid one or two of the processors having to do more work than the others. In some cases this imbalance of workloads may be dependent on the data supplied for the run(e.g. quicksort). In others the imbalance may be inherent in the chosen implementation (e.g. a prime number sieve). In almost any parallel algorithm, there will be some computation that cannot be performed concurrently, and this will further upset the work distribution. Under these circumstances, some processors will become idle, leading to longer running times, but less bus traffic. Our program suite includes two such programs, but the amount of idle time is such that a 16 processor system still completes them faster than any less powerful machine.

In most programs, explicit synchronisation between processes occurs infrequently compared to the time spent in other computations [EGG88]. However, after processes have synchronised, they may for a time run together through the same data structures (e.g. a work queue) and this can lead to beneficial or detrimental interference until the processes move apart. Changing the memory parameters can subtly alter the amount of time that the processes are interfering, and this can have noticeable effects on performance.

Changes in the layout of data, or in the times that it is accessed during a computation, can drastically change the running time. The classic example of this occurs when scanning through matrices. If a cache block contains consecutive elements from the same row, then running through a row will take maximum advantage of the prefetch mechanism, whereas a column will only use one word per block.

## SIMULATION

### Simulator Details

We have developed a high-level event driven simulator to model various multiprocessor systems. Behavioural models of the individual chips and bus wires are written in Modula-2 [WIR82], and they accurately reflect the detailed timing of the external logic signals. For instance, the processor model fetches instructions from the memory model by driving signals in the same way as the real chip. The whole system is generated from a set of high-level parameters such as the number of processors, cache associativity and wire delays.

The underlying model is one of nodes (circuit elements) communicating by sending values (64 bits) across contacts. This allows us to pass 32-bit bus values in one event, and to display them in a meaningful way to the user (e.g. hexadecimal values). As the interpretation of these values is defined from outside the simulator, it can be tailored to the application, for instance, by disassembling instructions when the values on the data bus are displayed.

All the models register extensive debugging commands with the user interface. For example, breakpoints can be set on processor addresses to stop the simulator and allow register dumps or single stepping, the values stored in caches and memories can be read or written, and individual addresses can be monitored to trace all changes. When investigating the performance of some algorithms, it has proved particularly instructive to watch the accesses to a lock and the data items it protects.

To save time, the memory model can interpret loadable images, and initialise itself directly, removing the need for a loader and simulated input device. The processor modeled is the Acorn RISC Machine (ARM) [FUR87] with a cycle time of 200 ns and is connected by a bus translator chip to the caches. The caches are our own design, they are write back and communicate with the global shared memory over buses that implement the Berkeley consistency protocol.

Running on a Sun260 workstation, a simulated single processor machine runs at around 35 ips (instructions per second). Machines with larger numbers of processors impose a greater load on the simulator, keeping the aggregate instruction throughput at 15 to 30 ips. Our benchmark programs require around 1 million cycles to complete, and take between 8 and 24 hours for each run.

### Programming Environment

The programs are written in C, with assembler libraries for booting, synchronisation and output. The main procedure takes two arguments representing the number of processors in the system, and the number of the processor that it is executing on. These numbers are computed by routines contained in the boot code. Each program can be linked for execution directly on the Archimedes workstation which compiles it, and debugged in single processor mode before being used in the simulation. After they have solved their particular problems, they use unimplemented instructions to signal the models to report statistics for that run, and they then proceed to verify that the results were correct. If the answers are correct, then a one line summary is entered in a collation file from which various performance graphs can be drawn. If the answers are incorrect, then the time is entered as zero to draw our attention to it, and the entry is ignored by subsequent tools. These checks have detected subtle errors in our C test programs, and faults in our simulated hardware that only rarely occur in particular configurations. The correct answers are obtained by running the programs on the real ARM in the Archimedes workstation.

### Simulated Machines

We simulated four simple programs runs on three bus layouts to compare their performance:

1) Wide-bus: A 128 bit wide bus with 16 processors.
2) 2-bus: Two 64 bit wide buses with 16 processors.
3) 4-bus: Four 32 bit wide buses with 16 processors.

All systems use caches as shown in figure 1. The cache size is 1 kbyte per processor, which means that in the 4-bus case each cache is 256 bytes. It is small to correspond with the small size of our programs. The total system cache is also constant because we are using 16 processors. The buses use separate paths for addresses, data, and control, and the master keeps control of the bus until its request is satisfied. Arbitration for the bus takes 50 ns. and a memory fetch 400 ns. (plus 200ns. for each additional word).

The cache block size is important in a shared memory architecture because it influences the amount of traffic on the bus and thus contention. For each of the above bus configurations we performed three runs of each program to determine the effect of block size on our measurements.

**Single Transfer.** The cache block size is equal to the bus width. In this case, on a cache miss, a block will be transferred in one bus cycle.

**Two-transfer.** The block size is now twice the bus width. Whenever data has to be moved between cache and memory, one address is sent, followed by two cycles of data transfer.

**Four-transfer.** The block size is four times the bus width. Each block will be fetched in four sequential memory transfers. We gain some advantage by only presenting the address information once, and by using memories with fast page modes. In the *Wide-bus* case we are fetching 16 words, which may be advantageous for some programs, and not for others. The cache block sizes (also the data transfer sizes) for the nine runs are shown in table 1.

| | Bus Width | | |
|---|---|---|---|
| Transfers | 1 | 2 | 4 |
| 1 | 1 | 2 | 4 |
| 2 | 2 | 4 | 8 |
| 4 | 4 | 8 | 16 |

**Table 1: Cache block sizes (words)**

## RESULTS

The results obtained are shown in the next four sections in bar chart form, one section for each program. Each bar represents the execution time of the program in microseconds (see figure 2). Thus a smaller bar represents a better processor performance. The text will refer to the bars by numbering them from the left, thus the wide-bus, 4-transfer case is bar 1, and the 4-bus, 1-transfer case is bar 9.

We also quote other statistics gathered from the simulations. Utilisation is given as the mean of the percentages of time that each individual bus is occupied by *any* processor. Average queue length is the mean number of processors that are requesting or have been granted the bus. We collect these statistics by observing the buses every 20ns., the period of the master clock from which all other clocks in the system are derived.

### Successive Over-Relaxation

This program repeatedly computes the value of grid locations by taking the average of the four surrounding points. Eventually, this method converges to a solution of Laplace's equation for the given boundary values. Our grid consists of 32 rows of 9 elements each, and we perform 25 iterations. For multiprocessor execution, we divide the grid equally into as many horizontal strips as there are processors. Each processor then updates every other element in its strip in turn, and increments its own iteration count. It then spins, waiting for its two neighbours to come to the same iteration number, then proceeds with the next wave of updates. At the edges of the strips, neighbouring processors are always trying to read the same locations, so the sharing overhcad is high.

216

The running times for this program are shown in Figure 2.

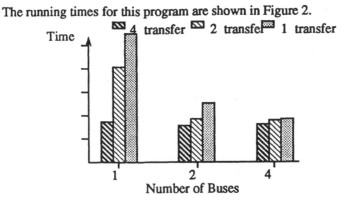

Figure 2 : Performance of SOR Program

Looking at bars 3, 6 and 9, the most striking feature of figure 2 is the very bad performance of the wide-bus machine with only one transfer per miss (bar 3). Normally, we would expect the prefetch given by a four-word block to enhance performance, but in this case it has dramatically reduced it. This is mainly due to the data for different processors being interleaved at one word grain in the regions where it is shared (a property of the software implementation). This leads to higher utilisation in the wide bus cases (greater block sizes): 99.8%, 89.7% and 41.6% for the 1, 2, and 4-bus cases respectively (bars 3, 6, and 9), leading to average queue lengths of 9.17, 3.49 and 0.88. The hit rates improve from around 90% on the narrow buses to 94% on the wide, not enough to overcome the effects of the much greater queue lengths.

The narrow bus machine with four transfers per miss (bar 7) does not suffer from this problem as it makes much better use of the memory (4 buses by 4 words = 16 words, transferred in 400 + 200 + 200 + 200 = 1000 ns.) than the wide bus with one transfer (bar 3, 4 words transferred in 400ns.). It also allows one processor to block its interfering neighbours for a longer period, but only on one bus, so the other buses become less congested, and other processors can proceed efficiently. Because the program causes a considerable amount of bus traffic, the buses become saturated if the memory is not used to best advantage, and we see 99.8% utilisation, 9.2 queue lengths for both the two- and single-transfer wide bus cases (bars 2 and 3). If we consider just the one-transfer cases, then we should see the effect of the greater prefetch as the buses become wider, as the time to satisfy a miss remains constant at 400ns.

## Matrix Multiplication

The matrix multiplication program multiplies two matrices (16 x 16 elements) stored as global arrays to produce the result matrix. Each processor calculates a part of the resultant matrix determined by its number, which is used to index the resultant array. This means that eventually each processor will fetch all elements of the first matrix and a column of the second matrix. Write invalidations in the blocks that hold the result should influence the performance of this program. The results obtained by the simulator are shown in figure 3.

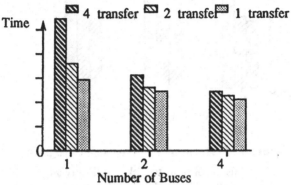

**Figure 3 : Performance of Prod Program**

There is a lot of read sharing in this algorithm, and fewer writes per instruction than the others, yet the average queue length in the wide bus case (single transfer, bar 3) was 6.45. This dropped to 1.93 and 0.92 in the 2-bus and 4-bus cases (bars 6 and 9). The main reason for the high contention on the wide bus is that each processor is responsible for computing every 16th element of the result. When one word is written, it invalidates the entire block, which contains the words being computed by three of the other processors, requiring extra bus transfers when they come to write their results. We therefore see this program being dominated by the effects of the wasted prefetch, with the smaller effect of the increased memory efficiency of multiple transfers playing a secondary role.

## Quicksort

The quicksort algorithm has been rewritten for concurrent execution on the multiprocessor. It is still based on recursively dividing the input list into two lists with elements smaller than and greater than a pivot. The first element of the list is used as pivot. In the beginning only one processor starts executing and the rest spin on a lock. When the list is divided the processor keeps one half of the list and gives the other to the next processor by clearing its lock. This is repeated until there are no more processors, when the execution is reduced into normal recursive quicksort. The list is stored as a global array of random numbers in memory. The performance of this program depends heavily on the input list which determines the load balancing of processors. The program was run sorting 1000 random numbers and the results are shown in figure 4

218

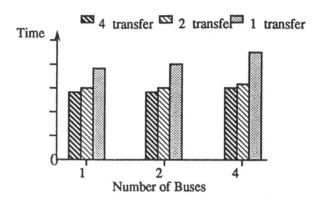

**Figure 4 : Performance of Quicksort Program**

Quicksort is the only program to take full advantage of the prefetch provided by the wide bus (bar 3), and runs slightly faster than with narrow buses in the single transfer mode (bar 9). When prefetch was added to the narrow bus case (bar 7), the program ran in only 70% of the time, outperforming the wide bus in all but the 4-transfer case (bar 1, 16 word blocks).

**Sieve**

This is a parallel implementation of the sieve of Eratosthenes. The main data structure is an array of 1024 integers, where the contents of array[i] indicate whether i is a prime or not. All processors start at the second element and move up the array looking for a zero. If they find one, they use a test-and-set instruction to mark the number as prime (a 1), and then proceed to mark all multiples as non-prime (a 2). When all processors have searched as far as the square root of the array size, the final processor scans the array, counting the number of primes (zeroes or ones).

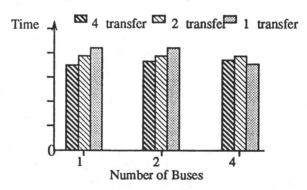

**Figure 5 : Performance of the Sieve Program**

Due to the restricted length of the sieve array, only eleven of the sixteen processors have any work to do, and after about 25% of the running time, the other five have found this and are idling. During the rest of the run, there can be considerable interference as processors rapidly mark off multiples of the remaining primes, so although the hit rate improves with prefetch, the invalidations also increase, leaving the running time largely unaltered. To show that bus bandwidth is indeed a bottleneck in this instance, we also show the mean queue lengths on the buses in figure 6.

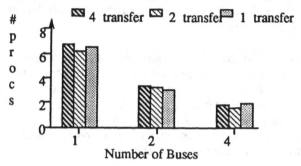

Figure 6 : Average Queue Lengths for the Sieve Program

Note that the queue length divided by the bus width remains roughly constant, so although the wide bus machines have greater latencies on a miss, their buses are transferring more data each time, and the overall performance becomes more a function of the efficiency of memory usage. We should therefore expect the multiple transfer machines to do much better (bars 1, 4, and 7), but due to the sparse nature of some of the accesses (e.g. marking every 29th element), the greater prefetch is sometimes wasted, and the improvement is not as great as might be hoped.

## DISCUSSION

Looking at the four sets of results together, we can try to find a machine configuration that is amongst the best for all programs. Single bus machines perform badly with the SOR program (1 and 2 transfer cases are bad), and with matrix multiplication in the 4-transfer case. Multiple bus machines with only single transfers perform badly for the highly sequential quicksort program. Thus we are left with the best all-round performers being a 4-bus machine with 2 or 4 single-word transfers on a miss, or a 2 bus machine with 2 dual-word transfers.

To help us to understand the factors influencing the running times; the processors, caches and memories gather detailed statistics about the bus accesses during the run. These are recorded in log files, and can be post-processed to display load balance, queue lengths, utilisations, hit rates, read/write ratios etc.

These programs represent only a few examples of the sort of behavior expected from the inner loops of parallel applications, but already some trends can be seen:

A large transfer unit is detrimental to programs that write shared data interleaved at a fine grain, as it can lead to unnecessary invalidations. An example would be updating items in a shared job queue or other list structure, where a change to one element could invalidate adjacent entries that were being worked on by other processors. This will lead to bad performance on wide bus machines with multiple transfers.

Buses with single transfers are not using the memory to best advantage (page modes, suppressed addressing of sequential blocks). Wide bus machines with single transfers are consistently slower than multiple bus machines with the same transfer unit. Compare the 1-bus 1-transfer, 2-bus 2-transfer, and 4-bus 4-transfer running times; all of these systems move data in four-word blocks, yet the 4-bus configuration is consistently faster.

From these observations, we expect that multiple bus machines will be worthwhile in environments where the very best performance of parallel algorithms is sought. They can provide high bandwidth to memory without the penalties of large transfer units, and with the added flexibility of concurrent transfers. When using wide bus machines for parallel applications, more care is required to make the best use of their potentially high bandwidth.

## CONCLUSION

We have run a selection of parallel programs on nine variations of shared memory multiprocessor architectures. The results have been encouraging, as the special characteristics of each program have led to predictable differences in performance on the nine machines. Our original thesis, that multiple narrow buses offer a high bandwidth with more flexibility than single wide buses, has been borne out by the poor performances observed in some wide-bus runs.

Our simulations have all used small programs operating over a relatively small range of addresses. Whilst they cannot be taken as typical examples of complete multiprocessor applications, they are representative of the inner loops of compute-intensive programs. The instructions of such pieces of code are always cached, and often constitute the major part of the running time, but the data they access might not be cached. If they are writing to shared data, or are reading large amounts of data, then they will generate bus traffic similar to that seen on our simulated systems.

With current technologies, multiple bus machines of a significant size are not cost-effective. The crossbar interconnect of 32-bit buses, with high-speed cache elements at each intersection, proves very difficult to implement.

As high-density interconnect systems become more widely used, the implementation of multiple buses will become easier, making such systems more attractive.

Wide-bus architectures, being more suitable for implementation on a conventional backplane, are now emerging in high-performance machines. It remains to be seen whether the unfavourable characteristics displayed by the SOR and matrix product programs can be avoided in practice.

## Acknowledgements

The authors would like to express their thanks to James Kenney and Kami Sehat of Cambridge University Computer Laboratory for writing the processor and cache models; Stuart Wray and Mark Chopping of Olivetti Research Laboratory, Cambridge for their work during the development of the multiprocessor simulations and programs described in this paper.

## References

[AGA88]    Agarwal A. and A. Gupta, "Memory-Reference Characteristics of Multiprocessor Applications under MACH," Proceedings of ACM Sigmetrics 1988.

[ARC86]    Archibald J. and J. Baer, "An Evaluation of Cache Coherence Solutions in Shared-Bus Multiprocessors," ACM Trans. on Computer Systems, 4,4, November 1986.

[BEL85]    Bell C.G, "Multis: A New Class of Multiprocessor Computers," Science, 228, April 1985.

[CHE88]    Cheriton D.R., A. Gupta, P.D Boyle and H.A Goosen, "The VMP Multiprocessor: Initial Experience, Refinements and Performance Evaluation," Proc. of 15th Intl. Symp. on Computer Architecture, Hawaii, June 1988.

[DAS85]    Das C.R, and L.N. Bhuyan, "Computation Availability of Multiple-Bus Multiprocessors", U of Southwestern Louisiana, 1985.

[DEC88]    Digital Equipment Corporation, "CVAX-based Systems", Digital Technical Journal no. 7, August 1988.

[EGG88]    Eggers S. and R. Katz, "Characterization of Sharing in Parallel Programs and its Applicability to Coherency Protocol Evaluation," Proc. of 15th Intl. Symp. on Computer Architecture, Hawaii, June 1988.

[FUR87]    Furber S. B and A. R Wilson,"The Acorn RISC machine - an architectural view", Electronics and Power, vol 33 no 6, pp 402-405 June 1987

[GOO83]    Goodman J. "Using Cache Memories to Reduce Processor-Memory Traffic," Proc. of the 10th Intl Symp. on Computer Architecture, Stockholm June 1983.

[GOO88]    Goodman J. and P.J. Woest, "The Wisconsin Multicube: A New Large-Scale Cache-Coherent Multiprocessor," Proc. of 15th Intl. Symp. on Computer Architecture, Hawaii, June 1988.

[GOT83]    Gottlieb A., et. al. "The NYU Ultracomputer--Designing an MIMD Shared Memory Parallel Computer", IEEE Trans. on Computers, VolC-32, Feb 1983.

[HIL86]   Hill M.D. et. al. "SPUR: A VLSI Multiprocessor Workstation," IEEE Computer, 19, 11 November 1986.

[KAT85]   Katz R.H. et. al., "Implementing a Cache Consistency Protocol," 12th international Symposium on Computer Architecture, IEEE, 1985, pp. 276-283.

[MCR84]   McCreight E, "The Dragon Computer System: An Early Overview," Tech. Report, Xerox Corp., September 1984.

[NGU88]   Nguyen T.M, Srini V.P, and A.M. Despain, "A Two-Tier Memory Architecture for High-Performance Multiprocessor Systems", Intl Conf. on Supercomputing, St. Malo, France, July 1988.

[PAT81]   Patel J. H, "Performance of processors-memory interconnections for multiprocessors", IEEE Trans on Computers, Oct 1981, pp 771-780.

[PAT82]   Patterson D.A., Garrison P., Hill M.D., Lioupis D., Nyberg C., Sippel T.N. & Van Dyke K.S., "Architecture of a VLSI cache for a RISC", 10th Intl. Symp. on Computer Architecture, 1982.

[ROS85]   Rose C.D, "Encore Eyes Multiprocessor Market," Electronics July 8, 1985.

[SAT80]   Satyanarayanan M. "Commercial Multiprocessing Systems ," IEEE Computer, 13, 5, May 1980.

[SEQ84]   Sequent Computer Systems, Inc. "Balance 8000" Technical Summary, Nov 1984.

[THA87]   Thacker C. and L. Stewart, "Firefly: A Multiprocessor Workstation", 2nd Intl. Conference on Architectural Support for Programming Languages and Operating Systems, pp 164-172, ACM, October 1987.

[WIL87]   Wilson A. W. Jr, "Hierarchical Cache/Bus Architecture for Shared Memory Multiprocessors," Proc of 14th Intl. Symp. on Computer Architecture, 1987.

[WIR82]   Wirth N., "Programming in Modula-2," Springer Verlag, New York 1982.

# CROSSBAR-MULTI-PROCESSOR ARCHITECTURE

## Vason P. Srini

Computer Science Division

University of California

Berkeley, CA 94720

## ABSTRACT

The crossbar-multi-processor (CMP) architecture is an interconnection of multis using a hierarchy of crossbars. It is intended to be the base architecture of an architectural framework that can be used to experiment with different processors, various directory protocols for communication among multis and memory to keep caches coherent, and different parallel programming paradigms. Each multi in the architecture provides low latency communication between a small (<8) number of processors. Communication between multis is supported by crossbars. To support a large number of multis a hierarchical connection of crossbars is employed. The CMP architecture combines the advantages of snooping cache schemes and directory schemes to keep the caches of a scalable multiprocessor consistent. The shared memory is distributed among the multis in the system. To reduce global interconnection traffic each cache also has a small associative store that contains a directory of locked data items in that processor.

Some of the components of the CMP have been designed and simulated. For example, a four processor multi using a variant of the Berkeley cache lock state protocol has been designed and parts of it simulated at the gate level. A 16 X 16 single-bit slice crossbar chip has been designed and simulated with a worst case latency of 40 ns using a 0.8 micron CMOS technology. A crossbar board for interconnecting 15 multis and another level of crossbar board has been designed and simulated. An outline of the CMP and its components are described in this paper.

Keywords: Cache coherence, crossbar, directory scheme, cache lock state

## 1. INTRODUCTION

The solution of large problems in aerospace, biological modeling, materials analysis, and image understanding requires computer systems that can perform in the TERAOP [26] range. To achieve such a level of performance the fastest circuit technology and massively parallel systems have to be employed. In addition, the parallel system must be programmable. This implies the development of parallel algorithms and efficient mechanisms to manage resources such as processors, memory, and communication channels. Parallel programs can be written using a message based model with explicit sends and receives for messages or a shared memory model with explicit ( fork and join) and implicit parallelism. Parallel programs can also be written in a dataflow like language with implicit parallelism. The underlying architecture for the parallel computer systems can be message based [31, 11] or shared memory. In this paper a shared memory architecture that can support thousands of processors is proposed. It is scalable in the spirit of the IEEE Scalable Coherent Interface (SCI) [38] specification.

## 1.1. Caches in Systems

Although many multiprocessors have been designed and built [44, 24, 30] during the past two decades, several fundamental problems are still open. The early multiprocessors, shown in Figure 1, are limited by the bandwidth to memory.

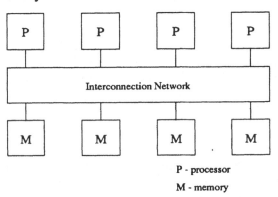

P - processor

M - memory

**Figure 1. A Multiprocessor System**

A subset of the processors busy-waiting on locks can shut out other processors from accessing memory modules. This memory interference can drastically lower the performance of the system. One way to reduce the interference and also increase the bandwidth is by employing caches between each processor and the interconnection network. The shared data in these caches must be made consistent. This cache consistency problem has been studied extensively [39, 9, 14, 16, 5]. A multiprocessor system employing snooping caches [16, 20], shown in Figure 2, has been proposed to solve the cache consistency problem for a small number (< 8) of processors. For high performance multiprocessor systems the bandwidth available on a single bus is insufficient.

Multiprocessing systems such as Cray X-MP and Y-MP achieve high performance by using pipelining techniques, fast circuitry, high-speed memory, and high bandwidth to memory. One key architecture component that is missing from the Cray machines is cache memory. Although one

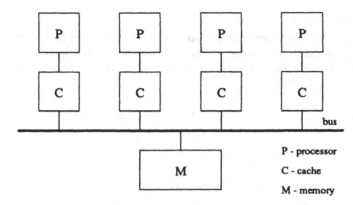

**Figure 2. Multiprocessor System with Snooping Caches on a Single BUS**

could argue that the instruction buffers, and backup registers B and T in Cray-1S can be treated as a form of instruction cache and programmable data cache, respectively, they are not caches in the general sense.

Previous studies [32] have shown that cache memory is a cost effective way to substantially improve performance. For example, the Convex's C-1 [42], a Cray-1S like processor, achieves one fifth the performance of a Cray-1S [28, 34] at one tenth of the cost. It uses a large cache (64K bytes), a slower technology (CMOS), a slower memory, and pipelining. The instruction and data caches in the Convex's C-1 play a key role in providing performance despite slow and limited bandwidth to memory.

For any shared memory multiprocessor architecture, the memory system is potentially a major bottleneck since the access time of a large, economically feasible memory system is 5 to 10 times slower than the processor cycle time, and this gap is much larger for supercomputers with very short processor cycle times. For example, the Cray-2 has a cycle time of 4.0ns but the fastest 1Mbit DRAM chip has a cycle time of 100ns.

In order to obtain high bandwidth to memory, current high-speed multiprocessor systems often contain a fully connected network such as crossbar, in the case of a small number of processors [44, 30] or an interconnection network such as the Omega network in Ultra computer [19] and shuffle exchange in Cedar [29], in the case of a large number of processors. These systems either do not employ caches due to the problem of multiple cache coherency associated with the particular interconnection network, or restrict the use of caches to read-only and non-shared read-write data. The medium-speed multiprocessors, usually called super-minis, contain caches with full dynamic coherency protocols. Because of the enormous hardware cost and complexity required to support synchronization and broadcasting schemes, these caches are connected to a single bus. In this case, the caches are efficiently utilized, but the single bus connection to memory is a major bottleneck as the number of caches/processors connected to the shared bus increases.

## 1.2. Crossbars and Caches

To reduce memory latency and to support a large number of processors, we propose a multi based system interconnected by multiple levels of crossbars. An example multiprocessor system using three levels of 4 X 4 crossbars is shown in Figure 3.

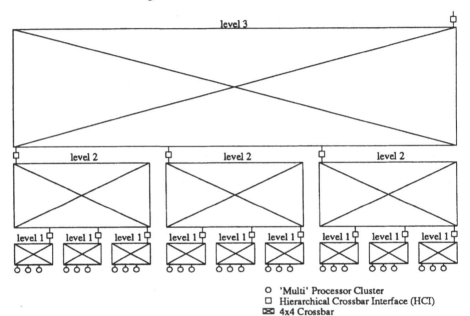

○  'Multi' Processor Cluster
□  Hierarchical Crossbar Interface (HCI)
⊠  4x4 Crossbar

**Figure 3. Crossbar-Multi-Processor (CMP) System**

The leaf nodes are the multis shown in Figure 2. The multis are connected to the crossbar using a multi crossbar interface (MCI). The physical memory is distributed among the multis. The memory latency is a variable (nonuniform memory access time). The memory latency time is the lowest in a multi. Accesses to memory blocks outside a multi but within the same level (local) will be faster than going through another level (remote) of crossbars. The actual values for local and remote latencies are dependent on the memory traffic, contention for a memory block, and the protocol used.

The motivation for the proposed architecture comes from the design and simulation of the Aquarius-II [12] architecture, the Wisconsin Multicube [17], the Multiple-Bus multiprocessor architecture [7], the VMP architecture [10], and others [38]. The key objective in developing the (CMP) architecture is to provide an architectural framework for experimenting with various processors, parallel programming paradigms (e.g. dataflow, logic programming, and object oriented programming), directory schemes and combinations of snooping caches and hardware/software supported directory schemes. Some important questions in the memory management, synchronization, and speedup of application programs can hopefully be answered with simulation experiments before building massively parallel systems.

The architectural framework consists of a base architecture, a snooping cache protocol for the multis, and directory schemes for maintaining caches consistent in the multis. Since there are many directory schemes [1] with different performance levels and hardware complexity, certain amount of experimentation is needed before picking a directory scheme. The intent of the architectural framework is to support this at the simulation level before building hardware.

The rest of this paper is divided into four sections. The multilevel crossbar system is discussed in Section 2. The cache coherency protocol for the multis is discussed in Section 3. The states needed to support multis connected to a crossbar is also described. The directory schemes that can be employed in maintaining cache coherency between the crossbar connected cluster of multis is discussed in Section 4. The simulation methodologies for studying memory management and protocol evaluation are discussed in Section 5.

## 2. MULTILEVEL CROSSBAR SYSTEM

The experience gained from the design and gate level simulation of the Aquarius-IIU [6] multiprocessor system has motivated the design of an architectural framework for a multiprocessor system with a large number of processors. A multi such as the Aquarius-IIU can exploit locality of memory references using caches and use the low-latency shared bus for communication between caches. The shared bus based multis have ben shown to be economical to build [40]. One of the limitations of a multi is the bus bandwidth. If there is heavy sharing of data between processors then four or more high performance processors such as the MIPS R3000 [22] on a bus can slow things down. This has been observed in simulating the parallel execution of Prolog programs on the Aquarius-IIU system [12]. Although systems such as Sequent's Symmetry [40] has been available with 30 processors on a bus, certain applications can saturate the bus and reduce performance.

Interconnecting multis using a low-latency crossbar can allow 64 to 160 processors to be used in a system assuming 4 to 10 processors per multi and a 16 X 16 crossbar. The unavailability of broadcast facility in a crossbar means that on a cache miss if a multi does not have the requested block there must be a directory that shows which multi has the block cached or which memory unit has the block. The directory can be centralized or distributed. It can be complete or partial, meaning that only some of the processors containing cached copies are in the directory. If a directory is distributed in such a way that each multi has a portion of the directory then the number of accesses to the crossbar can be reduced. The disadvantage of the distributed scheme is the extra traffic and time needed to invalidate the copies of a block on a write operation.

A directory scheme can be implemented as a distributed shared doubly linked list maintained by caches [38, 33]. For each block in memory there is a data structure for maintaining cache coherency. A part of the data structure is a linked list of caches containing copies of the block. The head of the linked list is stored in memory along with the block and state information.

The head points to the first cache that contains the block. Each cache containing a copy of the block has a a forward pointer to the downstream cache in the list and a backward pointer to the upstream cache in the list. Although this scheme is more complex than others [7] it is scalable. With a low latency interconnection network the communication time for maintaining cache coherency using a doubly linked list directory scheme can be kept within acceptable limits.

To accommodate hundreds and even thousands of processors a hierarchy of crossbars and a distributed directory scheme can be used. For example, in Figure 3, a 4 X 4 crossbar is used to connect three multis. The fourth port is used to communicate with clusters of other crossbars. The second level of 4 X 4 crossbar is used to connect three crossbar clusters and an optional third level. By employing n levels of p X p crossbars, n > 1, p >> 1, (p-1)**n multis can be connected. If h units of time is needed to communicate between levels, the longest delay involved in communicating between two multis is 2nh. With p = 16 and n =4 it is possible to connect 50,265 multis. It is shown in the next section that a 16 X 16 crossbar chip with a latency of 40 ns are possible. By employing these crossbars multis can communicate in less than one microsecond assuming that there is no contention in going between levels.

## 2.1. Crossbar Chip

One of the key components of the architecture in Figure 3 is the crossbar. It provides high bandwidth for communication between multis. A crossbar is a nonblocking type of interconnection network. Although crossbars have been used in computer systems for more than two decades, very few high performance off the shelf chips are available. Some VLSI designs based on an incremental design have been proposed by Franklin [15], Wann [43], and other designs are internal to corporations making signal processing systems. We have completed a high performance single stage fixed delay (assuming conflict free references) design for a 16 X 16 crossbar. The design employs a single-bit-slice approach with a maximum of 15 gate delays in the switch part ( not including delays in the pads and pad drivers) and a maximum of 210 pins. The chip is pad limited and has a size of 8mm X 8mm containing more than 40,000 transistors. It can be packaged in a 210 lead Pin Grid Array or surface mounted on a PC board using TAB technology.

The design and the functioning of the crossbar is explained using the pin out of a single-bit-slice crossbar chip [35] with 16 input ports and 16 output ports, shown in Figure 4. The input ports are connected to processors or multis and the output ports can be connected to memory units or multis or processors. Each input port contains four address pins (Pi), one address (PA), one data-out pin (PD), and one data-in (PDIN) pin. Each output port contains a data-in pin (MDOT), address pin (MA), and a data-out (MD) pin. All the pins are unidirectional. Processors can communicate words of data and address by using multiple single-bit-slice chips. For example, by stacking 33 single-bit-slice chips a 32-bit address/data can be sent to memory and a 32-bit data received from memory. The extra chip is for communicating

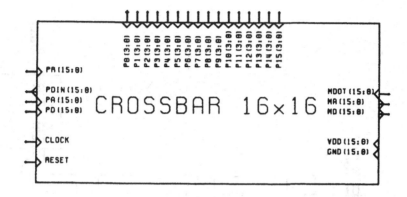

**Figure 4 Pin Out of Crossbar Chip**

control signals.

The design makes several simplifying assumptions. If two or more processors request the same memory unit, a fast arbitration method is used to select one of them. The selected processor will receive an acknowledge signal from memory. Other processor(s) will not receive acknowledge signals from memory. The processors are assumed to have the necessary logic to handle contention and retry at a later time. Each processor is assumed to supply the memory unit number along with an address and data in the case of a memory write or just an address in the case of a memory read.

The components of a single-bit-slice chip is shown in Figure 5. It contains an array of decoders, an array of arbiters, a crosspoint matrix, input drivers, and output drivers. The decoder receives a four bit input and produces a one on one of the 16 output lines if the decoder is enabled by the PR input from a processor. Each arbiter selects one out of sixteen inputs. The one of sixteen arbiter is constructed using a tree of one of two arbiters. We have designed an arbiter that selects one of the sixteen inputs in a fair manner. The fairness of the one of two arbiter can be checked by examining the following sequence of requests (REQ0 and REQ1) and grants (GRANT0 and GRANT1) in Table 1 from the time 4100.0 to 5600.0.

A processor (multi) wishing to read/write from one of the 16 processors (multis) supplies the address of the processor on the Pi address pins. The processor then sends the address of the desired location using the address pins of the stack of chips. For write operations the processor supplies data along with the address. For read operations the processor receives data from the selected processor on the data pins of the stack of chips. Each processor (multi) is connected to one output port (one data-in pin, one address pin, and a data-out pin) of a single-bit-slice chip. A processor receives an address followed by data from the data-out pins of the chips if a write is performed. For

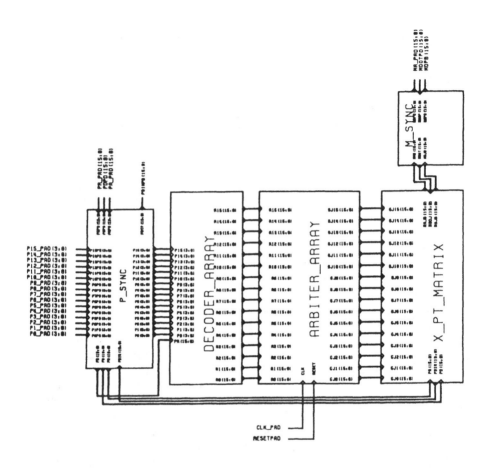

**Figure 5 Components of a Crossbar Chip**

a read operation, the processor reads the contents of the desired location and supplies it on the data-in pins of the chips.

Note that the proposed design is different from the incremental design [15, 43] in two respects. The flexibility of the incremental design is traded off for reduced gate delay. The complexity involved in contention handling is traded off to obtain a simple design. The price one has to pay for simplicity is degradation in performance when processor requests are skewed towards a subset of processors. Assigning tasks to processors so that memory references will not be skewed towards some subset of processors is still an open problem. It appears that reassigning tasks to other processors at runtime can mitigate the above problem. Further details of the crossbar design are in the paper by Srini [36].

# Table 1 Simulation Result of One of Two Arbiter

| TIME | ^REQ0 | ^REQ1 | ^GRANTC | ^REQC | ^GRANT0 | ^GRANT1 | ^CLK | ^CLKB | ^RESETB | ^SETB |
|---|---|---|---|---|---|---|---|---|---|---|
| 0.0 | Xr | Xr | Xr | X | X | X | 0 | 1 | 0 | 1 |
| 55.0 | Xr | Xr | Xr | X | 0 | 0 | 1 | 0 | 0 | 1 |
| 90.0 | Xr | Xr | Xr | X | X | X | 0 | 1 | 1 | 1 |
| 100.0 | 0 | 0 | 0 | X | X | X | 0 | 1 | 1 | 1 |
| 200.0 | 0 | 0 | 0 | 0 | 0 | 0 | 0 | 1 | 0 | 1 |
| 4100.0 | 1 | 1 | 1 | 1 | 1 | 0 | 0 | 1 | 0 | 1 |
| 4155.0 | 1 | 1 | 1 | 1 | 0 | 0 | 1 | 0 | 0 | 1 |
| 4190.0 | 1 | 1 | 1 | 1 | 0 | 0 | 0 | 1 | 0 | 1 |
| 4200.0 | 1 | 0 | 1 | 1 | 0 | 0 | 0 | 1 | 1 | 1 |
| 4204.0 | 1 | 0 | 1 | 1 | 1 | 0 | 0 | 1 | 1 | 1 |
| 4304.0 | 1 | 1 | 1 | 1 | 0 | 1 | 0 | 1 | 1 | 1 |
| 4404.0 | 1 | 1 | 1 | 1 | 1 | 0 | 0 | 1 | 1 | 1 |
| 4504.0 | 1 | 1 | 1 | 1 | 0 | 1 | 0 | 1 | 1 | 1 |
| 4604.0 | 1 | 0 | 1 | 1 | 1 | 0 | 0 | 1 | 1 | 1 |
| 4704.0 | 0 | 1 | 1 | 1 | 0 | 1 | 0 | 1 | 1 | 1 |
| 4804.0 | 1 | 1 | 1 | 1 | 1 | 0 | 0 | 1 | 1 | 1 |
| 4904.0 | 0 | 1 | 1 | 1 | 0 | 1 | 0 | 1 | 1 | 1 |
| 5104.0 | 1 | 1 | 1 | 1 | 1 | 0 | 0 | 1 | 1 | 1 |
| 5204.0 | 1 | 1 | 1 | 1 | 0 | 1 | 0 | 1 | 1 | 1 |
| 5304.0 | 1 | 0 | 1 | 1 | 1 | 0 | 0 | 1 | 1 | 1 |
| 5404.0 | 1 | 1 | 1 | 1 | 0 | 1 | 0 | 1 | 1 | 1 |
| 5504.0 | 1 | 1 | 1 | 1 | 1 | 0 | 0 | 1 | 1 | 1 |
| 5600.0 | 1 | 1 | 1 | 1 | 0 | 1 | 0 | 1 | 1 | 1 |

## 2.1.1. Simulation

Functional and timing simulation of the crossbar chip are performed to verify the design. The functional simulation is performed in two stages. Each component of the chip is simulated first. Then the entire chip is simulated. The patterns used for simulating the chip are generated by programs. These patterns correspond to single request, multiple requests with no conflict, and multiple requests with conflicts. The gate level simulator QUICKSIM of Mentor's IDEA station is used for functional and timing simulations.

To verify the fairness of the one of sixteen arbiter, it was simulated at the gate level using request patterns with the following characteristics:

a. Single request
b. Two simultaneous requests occurring on different one of two arbiters.
c. Two simultaneous requests occurring on the same one of two arbiter.
d. Four simultaneous requests.

e. Eight simultaneous requests.
f. Sixteen simultaneous requests.

The request patterns and the granted patterns are shown in Table 2. The first column shows the time. The second column shown the request pattern represented as hex characters, the third column shows the grant pattern. The remaining three columns show the values of clock and reset signals. The simulation was done using a a worst case cycle time of 100 ns for a 2.0 micron CMOS technology. The single phase clock of the chip rises at 55 ns and falls at 90 ns in each cycle. The flip-flops change state when the clock falls. The simulator output shows that the arbiter selects each of the processors once when all processors request for the same destination during 16 consecutive cycles starting from the time 7100.0 and ending at 8700.0. Using a 0.8 micron CMOS technology the worst case delay for the chip is estimated to be 40 ns.

## 3. CACHE COHERENCY IN A MULTI

Many proposals for multiprocessor cache coherency [1, 21, 27] using a variety of protocols are available. These protocols require monitoring the bus and broadcasting the data to caches and to memory. Bitar [5] has extended Goodman's snooping cache for more efficient locking. Bitar's scheme employs a cache lock state that reduces traffic on the bus, in addition to having one less memory access than the conventional test-and-set scheme for scalars. This scheme requires 3 state bits associated with each cache block and allows for cache-to-cache transfers for update or invalidate. Such a scheme is vital to fast synchronization accesses. This protocol has been simulated at the instruction level [8] and also at the gate level [6] for a four processor Aquarius-IIU multi. The finite state machine for the cache controller and snoop controller implementing the protocol has a total of around 180 states. The protocol has been extended by adding cache states for handling requests from other multis using the crossbar. Since only a small portion of the address space is needed for synchronization variables such as locks, counting semaphores, event queues, rendezvous points, and other shared items, the states connected with locking and unlocking are separated from the protocol. Each cache has an associative storage for keeping track of shared words in a directory called lock directory [18]. For example, if the cache holds 64K blocks then the lock directory will be designed to hold 0.5K entries. The associative storage will be implemented using RAM chips, a hash and compare scheme, insert operation, and extract operation. In addition to the address and data in the lock directory there is also a three bit state information for each entry. Before outlining the protocol some of the assumptions are described. Let p, the crossbar dimension be a power of 2 so that routing decisions can be made using bit masking operations. Let n be the number of levels. Each multi is assigned a portion of the address space. Let $2 ** a$ be a multi's address space.

### Table 2 Request/Grant Pattern of an Arbiter

| TIME | ^PREQ | ^PGRNT | ^CLK | ^RESET | ^SET |
|---|---|---|---|---|---|
| 200.0 | 0001 | 0000 | 0 | 0 | 0 |
| 212.0 | 0001 | 0001 | 0 | 0 | 0 |
| 300.0 | 0002 | 0001 | 0 | 0 | 0 |
| 302.0 | 0002 | 0002 | 0 | 0 | 0 |
| 400.0 | 0004 | 0002 | 0 | 0 | 0 |
| 407.0 | 0004 | 0004 | 0 | 0 | 0 |
| 500.0 | 0008 | 0004 | 0 | 0 | 0 |
| 502.0 | 0008 | 0008 | 0 | 0 | 0 |
| 600.0 | 0009 | 0008 | 0 | 0 | 0 |
| 607.0 | 0009 | 0001 | 0 | 0 | 0 |
| 755.0 | 0009 | 0008 | 1 | 0 | 0 |
| 790.0 | 0009 | 0008 | 0 | 0 | 0 |
| 855.0 | 0009 | 0001 | 1 | 0 | 0 |
| 955.0 | 0009 | 0008 | 1 | 0 | 0 |
| 1000.0 | 000A | 0001 | 0 | 0 | 0 |
| 1004.0 | 000A | 0002 | 0 | 0 | 0 |
| 1055.0 | 000A | 0002 | 1 | 0 | 0 |
| 1155.0 | 000A | 0008 | 1 | 0 | 0 |
| 1255.0 | 000A | 0002 | 1 | 0 | 0 |
| 1355.0 | 000A | 0008 | 1 | 0 | 0 |
| 1400.0 | 000C | 0002 | 0 | 0 | 0 |
|  |  |  |  |  |  |
| 7100.0 | FFFF | 0000 | 0 | 0 | 0 |
| 7113.0 | FFFF | 0100 | 0 | 0 | 0 |
| 7201.0 | FFFF | 0001 | 0 | 0 | 0 |
| 7301.0 | FFFF | 1000 | 0 | 0 | 0 |
| 7401.0 | FFFF | 0010 | 0 | 0 | 0 |
| 7501.0 | FFFF | 0400 | 0 | 0 | 0 |
| 7601.0 | FFFF | 0004 | 0 | 0 | 0 |
| 7701.0 | FFFF | 4000 | 0 | 0 | 0 |
| 7801.0 | FFFF | 0040 | 0 | 0 | 0 |
| 7901.0 | FFFF | 0200 | 0 | 0 | 0 |
| 8001.0 | FFFF | 0002 | 0 | 0 | 0 |
| 8101.0 | FFFF | 2000 | 0 | 0 | 0 |
| 8201.0 | FFFF | 0020 | 0 | 0 | 0 |
| 8301.0 | FFFF | 0800 | 0 | 0 | 0 |
| 8401.0 | FFFF | 0008 | 0 | 0 | 0 |
| 8501.0 | FFFF | 8000 | 0 | 0 | 0 |
| 8601.0 | FFFF | 0080 | 0 | 0 | 0 |
| 8701.0 | FFFF | 0100 | 0 | 0 | 0 |
| 8902.0 | 0000 | 0000 | 0 | 0 | 0 |

| TIME | ^PREQ | ^PGRNT | ^CLK | ^RESET | ^SET |

## 3.1. Cache Line States

The protocol under development specifies that each cache block can be in one of 7 states. Some of these states are source states meaning that they can respond to the request for a copy of the block.

*Invalid:*

The block doesn't contain any valid data.

*Local Read Shared:*

The block contains valid data with only read privilege. Copies of the block only exist in this multi. Other multis connected by one or more levels of crossbar does not contain a copy of this block and so a global access is not needed. It is not the source.

*Local Read Shared Source :*

The block contains valid data with read privilege, and is the source for the block. The data in the block is the same as the one stored in memory. Copies of the block only exist in this multi. Other multis connected by one or more levels of crossbar does not contain a copy of this block and so a global access is not needed.

*Global Read Shared:*

The block contains valid data with only read privilege. Copies of the block may exist in this multi and other multis connected by one or more levels of crossbar. A global access is needed if the state of the block is to be changed. It is not the source.

*Global Read Shared Source :*

The block contains valid data with read privilege, and is the source for the block. The data in the block is the same as the one stored in memory. Copies of the block exist in this multi and other multis connected by one or more levels of crossbar. A global access is needed if the state of the block is to be changed.

*Exclusive and Clean:*

The block contains valid data with read and write privileges, and is the source for the block. The data in the block is the same as the one stored in memory.

*Exclusive and Modified :*

The block contains valid data with read and write privileges, and is the source for the block. The data in the block is not the same as the one stored in memory.

The associative storage containing the lock directory has the following states for each entry. If one or more caches in the same multi are busy waiting on a locked word and no other multi is busy waiting for the word then during unlock operation a broadcast is done on the bus for the multi. One of the waiters will arbitrate for the word and gain control. There is no need to communicate with the crossbars. This optimization is supported by the local locked waiter state.

*Locked:*
> The entry contains valid data with write privileges, and has a lock on the word. The block is the source. There is no processor waiting for the word.

*Locked with Local Waiters:*
> This state is the same as the Locked state, except that there are also processes in one or more of the processors of the multi busy-waiting on the block containing the word. There are no processes on other multis busy-waiting on the block.

*Locked with Global Waiters:*
> This state is the same as the Locked state, except that there are also processes in one or more multis busy-waiting on the block containing the word. Global communication on the crossbars is needed when the word is unlocked.

*Busy-waiting:*
> The word is locked by some other processor. This state is provided so busy-waiting can take place locally and thus reduce bus traffic.

*Pending:*
> This a transit state of a shared word. The cache unit is waiting for a response from another cache .

*Unlocked*
> The word is unlocked and is available for the next request. The cache is the source for the block containing the word.

A processor accesses its cache when it executes read, write, lock, or unlock instructions. The cache performs the necessary actions and changes state based on the input and present state. The details of the finite state machine are under development.

### 3.1.1. Locking and Unlocking

The *lock* operation is given the address of a lock and returns the value read from the address, once the lock is obtained. Similarly, the *unlock* operation will write a value to an address before unlocking it. If a processor attempts to read, write, or lock a block that is currently locked it will begin busy-waiting. To support efficient busy-waiting the lock directory has an entry for the requested word with its state set to busy-waiting. This way no bus traffic or communication on the crossbar is needed while busy-waiting. The attempt to access a locked word will cause the lock directory holding the lock to enter the locked with local waiters state if the request comes from the same multi holding the lock or enter the locked with global waiters state if the request is coming from another multi. When the processor releases the lock the cache knows that a broadcast is required on the local bus in the case of locked with local waiters and additional communication using the crossbars in the case of locked with global waiters state to wake up all of the waiters.

All processes that are waiting on a lock will wake up and arbitrate for the bus after the unlock broadcast. The highest priority processor wins the arbitration and obtains the block next.

## 4. DIRECTORY SCHEME

Directory based cache coherence schemes have been proposed for large multiprocessor systems since an arbitrary interconnection network can be used. The schemes employ a data structure called directory for the blocks in main memory. Each directory entry usually contains a state field indicating whether the block is clean (fresh) or dirty (stale), list of caches having copies of the block, and the block. The cache entry for each block contains an address tag, state of the block, and the block. The states of a cache block have been discussed earlier in Section 3.1. The directory schemes proposed in the literature [39, 9, 3, 1, 7] differ in the way the directory is organized. Most of the schemes disallow dirty blocks from residing in more than one cache. Except for the schemes by Archibald [3] and Carlton [7] no broadcast is involved to invalidate caches.

Three classes of directory schemes are proposed for the CMP architecture to keep caches consistent across multis using the hierarchical network of crossbars. Since main memory is distributed across the multis the directories will be distributed. Only an outline of the directory schemes is included since the details are under development.

### 4.1. Restricted Directory

The first class of directories is a restricted directory scheme. For each block of memory the fields are:

a.  Three address fields for specifying the addresses of three multis that share the block.

b.  An overflow bit.

c.  A link to an overflow area if more than three multis share the block.

d.  The state of the block.

e.  The data for the block.

For a CMP with a crossbar dimension of $p$ and $n$ levels, the address field of a multi needs $n(\ln p)$ bits. The size of the link field depends on implementation. A block can be in one of four states. It is encoded using 2 bits. These states are similar to those proposed by Archibald [3] and Carlton [7]. The states are the following:

a.  uncached - No cache in any of the multis contains a copy of the block.

b.  write cached - Exactly one cache in a multi contains a modified copy of the block.

c.  read cached - Zero or more multis have a copy of the block. The addresses of the multis are in the address field.

d.  unavailable - The processing of a request for the block is in progress.

Several variations to the above scheme are possible. Instead of having an overflow bit and a link field the number of multis that can read share a block can be limited to four and an associative searching can be used. A scheme like this is used in ALEWIFE [2] multiprocessor project where the number of invalidations over a large collection of programs has been observed to be <= 4.

On a cache miss the main memory of a multi receives the address of the block. If it is not the home multi for the address the crossbar interface is used to send the request to the home multi ( See Figure 3). The response is provided by the home multi to the requesting multi.

## 4.2. Linked Directory

The second class of directories is based on a doubly linked list of caches containing copies of a block. It is similar to the protocol suggested in the SCI [38] specification. For each block of memory the directory entry has the following fields:

a.  The head of a list that points to the first cache containing a copy of the block.

b.  The state of the block.

c.  The data for the block.

The state field of a block has 2 bits encoding the following states:

a.  uncached - No cache has a copy of the block.

b.  read cached - Zero or more multis have a copy of the block. The head of the list of multis is in the head field.

c.  write cached - Exactly one cache in a multi has a modified copy of the block. The address of the multi is in the head field.

d.  unavailable - The processing of a request for the block is in progress.

Each entry in a cache has the following fields:

a.  Memory address for the block (address tag).

b.  The state of the block in the cache.

c.  A forward pointer to the downstream cache in the list of cached copies.

d.  A backward pointer to the upstream cache in the list of cached copies.

e.  The list state.

f.  The data for the block.

The states of a cache are those described in Section 3.1 The list state can be one of the following: head, tail, middle, only member, or candidate for exclusion from the list. On a cache miss the main memory of a multi receives the address of the block. If the home multi for the addressed block is not this multi then the crossbar interface is used to send the request to the home multi. The home multi responds to the request from its memory or by chasing the linked list of caches.

### 4.3. Software-Assisted Directory

The third class of directories is a combination of software and hardware to achieve cache coherency across multis. The objective is to reduce the need for fast invalidates and to keep the cache coherence overhead low. A compiler is expected to detect potential coherence problems and produce code to enforce cache coherence in parallel programs. Cache invalidation can be postponed as long as the compiler decides it is safe. Shared variables not handled by the compiler are kept coherent by the directory scheme. Time stamping and version control can also be used to assist the compiler [41, 4]. The two classes of directory schemes discussed earlier can be used with this approach. Additional hardware may be needed to check version numbers and time stamps.

## 5. SIMULATION METHODOLOGY

To obtain reasonable estimates on performance, memory traffic, and contention on the interconnection network an instruction set architecture (ISA) level simulator is needed. By running benchmark programs on the ISA level simulator with extensive instrumentation performance measurements can be made. Although trace driven simulation can give first order approximation to performance measures the accuracy of the running of benchmark programs on the simulator is desired. To develop an ISA level simulator for the CMP architecture and to allow experimentation with the architectural framework many factors must be considered. Some of them are now discussed.

**Flexibility:** The simulator for a parallel system consists of an execution model and an architecture. It should be possible to change the execution model or the architecture within specified guidelines.

**Modularity:** The simulator should be composed of modules. There should be a clean separation between the modules dealing with the execution model and the architecture.

**Portability:** The simulator should be written in a portable general purpose language such as C. The calls to the operating system and other system dependent modules should be clearly identified.

**Simulation Time:** ISA level simulation is usually time consuming. For uniprocessor simulations 5,000 to 10,000 cycles are needed on the host machine to simulate one cycle of the target machine [23]. Since parallel systems are more complex than uniprocessor systems the simulator execution time is bound to get worse. Byte coding and direct compilation on the host might have to be used to reduce the space needed and simulation time.

The key modules needed to simulate the CMP are now outlined. The CMP simulation system is even driven with the events ordered by time stamps. It consists of a control module, an execution model module, hierarchical crossbar module, memory module, multi module, task module, and processor module. The control module manages events by prioritizing events, inserting and deleting events from queues. It also starts all the event servers. The execution model module creates and maintains tasks. The scheduling of tasks to processors and terminating completed tasks are also done by this module. The simulation of the directory protocol, communication through the crossbars, and contention handling are performed in the hierarchical crossbar module.

Dynamic memory management is an important activity in parallel systems. The management of the address space assigned to a task and managing the main memory are done by the memory module. The multi module combines snooping cache protocol simulation, cache simulation, and bus simulation. These simulations are bound together by a separate event scheduler. There are well defined interfaces between these modules allowing any one of them to be modified without the need to change the other. It uses the processor module to simulate a processor. An example for the multi module is the Multisim developed by Carlton as a part of the Aquarius Project [8].

The processor model emulates a given processor architecture at the instruction set level (ISA level). The memory requests to the cache, memory in the local multi, and memory in another multi are all generated in this module. The task module uses the processor module for simulating the execution of a task and the multi module to simulate the communication within a multi.

The modules and the simulation features discussed in this section are being implemented in Berkeley for the Parallel Prolog Processing (PPP) execution model and the Aquarius-II architecture [13, 12].

## 6. DISCUSSION

The CMP architecture is still under development. Although parts such as the crossbar and the snooping cache protocol have been completed the directory scheme is yet to be implemented. The plan is to implement a restricted directory scheme with four address fileds for each directory entry. An ISA level simulation system will be developed based on the methodology suggested in this paper and the work on Aquarius-II system [23]. There are two plans for the processor module simulation. One is to use a Berkeley developed VLSI processor for symbolic and numeric processing. The other approach is to use a dataflow processor that performs efficient token matching [25, 37]. The multi module will be a modification of the Multisim using the snooping cache protocol outlined here with the lock directory. There will be four processors per multi. The snooping bus will use the signals of the VME bus. The execution model currently under investigation is the AND/OR process model of Prolog. The dataflow model is another candidate. The 16 X 16 crossbar system and three levels of crossbar will be used as the hierarchical crossbar system.

240

## ACKNOWLEDGEMENT

I am thankful to Tam Nguyen, Bruce Holmer, and Mike Carlton for discussions on the CMP architecture and simulation; Philip Bitar for discussions on the cache coherency protocol; Barry Fagin for answering questions on the PPP execution model; Peter VanRoy for discussions on the compiler; and Darren Busing and Georges Smine for the gate level simulation of the Aquarius-IIU architecture. The comments by Al Despain and Yale Patt and the help provided by Tara Weber, Linda Bushnell, and others of the Aquarius Group are appreciated.

This work is partially funded by the Defense Advance Research Projects Agency (DARPA) and monitored by the Office of Naval Research under contract No. N00014-88-K-0579. Equipment and other support for the project have been provided by DEC, NCR, Apollo, ESL, and Xenologic.

## References

1. A. Agarwal, R. Simoni, J. Hennessy, and M. Horowitz, "An Evaluation of Directory Schemes for Cache Coherence," *Proceedings of the 15th International Symp. on Computer Architecture*, pp. 280 - 289, June 1988.

2. A. Agarwal and M. Cherian, "Adaptive Backoff Synchronization Techniques," *Proceedings of the 16th International Symposium on Computer Architecture*, pp. 396 - 406, Jerusalem, Israel, May 1989.

3. J. Archibald and J. Baer, "Economical," *Proceedings of the 11th International Symposium on Computer Architecture*, pp. 355 - 361, June 1984.

4. J. Baer, "Self-invalidating Cache Coherence Protocols," *ISCA Workshop on Cache and Interconnect Architecture in Multiprocessors*, Eilat, Israel, May, 1989.

5. P. Bitar and A. Despain, "Multiprocessor Cache Synchronization Issues, Innovations, Evolution," *Proceedings of the 13th Intl. Symposium on Computer Architecture*, pp. 424-433, Tokyo, Japan, June 1986.

6. D. R. Busing, V. P. Srini, G. E. Smine, M. J. Carlton, and A. M. Despain, "The Aquarius-IIU System," *Proceedings of the First International Conference on System Integration*, Morristown, NJ, April, 1990.

7. M. Carlton, *Cache Coherency for Multiple-Bus Multiprocessor Architecturea*, p. Appendix 2, Aquarius Project Report, CS Division, Univ. of California, Berkeley, CA, April 1989.

8. M. Carlton, B. K. Holmer, and T. M. Nguyen, *Multisim: A Multi Simulator*, Aquarius Project Internal Report, CS Division, Univ. of California, Berkeley, CA, April 1988.

9. L.M. Censier and P. Feautrier, "A New Solution to Coherence Problems in Multicache Systems," *IEEE Transactions on Computers*, vol.

Vol. C-27, No. 12, pp. 1112 - 1118, Dec. 1978.

10. D. R. Cheriton, H. A. Goosen, and P. D. Boyle, "Multi-Level Shared Caching Techniques for Scalability in VMP-PC," *Proceedings of the 16th International Symposium on Computer Architecture*, pp. 16 - 24, Jerusalem, Israel, May 1989.

11. W. J. Dally, "Wire-Efficient VLSI Multiprocessor Communication Networks," *Proceedings of the 1987 VLSI Conference*, pp. 391 - 415, Stanford, CA, March 1987.

12. T.M. Nguyen, V.P. Srini, and A.M. Despain, "A Two-Tier Memory Architecture for High-Performance Multiprocessor Systems," *Proceedings of the International Conference on Supercomputing*, Saint-Malo, France, July 1988.

13. B.S. Fagin, "A Parallel Execution Model for Prolog," *Ph. D. Thesis, University of California*, CS Division Report No. UCB/CSD 87/380, Berkeley, CA, Nov. 1987.

14. S. Frank, "Tightly Coupled Multiprocessor System Speeds Memory-Access Times," *Electronics*, Jan. 12, 1984.

15. M.A. Franklin, D.F. Wann, and W.J. Thomas, "Pin Limitations and partitioning of VLSI Interconnection Networks," *IEEE Transactions on Computers*, Nov. 1982.

16. J. Goodman, "Using Cache Memories to Reduce Processor-Memory Traffic," *Proceedings of the 10th Intl. Symposium on Computer Architecture*, Stockholm, Sweden, June 1983.

17. J. R. Goodman and P. Woest, "The Wisconsin Multicube: A New Large-Scale Cache-Coherent Multiprocessor," *Proceedings of the 15th International Symp. on Computer Architecture*, June 1988.

18. A. Goto, A. Matsumoto, and E. Tick, "Design and Performance of a Coherent Cache for Parallel Logic Programming Architecture," *Proceedings of the 16th International Symposium on Computer Architecture*, pp. 25 - 33, Jerusalem, Israel, May 1989.

19. A. Gottlieb and et. al., "The NYU Ultra Computer," *IEEE TC*, vol. C-32, No. 2, pp. 175-189, February 1983.

20. M. Hill and and Others, "Design Decisions in SPUR," *IEEE Computer*, pp. 1 - 22, Nov. 1986.

21. R.H. Katz, S.J. Eggers, D.A. Wood, C.L. Perkins, and R.G. Sheldon, "Implementing a Cache Consistency Protocol," *Proceedings of the 12th Intl. Symposium on Computer Architecture*, pp. 276-283, Boston, June 1985.

22. J. Mashey, "MIPS RISC Architecture," *HOT Chips Conference*, Stanford University, Stanford, CA, June 1989.

23. T. M. Nguyen and V. P. Srini, "The Validation of a Multiprocessor Simulator," *Proceedings of the First International Conference on System Integration*, Morristown, NJ, April, 1990.

24. E.I. Organick, *Computer Systems Organization: The B5700/6700 Series,* Academic Press Inc., New York, 1973.

25. G. M. Papadopoulos, *Implementation of a General Purpose Dataflow Multiprocessor,* Ph. D. Thesis, Dept. Of Electrical Engineering and Computer Science, MIT, Cambridge, MA, July, 1988.

26. H. J. Raveche, D. H. Lawrie, and A. M. Despain, "A National Computing Initiative," *Distributed by the Society of Industrial and Applied Mathematics,* SIAM Workshop, Leesburg, VA, Philadelphia, 1987.

27. C. V. Ravishankar and J. Goodman, "Cache Implementation for Multiple Processors," *IEEE Spring Compcon Conference,* San Francisco, February 1983.

28. R.M. Russell, "The Cray-1 Computer System," *Communications of the ACM,* vol. Vol. 21, No. 1, pp. 63 - 72, Jan 1978.

29. D. Gajski, D. Kuck, D. Lawrie, and A. Sameh, "Cedar - A Large Scale Multiprocessor," *Proceedings of the 1983 Parallel Processing Conference,* pp. 524 - 429., Michigan, Aug. 1983.

30. M. Satyanarayanan, *Multiprocessors - A Comparative Study,* Prentice-Hall, Inc., 1980.

31. C. Seitz, "Concurrent VLSI Architectures," *IEEE Transactions on Computers,* pp. 1247 - 1265, Vol. C-33, No. 12, Dec. 1984.

32. A.J. Smith, "Cache Memories," *Computing Surveys,* vol. 14, No. 3, pp. 473-530, Sept. 1982.

33. G. S. Sohi, "Cache Coherence Mechanisms for Multiprocessors with Arbitrary Interconnects," *ISCA Workshop on Cache and Interconnect Architecture in Multiprocessors,* Eilat, Israel, May, 1989.

34. V.P. Srini and J.F. Asenjo, "Analysis of Cray-1S Architecture," *Proceedings of the 10th Intl. Symposium on Computer Architecture,* pp. 194-206, Stockholm, Sweden, June 1983.

35. V.P. Srini, "An Architecture for doing Concurrent Systems Research," *Proceedings of the National Computer Conference,* Chicago, July 1985.

36. V.P. Srini, "A Low-Latency Crossbar Chip for Multiprocessors," *Patent Application, University of California,* Berkeley, CA, Jan. 1988.

37. V. P. Srini, "A Fault-Tolerant Dataflow System," *IEEE Computer Magazine,* pp. 54 - 68, March 1985.

38. P. Sweazey, "Directory-based Cache Coherence on SCI," *ISCA Workshop on Cache and Interconnect Architecture in Multiprocessors,* Eilat, Israel, May, 1989.

39. C.K. Tang, "Cache System Design in the Tightly Coupled Multiprocessor System," *Proceedings of the National Computer Conference,* vol. Vol. 45, pp. 749 - 753, 1976.

40. S. Thakkar, "The Performance of Cache Coherence Protocols," *ISCA Workshop on Cache and Interconnect Architecture in Multiprocessors,* Eilat, Israel, May, 1989.

41. A. Veidenbaum, "Compiler-assisted Cache Management in Multiprocessors," *ISCA Workshop on Cache and Interconnect Architecture in Multiprocessors*, Eilat, Israel, May, 1989.

42. S. Wallach, "The Convex C-1 64-bit Supercomputer," *Digest of Papers, Spring COMPCON 85*, pp. 122-126, San Francisco, Feb. 1985.

43. D.F. Wann and M.A. Franklin, "Asynchronous and Clocked Control Structure for VLSI- Based Interconnection Networks," *IEEE Transactions on Computers*, March 1983.

44. W. Wulf and C. Bell, "C.mmp - A multi-Miniprocessor," *AFIPS Proc. (FJCC)*, vol. 41, Part 2, pp. 756 - 777, 1972.

# "CHESS" Multiprocessor
# A Processor-Memory Grid for Parallel Programming

**Dimitris Lioupis** ,
Olivetti Research Ltd.
24A Trumpington St.
Cambridge CB2 1QA
ENGLAND

**Nikos Kanellopoulos**
University of Patras
Dept. of Computer Engineering
Patras
GREECE

## ABSTRACT

In this paper we describe the architecture of a parallel computer named "CHESS" designed for the parallel execution of imperative languages. It features a grid of processors and memories which connect with each other to form a processing surface onto which a program is mapped. The grid can be implemented using standard bus technology and 4N caches. A diffusion algorithm distributes the work load and minimizes long haul communications between processors. The resulting computer architecture provides a uniform picture to the user and a familiar programming model with increased performance.

Keywords: **Processor-Memory Interconnection, Processing Surface, Multiprocessor**.

## 1. INTRODUCTION

Multiprocessors are used today to provide better performance than earlier machines, at lower cost. Many existing products, such as Sequent [SEQ84], Firefly [THA87] and Encore [ROS85] are based on a shared bus architecture which provides a good improvement in performance combined with an easy to use programming model, due to shared memory. The shared bus, however, constitutes a bottleneck in these architectures which limits the number of processors that can be connected to the bus and thus limiting maximum performance.

The goal of computer architects is to provide a scalable architecture with a good programming model. Grids of processors, each with a private memory, fulfill the scalability requirement but are difficult to program because memory is distributed. Thus shared data must be passed around as messages with consequent degradation in performance.

Our aim is to design a type of architecture which scales as well as the grid architecture but which also allows more connectivity between processors and memory modules to reduce the problem of private memory modules. Because of shared memory the same programming model of shared bus multiprocessors can be used simplifying the programming task. In such an architecture, work which needs to share data will be allocated to processors with access to the same memory module. When this is not possible then processors can still access data from remote memories by message passing but with reduced performance.

In this paper we propose a computer architecture which allows increased connectivity between processors and memory modules by means of a processor memory grid. Processors share data through shared memory modules and communicate with each other through memory by passing pointers. This reduces the copying of the shared data and also provides a uniform way of both sharing data and passing messages to other processors.

The remainder of the paper is organised as follows. In the next section we give a brief description of the proposed architecture and compare it with existing designs. In section 3 we describe the programming model of this architecture. Section 4 has an overview of the diffusion algorithm. The way a grid of processors and memories can be implemented using standard shared bus technology is included in section 5. Section 6 contains our plans for the future and we conclude in section 7.

## 2. ARCHITECTURAL DESCRIPTION

The proposed architecture is a distributed memory architecture which can support a large number (>100) of processors. Each processor is connected to four memory modules as shown in figure 1. Each memory module has four ports. It will be shown later how these ports are implemented.

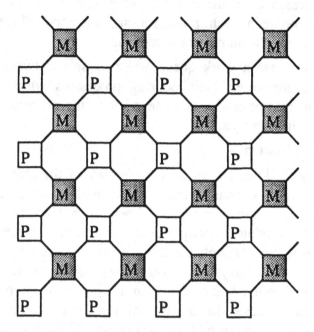

Figure 1 : The "CHESS" Computer Architecture

The above grid is wrapped around in both directions to form a torus. Its size can be increased in either direction to allow more processors and memories to be interconnected. The symmetric shape of the torus allows work to be started anywhere on the processing surface depending on the load of the processors in the area. Work is allocated by the operating system which has knowledge of the load and resources of the system. When a processor is given a granule of work it can proceed with execution, until either a distant data is needed or a new work granule is generated. In both cases the OS is called to resolve the situation. Requests for data are directed to the nearest processor which has access to this data by using its global address to obtain the direction toward which each request must be routed.

## 2.1. Processor

The processor is a standard part microprocessor. It executes instructions located in the four surrounding memory modules which are considered as four banks of the same memory. There is no extra local memory on each processor but because of the speed difference between processors and memories a cache memory is needed to act as a buffer between each processor and memory. There are 4N caches where N is the number of processors.

Each processor has a work queue which is split between the four neighbouring memories. Neighbouring processors which have access to these memories can allocate work to the processor by writing in one of these queues.

## 2.2. Memory System

The memory modules constitute the memory of the machine. They can be built from standard parts and are used to store instructions and data. As can be seen in figure 1, memory is distributed. However all memory modules belong to the same address space. An item can be accessed via its global address by any processor. If this item resides in the processor's neighbouring memory then the processor can access it directly. If the item is in another memory module then the processor requests the transfer of the item by transmitting a message to the corresponding processor. Messages are passed through memory. A processor copies from one memory module to another and then passes a pointer to the destination processor. This memory to memory copying can be done by the processor or alternatively by a Direct Memory Access controller which employs cycle stealing to avoid loading the processor.

There are two difficulties associated with such a memory hierarchy:

a) *global memory consistency*,

   keeping different copies of the same data consistent between distant memory modules. We propose to solve this problem by the weak coherence scheme similar to the Carnegie Mellon ideas described in [BIS88], and formally defined by Dubois [DUB86]. Multiple copies of the same data are allowed to exist in the machine but operations on them (e.g.: write) are preceded by synchronisation operation. Coherence operations are performed only when necessary, thus reducing coherence cost.

b) *cache consistency*,

   keeping caches connected to the same memory module consistent. Caches are connected to a particular memory module through a shared bus. Consistency is achieved by the well developed snooping algorithms used in shared bus architectures described in [HIL86] [ARC86] and others.

## 2.3. I/O

There are two types of I/O in a computer system: communication with the outside world and paging. The former consists of slower communications with terminals and back-up memories such as tape drives where the latter requires faster access to large amount of frequently used data. We address the two cases differently in our architecture.

For the slow communication channels where latency and response time is important we dedicate a parallel ring which joins all processors with all the slow I/O devices. Any processor can perform terminal I/O which helps to maintain symmetry.

Because of virtual memory, pages must be swapped between fast disks and memory modules. In a multiprocessor environment with a large number of processors it is not practical to have a centralized disk, where all pages are swapped, because this disk will soon become the bottleneck. During the execution of a program, a page is swapped in and out of the same memory module. We propose to use one disk per cluster of 4 processors and 4 neighbouring memories where all the pages from these memory modules are swapped. From the results of recent work at Berkeley multiple disks can be used for I/O, but reliability becomes an issue [PAT88]. We allow some redundancy in case of failure. A memory is always backed-up in its cluster disc by one of the processors in the cluster, unless the disk is faulty. In this case another processor of a different cluster can perform the paging to a neighbouring disk at no extra cost since a memory is connected to 4 processors which have access to other cluster disks. By distributing the disks around the processor array we solve the bottleneck and increase bandwidth to back-up memory by allowing multiple paths.

## 3. PROGRAMMING MODEL

The machine can be programmed in both functional and imperative languages. We concentrate here on the actual model which applies to both. The basic idea behind the programming model is to avoid long haul communications by data copying. This is achieved in conjunction with the diffusion algorithm by allocating work to the processor which has access to either all or most of the data a work granule might need.

Work is divided (by the compiler or a post-processor) into self-contained granules of 50-500 lines of code. Each granule contains the code to be executed and a header which indicates the needed resources for its execution. Initially the program is loaded into the memory modules according to the data dependencies of the granules and processor work queues amended accordingly. In effect, the execution graph of a program is mapped onto the processor array and is allowed to expand or contract during execution.

A granule is assigned to a processor according to the resources it needs and depending on the load of the processor. Assigning work means that the code is copied into one of the processor's four neighbouring memories (if it is not already there) and a pointer inserted into its work queue. Processors execute any work that is active in their work queues. If more work is generated by forking a process then it might be executed by the same processor or it might be diffused to another processor by the diffusion algorithm described in the next section.

## 4. DIFFUSION ALGORITHM

In the "Chess" architecture shared data can reside in a shared or a distant memory module. For the efficient execution of programs it is imperative that processors have fast access to shared data. If processes with shared data are kept around the memory module which contains the data, the load on the array might not be balanced. If processes with shared data are spread out into many distant processors the communication overhead is increased. The diffusion algorithm makes the trade-off between even load distribution and cost of communication.

The diffusion algorithm is based on the global load notion similar to the pressure algorithm described in [KEL84]. It has knowledge of the load of the system and the topology of the array. Each processor has a table in all four memory modules it connects to, which contains three types of information:

a) the number of the 4 neighbouring memory modules

b) the id numbers of the 8 processors which are connected to these memory modules,

c) the load of each of these processors including the processors own load.

The load of a processor is calculated by the number of outstanding work granules in a processors queue and the load of its neighbours. Every time a load changes, each processor updates its own load as necessary.

When a new granule of work is to be assigned to a processor the diffusion algorithm checks the granules data requirements and the load of the surrounding processors. If the granule of work does not share any data with another granule then it can be assigned to any neighbouring processor (the least loaded will be selected). If the granule requires data which reside in the surrounding memory modules then a cost function is evaluated to decide if the work is to be migrated or kept in the processors connected to the memories containing the data. Usually the work will be allocated to a neighbouring processor which has access to the memory modules containing the shared data. If this is not possible, then the work will be assigned to the least loaded neighbour and the shared data will be copied to one of its memory modules. Copying data is performed by memory to memory transfer and it should be fast.

## 5. PHYSICAL IMPLEMENTATION

In this section we show how the "Chess" architecture can be implemented with standard technology. We only employ standard parts and techniques used in shared bus architectures to obtain the grid of processors and memories as described earlier in the paper.

To understand how we can implement an array of processors with a grid of buses it is helpful to note that a four port memory is implemented by a bus with four cache memories. Each cache acts as a port to the memory module. The grid interconnection is implemented by a mesh of buses. A 16 processor grid is shown in figure 2.

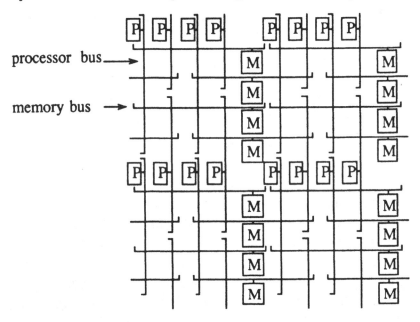

Figure 2 : Physical implementation of the processor grid using buses

As can be seen in figure 2 processors connect to four memory modules through four separate buses. In each intersection of the buses there is a cache memory which is not shown in the diagram. By shifting two of the four memory and processor buses two places we can achieve the connectivity of the grid. Each memory module connects to four processors and each processor connects to four memories as in the grid arrangement shown in figure 1. Each memory bus can easily accommodate the traffic of four processors since the processor requests are buffered by the caches. The use of cache memories provides true four ported access to each memory module and allows the processors to execute at maximum speed.

The above arrangement is very regular and very easy to build. It is the replication of a four processor - four memory cluster shown in more detail in figure 3. The processor-memory cluster consists of two basic boards; namely, the *processor board* and *memory board*. The processor board has two versions. The first consists of a processor with four caches connected on a continuous bus, while the second is the same processor board with the processor bus divided in two and two extra edge connectors on top and bottom which are used to join the two halves on separate boards. The memory board contains four memory modules.

Both processor and memory boards have four edge connectors to connect to the memory buses. Each of the memory buses are implemented on a backplane with connectors at appropriate places to allow the processor and memory boards to plug in. Also connectors at the end of split memory buses allows connection to their corresponding half on the other side of the backplane.

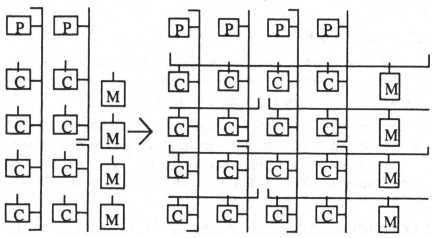

Figure 3 : A processor-memory cluster

The processor-memory (P-M) cluster shown above is used to implement a processor memory grid torus by compressing the torus in two dimensions. The resulting interconnection is shown in figure 4.

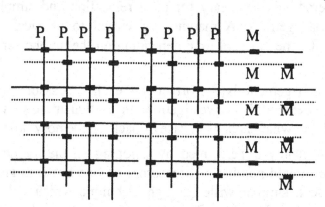

Figure 4 : Physical implementation of two P-M clusters

The continuous line memory buses belong to one processor-memory cluster (at the front of the torus) and the dotted line to another (inside back side of torus). To form a 16 processor multiprocessor the mirror image of the above interconnection is implemented on the reverse side of the backplane. The buses that are divided in half are connected with their corresponding halves on the other side of the backplane by a short length of ribbon cable and edge connectors. The basic module shown in figure 4 can be repeated as many times as necessary to form a multiprocessor with a large number of processors.

## 6. FUTURE WORK

Our work was concentrated on the design and implementation of the "Chess" architecture. We must resolve many other issues which will be decisive on the success of the project.

Our next step will be to build a simulator to allow the execution of programs written in C. With the simulator we will be able to see if it is possible to execute programs with shared data without much communication overhead and test the effectiveness of the diffusion algorithm.

Many operating system issues are unresolved and need to be studied. The overhead of calling the OS must be very small since it is called frequently for load balancing. We envisage a distributed kernel which runs in every processor but it is not clear how all the tables and data structures will be implemented.

Virtual memory is necessary for code relocation and simplifies our memory management. A mapping of virtual to physical addresses must be performed at boot time depending on the number of memory modules.

Memory management is performed by each processor on demand basis and needs further investigation. In particular how is it to be performed and what happens in case of back-up memory failure.

Cache consistency is performed by snooping on the memory buses. Due to the limited number of processors on one bus it might be possible to use a simpler write through technique which will simplify the design and reduce cost. The effect of write through versus write back techniques on the bus bandwidth must be examined.

## 7. CONCLUSION

We have designed a computer architecture which exhibits good properties of programmability and extensibility. It can be implemented using standard technology and can provide a multiprocessor with a large number of processors. A grid of processors interconnected with memories promises good performance on programs with shared data and a simple programming model. It remains to be seen if a processing surface thus produced can be useful for parallel programming

## 8. ACKNOWLEDGEMENTS

The authors would like to express their thanks to Alan Jones, Andy Hopper, Kami Sehat and Stuart Wray of Olivetti Research Laboratory, Cambridge for their comments and encouragement on the architecture described in this paper.

## References

| | |
|---|---|
| [AGA88] | Agarwal A. and A. Gupta, "Memory-Reference Characteristics of Multiprocessor Applications under MACH," Proceedings of ACM Sigmetrics 1988. |
| [ARC86] | Archibald J. and J. Baer, "An Evaluation of Cache Coherence Solutions in Shared-Bus Multiprocessors," ACM Trans. on Computer Systems, 4,4, November 1986. |
| [BEL85] | Bell C.G, "Multis: A New Class of Multiprocessor Computers," Science, 228, April 1985. |
| [BIS88] | Bisiani R., Nowatzyk A., & Ravishankar M., "Coherent Shared Memory on a Message Passing Machine", Carnegie Mellon University, Computer Science Report # CMU-CS-88-204, December 1988. |
| [DAS85] | Das C.R, and L.N. Bhuyan, "Computation Availability of Multiple-Bus Multiprocessors", U of Southwestern Louisiana, 1985. |
| [DUB86] | Dubois M., Scheurich C., and Briggs F., "Memory Access Buffering in Multiprocessors", 13th ISCA, pages 434-442, IEEE, June 1986. |
| [EGG88] | Eggers S. and R. Katz, "Characterization of Sharing in Parallel Programs and its Applicability to Coherency Protocol Evaluation," Proc. of 15th Intl. Symp. on Computer Architecture, Hawaii, June 1988. |
| [PAT88] | Patterson D.A., Gibson G. & Katz R.H. "A Case for Redundant Arrays of Inexpensive Disks (RAID)" ACM SIGMOD, Chicago, June 1-3, 1988. |
| [GOO83] | Goodman J. "Using Cache Memories to Reduce Processor-Memory Traffic," Proc. of the 10th Intl Symp. on Computer Architecture, Stockholm June 1983. |
| [HIL86] | Hill M.D. et. al. "SPUR: A VLSI Multiprocessor Workstation," IEEE Computer, 19, 11 November 1986. |
| [KEL84] | Keller R.M. & Lin F.C.H., "Simulated Performance of a Reduction-Based Multiprocessor", Computer 17(7), July 1984. |
| [ROS85] | Rose C.D, "Encore Eyes Multiprocessor Market," Electronics July 8, 1985. |
| [SAT80] | Satyanarayanan M. "Commercial Multiprocessing Sys- |

tems ," IEEE Computer, 13, 5, May 1980.

[SEQ84]     Sequent Computer Systems, Inc. "Balance 8000" Technical Summary, Nov 1984.

[THA87]     Thacker C. and L. Stewart, "Firefly: A Multiprocessor Workstation", 2nd Intl. Conference on Architectural Support for Programming Languages and Operating Systems, pp 164-172, ACM, October 1987.

[WIL87]     Wilson A. W. Jr, "Hierarchical Cache/Bus Architecture for Shared Memory Multiprocessors," Proc of 14th Intl. Symp. on Computer Architecture, 1987.

# Software-directed Cache
# Management in Multiprocessors

**Hoichi Cheong & Alexander V. Veidenbaum**

*Center for Supercomputing Research and Development*

*University of Illinois at Urbana-Champaign*

*104 South Wright Street*

*Urbana, Illinois 61801*

*Abstract*

*We discuss three different software-assisted cache coherence enforcement schemes for large shared-memory multiprocessor systems using interconnection networks. All three rely on a compiler to detect potential coherence problems and generate code to enforce coherence in a parallel program. The main goals are to maintain coherence without any interprocessor communication and to keep coherence enforcement overhead low. The former is achieved by using compile-time knowledge of the parallelism and data dependences in a program. The latter is achieved by using special hardware to invalidate stale cache blocks in time independent of the number of such blocks. Cache words are allowed to become inconsistent with memory as long as the compiler decided it is safe to do so. This allows invalidation to be delayed beyond the time a new copy of a cache word has been generated till the time the word has to be invalidated. The three schemes differ in the complexity and the power of the compiler detection algorithms, the complexity of the additional hardware, and the run-time support the hardware provides for deciding what to invalidate. Each scheme improves over the previous one in terms of the amount of unnecessary invalidation and achieves higher hit ratios.*

Keywords: **Software-directed cache coherence, parallel task execution, fast-selective invalidation, version control.**

# 1  INTRODUCTION

Multiprocessor architecture has assumed an important role in high speed computing in recent years as a way to increase performance over that of uniprocessor systems. However, as the number of processors is increased, the time for data and instructions to travel between the shared memory and the processors, the memory latency, increases due to the limited throughput of the interconnection media and memory conflicts.

The memory access latency can be reduced by a cache memory. However, before private caches can be used in large-scale multiprocessor systems, the cache coherence problem needs to be solved. In this paper, we discuss why hardware-based cache coherence strategies are not adequate for large-scale multiprocessor systems. Then, we present three different software-based strategies that share the same goals and general approach.

## 1.1  Drawbacks of the Hardware-based Schemes

Several algorithms have been proposed for cache coherence enforcement in multiprocessor systems. Most of them apply only to bus-based systems [1, 2, 3, 4, 5]. Others use a directory scheme, either centralized [6] or distributed [7, 8], to maintain coherence. The bus-based cache coherence strategies rely on monitoring the bus accesses and are not scalable to a large number of processors. Neither can they be applied to systems using multistage interconnection networks instead of a bus. The directory schemes are not scalable because the memory latency and the amount of storage required grows proportionally to system size. The central directory requires an unacceptable amount of storage for ownership identification. For distributed directories, store controllers have to broadcast to every cache unit both cache line status changes and requests for up-to-date words. In both cases directory schemes require complicated protocols and can cause latency to increase dramatically.

We are interested only in strategies suitable for shared memory multiprocessor systems with multistage interconnection networks and a large number of processors. A scalable, efficient cache coherence scheme for large-scale systems needs to (1) eliminate the run-time communication, and (2) reduce the hardware overhead necessary to enforce coherence, which existing hardware schemes are not capable of. The first requirement can be achieved by using compile-time program analysis rather than relying entirely on run-time detection and enforcement. The latter requirement can be achieved by using special hardware to perform invalidation in time independent of the number of invalidated lines. These attributes are the essence of the three software-based schemes we developed which are discussed in this paper. The observation that is central to all of these schemes is that the contents of private caches and the shared memory can be different as long as incorrect data are not used by a processor. This observation relaxes the requirement used in hardware-based schemes, that every write to a data element, namely, a scalar variable or an element of an array variable, must be made known to all caches that contain a copy of the data element, and therefore, it eliminates the need for communication.

## 1.2 A Parallel Task Execution Model and Task Graph

We will concentrate on maintaining cache coherence in the execution of parallel programs. We assume that the execution of a parallel program (parallelized from a sequential program [9] or written in a parallel language) is represented by tasks each executed by a single processor. Tasks that are independent [10] of each other can be scheduled for parallel execution. Tasks that are dependent will be executed in the order defined by program semantics. The execution order of dependent tasks is enforced through synchronization.

The dependence relationship among tasks and hence the execution order can be described by a task graph. A task graph, $G = \{E, T\}$, is a directed graph where $E$ is a set of edges and $T$ is a set of nodes. A node, $T_i \in T$, represents a task and a directed edge, $e_{i,j} \in E$, represents that some statements in $T_j$ depend on other statements in $T_i$ (Figure 1a). $T_i$ in such a case is called the parent node of $T_j$, and $T_j$ the child node of $T_i$.

Task nodes are combined into a single node using the following criterion: Two nodes $T_i$ and $T_j$ connected by an edge $e_{ij}$ can be combined into one node if $T_i$ is the only parent node of $T_j$, and $T_j$ is the only child node of $T_i$.

The task graph can be divided into levels $L = \{L_0, \ldots L_n\}$, where each $L_i$ is a set of tasks such that the longest directed path from $T_0$, the starting node, to each of the tasks in the set has $i$ edges (Figure 1b). Tasks on the same level are not connected by any directed edges. Therefore, no write accesses or read-writes to the same data element (element for short) by

Figure 1. An example of a task graph.

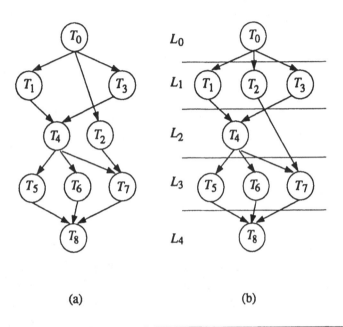

(a)                              (b)

different processors are performed by tasks on the same level. Such tasks on the same level can be executed in parallel without inter-task synchronization.

Let us assume that parallelism in a program is expressed in terms of parallel loops. A parallel loop specifies starting execution of iterations of the loop by multiple processors. In a *Doall* type of parallel loop, all such iterations are independent and can be executed in any order. In a *Doacross* type of loop, there is a dependence between iterations. In terms of tasks, one or more iterations of a *Doall* loop are bundled into a task. In a *Doacross* loop, one iteration is a task, and there is synchronization between tasks. We'll use both ways of describing parallelism interchangeably.

In general, tasks with inter-task dependence can also be executed in parallel provided synchronization preserves the correct semantics. For clarity, the following discussion focuses on parallel task execution without inter-task dependence. However, the cache coherence schemes to be discussed in this paper can be applied to the parallel execution with inter-task synchronization.

## 2   A SIMPLE INVALIDATION APPROACH

The first scheme [11] is characterized by small hardware overhead and low complexity of the compiler algorithm to maintain cache coherence. It assumes the value in the shared memory is always current. It defines an incoherence as a condition in which:

1.   a processor performs a memory fetch, and
2.   there is a cache hit, but the cache has a value different from that in memory.

An incoherence cannot occur if the access is a store. Note that we require a processor to try to fetch X; otherwise the fact that the memory and the cache have different values is not an error. The necessary conditions for the cache incoherence to occur on a fetch of X are:

1.   a value of X is present in the cache of processor $P_j$, and
2.   a new value has been stored in the shared memory by another processor since the access by $P_j$ that brought X into the cache.

The above conditions can be formulated in terms of data dependences [10], and a compiler can then check for a dependence structure which may result in coherence violations. This is rather complex, however, because the test will have to be performed for every read reference. In addition, the data dependence information does not specify whether the references involved are executed by different processors. To simplify the analysis and to get the processor information, we propose to use the parallel loop type. The compiler has already performed data dependence analysis to determine the loop type, and processor assignment is part of the loop execution model. (If other types of parallelism are being exploited, they can be taken care of in a similar fashion.) Let us consider programs with *Doall* and *Doacross* loops. By definition, any dependence between two statements inside a *Doall* loop is not across iterations, but there are cross-iteration dependences in *Doacross*. It follows that a statement $S_i$ in a *Doall* dependent on a statement $S_j$ in the same loop is executed on the same processor as $S_j$. In a *Doacross* loop, two statements with a cross-iteration dependence are executed on different processors, whereas statements with a dependence on the same iteration are executed on the same processor.

## 2.1 A Cache Management Algorithm

Let us assume that the following instructions are available for cache management:

*Invalidate*       This instructions invalidates the entire contents of a cache.

*Cache_on*       This instruction causes all global memory references to be routed through the cache.

*Cache_off*       This instruction causes all global memory references to bypass the cache and go directly to memory.

In addition, the cache state, on or off, must be part of the process state and has to be saved/restored on context switch. Processes are created in the cache-off state.

The algorithm uses loop types for its analysis as follows.

1. A *Doall* loop does not have any dependences between statements executed on different processors. Therefore any shared memory access in such a loop can be cached.
2. A serial loop is executed by a single processor, and shared memory accesses can be cached.
3. *Doacross* or recurrence loops do have cross-iteration dependences. Therefore conditions for incoherence can be true, and shared memory accesses should not be cached.

The general idea is to turn caching on and off as loop boundaries are crossed. Conditions for incoherence can only occur and need to be avoided at loop boundaries where processor reassignment occurs. Coherence enforcement is accomplished by invalidating each cache to guarantee that no old data are present.

The algorithm is presented in [11]. The correctness of the algorithm is proven by showing that the conditions necessary for an incoherence to occur are not satisfied in programs processed by the algorithm.

## 2.2 Improving the Cache Management Algorithm

In this section we describe possible extensions of the cache management algorithm. The first one allows caching to be used in *Doacross* loops. The second and third attempt to reduce the number of cache invalidations by doing a more detailed dependence and flow analysis.

### 2.2.1 Caching of data inside *Doacross* loops

A *Doacross* loop is executed by assigning successive iterations to different processors (modulo the number of processors available). The cross-iteration dependences that exist in a *Doacross* are thus between statements executed by different processors. Synchronization primitives have to be used between these processors to ensure that dependences are satisfied e.g., the classical P and V primitives.

A straightforward solution is to issue an "Invalidate" instruction after the V by each processor executing a statement depending on a statement executed by another processor. Since the shared memory has the current value after the V instruction and the cache does not have anything, the value will be fetched out of global memory. Otherwise the *Doacross* loops can be treated the same way as the *Doall* loops by the cache management algorithm. The most interesting case of *Doacross* is one with other loops nested in it. In such a case the proposed extension will work quite well.

### 2.2.2 More sophisticated detection of conditions

The simplified algorithm we presented does not really look for the dependence structure implied by the necessary conditions. Specifically, it does not check the existence of a statement bringing a variable into a cache prior to the execution of the two statements with a dependence on two different processors. An incoherence cannot occur if such a statement does not exist. In such a case it is not necessary to invalidate the contents of a cache.

Consider a *Doacross* loop with caching enabled. Assume each processor executing this loop performed an Invalidate instruction just after it entered the loop. Let us now consider a statement $S_i$ that uses a variable X generated in another iteration of the *Doacross*. If we examine all the flow of control paths from the first statement in a loop to $S_i$ and determine there are no generations or uses of X on any of them, then we do not have to invalidate X in the cache before $S_i$ (a single assignment condition). If the above is true for all the cross-iteration dependences in the loop, we do not need an Invalidate instruction in this *Doacross*.

This technique can be extended to analyze the whole program to avoid invalidating after every parallel loop.

### 2.2.3 Data dependence analysis

The algorithm uses data dependence information indirectly, through loop types. A beginning and end of a parallel loop are synchronization points it detects and uses to issue cache management instructions. This synchronizes all dependences from statements in such loops to statements outside of such loops. However, this synchronization point may be located much earlier than the statement using the data. Another synchronization point may exist later in the program that takes care of an earlier one. Using dependence analysis, we can try to find the latest point for each loop at which to enforce coherence.

## 3   THE FAST-SELECTIVE INVALIDATION SCHEME

The goal of the fast-selective invalidation scheme [12, 13] is to avoid invalidating non-stale cache lines while keeping the time cost of invalidations independent of the number of items to be invalidated. The general ideas of the scheme are introduced along with an example. Assumptions and requirements to implement the scheme will be discussed. Then, the main idea of compiler-assisted reference marking is presented.

### 3.1 General Ideas

Every read reference to shared memory in a program is classified by the compiler as either *memory-read* or *cache-read*. The reference is marked according to the classification and different memory operand fetches will be generated according to the classifications. Read references are marked *cache-read* if the cache resident copy is guaranteed to be up to date. Read references will be marked as a *memory-read* if the cache resident copy referenced may have become stale.

Consider the example in Figure 2. Assume all processors executing the program start with an empty cache. Each loop corresponds to a task level, and an iteration or a group of consecutive iterations is a task. Read accesses to the elements of $W$ are marked *cache-reads*, because $W$ is read-only. Accesses to $Y$ are also *cache-reads*, because the writes to $Y$ do not have existing copies to turn stale. Accesses to $X$ before the write in the second loop are *cache-reads*, because they precede all writes to the $X$ elements; accesses in the third loop are *memory-reads*, because they may access copies loaded in the first loop but turned stale by the write in the second loop.

Figure 2. A program example.

```
doall i = 1, n
   Y(i)= .
       = W(i)... Y(i) /* cache-reads */
       .
       = ... X(i) /* cache-read */
       .
enddo
doall j = 1, n
/* an invalidate-cache would be inserted here to set
the change bits */
       .
       = W(i)... Y(j) /* cache-reads */
  X(j) = ...
       .
enddo
/* an invalidate-cache would be inserted here to set
the change bits */
doall k = 1, n
       = W(k)       /* cache-read */
       = ... X(k) /* memory-read */
       .
       = ... Y(k) /* cache-read */
       .
enddo
```

The cache controller treats a *cache-read* as a read in a uniprocessor conventional cache. A *Cache-read* implies that cache data accessed will not be invalidated; therefore, invalidation in this scheme is selective.

Since a *memory-read* implies reading a potentially stale copy, an up-to-date copy will be loaded. A simple approach will treat the *memory-read* as a default miss and use the global memory copy. However, in the case of multiple *memory-reads* to the same data element in a task, default misses on all of them are wasteful, because the first one will deposit an up-to-date copy into the cache. Similar waste occurs if a write to the data element precedes *memory-reads* in the task. These can be avoided as follows.

A status bit called the *change* bit is added to each cache word. The *change* bits are set true (in one clock) at each task level boundary by the processor crossing the boundary. An individual bit is reset by a read miss or a write. A *memory-read* to a cache word with a true *change* bit is a default miss, but it will be treated as a conventional cache access with a false bit.

Therefore, the status of the bit can distinguish the first *memory-read* or the *memory-reads* following a write from other accesses to the same data element in the same task. An invalidate instruction can be used to set the *change* bits, and it will be inserted in the program as in the simple invalidation scheme of the last section.

The scheme is selective because it deals with individual references. It is fast because a single instruction taking one or two clocks can reset all *change* bits using fast, resettable SRAMs.

## 3.2 Assumptions and Requirements

We assume the parallel program execution model represented by the task graph introduced earlier. In addition, the following assumptions and requirements are used:

*Write-policy*   We use a write-through policy even though the coherence enforcement scheme can be adapted to a variety of write-miss and allocate policies.

*Line-fetching*   The cache issues a line request for multiple words on a read miss. Line fetching may cause cache coherence problems when different words of a line are accessed by two processors. Details to handle these cases are discussed in [12]. In the following, a line size of one word is assumed.

### 3.2.1 Cache operation

*Valid and change bits*   Associated with each cache word are a *valid* bit (similar to the valid bit in the traditional sense) and a *change* bit. The function of the *change* bit has already been described. The *valid* bit is used to provide the processor with a clean cache. The processor will issue a clear-cache instruction to reset the bits. When it is reset (false), it implies that nothing has been loaded/stored in the cache word and will cause a default miss. A load or store operation sets the *valid* bit of an individual cache word.

The cache controller decides whether a memory operand access is a cache hit or a miss from the classification of the accesses and the status bits. A cache hit is a function of four Boolean variables:

1.  matched (true for address tags matched and false otherwise),

2. cacheread (true for cache-read and false for memory-read),
3. change (true for a set *change* bit and false for a reset *change* bit),
4. valid (true for a set *valid* bit and false for a reset *valid* bit).

$$Hit = matched \cap valid \cap \left(cacheread \cup \overline{\left(cacheread \cap \overline{change}\right)}\right)$$

## 3.3 Reference Marking Scheme

We rely on a parallel Fortran compiler such as Parafrase [14] to insert the invalidate-cache instruction at appropriate places in the instruction stream and also to identify and mark references as *cache-read* or *memory-read*. The algorithm for the former task is discussed in [11]. The reference-marking scheme is discussed next; a more detailed discussion can be found in [12].

The marking of read references is based on the order of the read and write accesses and the task level boundaries. Flow analysis [13] is used to carry out such marking (a similar use of flow analysis is also proposed independently by Cytron et al.[15]).

The reference-marking algorithm is applied to one subroutine at a time. Processors are assumed to start a subroutine with a clean cache (the clear-cache instruction is issued upon entry to each subroutine). References to read-only variables within a subroutine are marked cache-read. For variables that are both read and written within the subroutine, all references to a variable which precede the first write to that variable are marked cache-read. The remaining read references are marked according to the following rule:

In the parallel execution graph, for each task level $L_i$ that contains a write to an element, if accesses to the element exist in preceding levels, all read references to the element in task levels subsequent to level $L_i$ should be marked memory-read. The rest of the read references should be marked cache-read.

The above rule is based on the fact that an existing cache copy of an element will be turned stale by a write access to the element from another processor. When read references to the same element are issued by processors other than the one that writes, the read references are not guaranteed to access a non-stale cache copy; hence the read references are marked memory-read.

### 3.4 Summary

The fast-selective invalidation scheme does not invalidate cache copies for read-only (*W* in the example) and read-write (*Y* and *X*) variables that are accessed by *cache-reads*. Therefore, it is a selective scheme. It preserves more temporal locality than indiscriminate invalidation approaches, which invalidate at least all cache copies of read-write variables at each loop boundary. Because misses due to stale cache copies do not require additional processor invalidation operations, it is different from conventional approaches in which a processor has to invalidate stale cache copies sequentially, and hence the name "fast." Other methods [15, 16, 17] aimed at selective invalidation either do not achieve the same level of selective invalidation or require sequential invalidation ( for detailed discussion, see [18]).

Overall, this scheme is still not selective enough. Relying only on the compile-time detection, the scheme is forced to be conservative. Even though temporal locality exists across task levels, it cannot be exploited by *memory-read* references. More selective invalidation methods, and hence better temporal locality, are the target of the next coherence maintenance scheme.

## 4   THE VERSION CONTROL SCHEME

This scheme uses version numbers to record the state of existing cache copies to detect and to avoid stale accesses. Consider two tasks at different levels that both contain writes to the same variable. The order of such writes from different tasks is determined by the task execution graph. The writes to a variable in one task are said to produce a different version of the variable than the writes in the other task. Each cache copy of a variable in the system must belong to a particular version.

Multiple writes to a variable within a task are considered to produce only one version because only the value of the last write to a variable will ever be read by other tasks, and only by tasks at subsequent task levels. Thus, at the end of a task execution, only one new version has been produced for each variable written within the task.

For the scheme to be practical, an array is considered a single variable. Even though tasks may write to only a part of an array, a new version is nevertheless assigned for the entire array. If an array is written to by multiple tasks on the same task level, the writes altogether produce only one new version.

A version of a variable produced in a task is the current version of the variable until a task on a subsequent level produces the next version. The current version of the variable contains the up-to-date value to be used until the generation of the next version.

An integer called the Current Version Number ($CVN$) is used to distinguish the different versions of a variable (scalar or array). Each processor maintains its own $CVN$ for each variable used in the program in a separate local memory. Since each array needs only one $CVN$, the local memory is small.

Each cache word is tagged with a birth version number ($bvn$) field. When the cache word is loaded from the global memory, the corresponding $CVN$ of the variable is copied into the $bvn$ field of the cache word. When a cache word is written, the $bvn$ field of the cache word will be set to the new version number of the variable, that is, $CVN$ plus one. The $bvn$ of the cache copy is checked against the $CVN$ of the variable when the copy is read. A cache copy with a $bvn$ less than the $CVN$ of the variable is a stale cache copy. When this is detected, a cache miss will be generated, and the up-to-date value will be loaded from the global memory.

$CVN$s of all variables written on a task level are incremented by one when the tasks of that level are completed. Every processor participating in the execution of the program is required to update their $CVN$s. Hence, the cache copy written by a processor will have its $bvn$ equal to the new $CVN$. On a subsequent task level, the up-to-date cache copy will be recognized by the equality of the $CVN$ and the $bvn$, and will not be invalidated. Therefore, intertask temporal locality is preserved.

The version scheme consists of three tasks: (1) proper maintenance of the $CVN$s, (2) tagging each cache copy with a $bvn$, and (3) run-time comparison of the $bvn$ of a cache copy and the $CVN$ of the variable. We show how these tasks can be achieved with minimal time cost to the system, given adequate hardware support.

The most important part of the scheme is how to update the $CVN$ of a variable efficiently when a new version is created. The updates of the $CVN$s in each processor can be done independently without communication overhead, and with little computational overhead. In the following subsections, we will describe how to keep track of different versions of a variable, the hardware necessary to support an implementation of the version control scheme, and the implementation issues.

## 4.1 Version Update

Let us restrict the discussion to acyclic task execution graphs (a detailed discussion on cyclic task graph can be found in [18, 19]). A set of variables $Var_i$ that the tasks can write to at level $i$ can be computed at compile-time and used to update the CVNs of these variable at run-time. When a processor finishes a task at level $i$ and is ready to execute a task at level $i+k$, it needs to increment the CVN of each variable that could have been modified on level $i$ and the levels that the processor skips, that is, $\bigcup_{j=0}^{j=k-1} Var_{i+j}$. Provided a variable is written at any level from $L_{i+1}$ through $L_{i+k-1}$, the CVN of the variable will always be larger than the bvn of the cache copy of the processor. The processor thus knows whether or not its cache copies are up to date.

The CVNs of the same variable kept by different processors do not have to agree. The fact that the bvn of the copy is less than the CVN of the variable, not the exact difference of the two number, is sufficient for maintaining cache coherence. Therefore, the processors can manage the CVNs independently.

## 4.2 Hardware Support

The version control coherence scheme requires the following hardware support.

1. A *version manager* to maintain the CVNs of each variable in a fast local memory. A CVN is addressed by an identity (ID) number assigned to each variable at either compile time or link time. The version manager executes instructions issued by the processor to increment CVN or to reset all CVNs.
2. A field in the memory address for each reference to store the identity number (ID) of the variable.
3. A field in each cache word that contains the bvn. All bvns can be reset by a processor instruction.

Before a program execution starts, the *CVN*s are reset to zero, the cache words are invalidated, and the *bvn* field in each cache word is reset to zero. A simplified view of the hardware block diagram is illustrated in Figure 3.

In parallel with the cache read operation, the ID number in the address is used to retrieve the *CVN* from the version manager's memory. The retrieved *CVN* is compared with the *bvn* of the cache copy. The comparison of the *CVN*s and the *bvn* is carried out in parallel with the tag comparison of the cache access. Also, the loading of an up-to-date copy from the global memory and the loading of the correct *CVN* into the version field of the cache word can be done in parallel.

When a missed cache word is brought into the cache, its *bvn* is set to the *CVN* of the variable. Hence, the correct version number will be written to the *bvn* field of the up-to-date cache copy read from the global memory.

Figure 3.   Hardware support for version control.

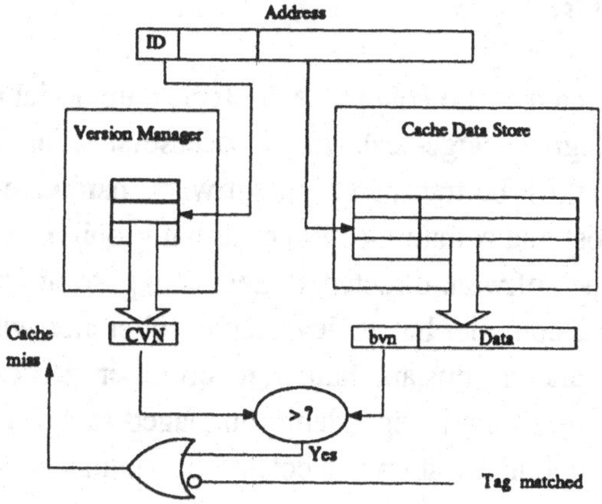

A write operation will update the cache word and update the *bvn* field of the cache word with the *CVN*s plus one. The suboperations associated with a cache write can be carried out in parallel.

### 4.3 Summary

Using version numbers, a processor is able to distinguish the up-to-date cache copies written by the processor itself from other copies that may have been written by other processors. The temporal locality of such cache copies is preserved across task level boundaries until the version numbers show that these copies may have been written by other processors. Neither schemes with indiscriminate invalidation nor the fast-selective invalidation can preserve this temporal locality. The temporal locality within a task level, and the limited intertask temporal locality preserved by *cache-read* references are both preserved by using a version of a variable. Therefore, the version control scheme delivers better hit ratio (for performance comparison, see [12, 19]).

While each processor has to spend time communicating with its version manager, this does not add to the global traffic. No communication between processors is required. A study on the scheme shows that the number of operations that a processor needs to execute to maintain its version numbers is negligible[19, 18].

## 5 CONCLUSION

Software-directed cache coherence strategies are a viable alternative for cache system design in large-scale multiprocessors. While adhering to the notion that cache must be transparent to software, hardware-based strategies incur hardware cost and communication cost that prohibit expansion to large-scale systems. The software-directed strategies expose multiprocessor cache management to the compiler but achieve cache coherence with independently managed caches and a constant hardware cost per processor. The most important advantage of the independently managed caches is the elimination of interprocessor communication for coherence maintenance.

## 6 ACKNOWLEDGMENT

This work is supported in part by National Science Foundation under Grant No. US NSF MIP-8410110, the U.S. Department of Energy under Grant No. US DOE DE-FG02–85ER25001, NASA Ames Research Center Grant No. NASA NCC 2–559, and IBM Corporation.

# References

[1] J. R. Goodman. Using cache memory to reduce processor-memory traffic. *Proc. 10th Annual Int'l. Symp. on Computer Architecture*, pages 124–131, 1983.

[2] E. McCreight. The dragon computer system: An early overview. Technical report, Xerox Corp, September 1984.

[3] Mark S. Papamarcos and Janak H. Patel. A low-overhead coherence solution for multiprocessors with private cache memories. *Proc. 11th Annual International Symposium on Computer Architecture*, pages 348–354, June 5-7, 1984.

[4] Larry Rudolph and Zary Segall. Dynamic decentralized cache schemes for MIMD parallel processors. *Proc. 11th Annual International Symposium on Computer Architecture*, pages 340–347, June 5-7, 1984. Also, Rpt. No. CMU-CS-84-139, Dept. of Computer Sci., Carnegie-Mellon U., 1984.

[5] Randy H. Katz, Susan J. Eggers, D. A. Wood, C. L. Perkins, and R. G. Sheldon. Implementing a cache consistency protocol. *Proc. 12th Annual International Symposium on Computer Architecture*, pages 276–283, June, 1985.

[6] C. K. Tang. Cache system design in the tightly coupled multiprocessor system. *Proc. NCC*, 45:749–753, 1976.

[7] L. M. Censier and P. Feautrier. A new solution to coherence problems in multicache systems. *IEEE Trans. Computers*, C-27(12):1112–1118, December, 1978.

[8] James Archibald and Jean-Loup Baer. An economical solution to the cache coherence problem. *Proc. of the 11th Annual Int'l. Symp. on Computer Architecture*, pages 355–362, June 5-7, 1984.

[9] M.J. Wolfe. Optimizing compilers for supercomputers. Technical report, Department of Computer Science, University of Illinois at Urbana-Champaign, Oct., 1982. Ph.D. Thesis.

[10] Utpal Banerjee. Data dependence in ordinary programs. Technical Report No. 76-837, Univ. of Illinois at Urbana-Champaign, Dept. of Computer Sci., Nov., 1976. M.S. thesis.

[11] Alexander Veidenbaum. A compiler-assisted cache coherence solution for multiprocessors. *Proc. 1986 International Conference on Parallel Processing*, pages 1029–1036, August 1986.

[12] Hoichi Cheong and Alex Veidenbaum. A cache coherence scheme with fast selective invalidation. *Proc. 15th Annual International Symposium on Computer Architecture*, page 299, June 1988.

[13] Hoichi Cheong and Alexander V. Veidenbaum. Stale data detection and coherence enforcement using flow analysis. *Proc. 1988 International Conference on Parallel Processing*, I, Architecture:138–145, August 1988.

[14] David J. Kuck, Robert H. Kuhn, Bruce Leasure, and Michael Wolfe. The structure of an advanced vectorizer for pipelined processors. *Computer Software and Applications Conference (COMPSAC80)*, pages 709–715, October 1980.

[15] Ron Cytron, Steve Karlovsky, and Kevin P. McAuliffe. Automatic management of programmable caches. *Proc. the 1988 International Conference on Parallel Processing*, II, Software:229–238, August 1988.

[16] Kevin P. McAuliffe. Analysis of cache memories in highly parallel systems. Technical Report No. 269, Courant Institute of Mathematical Sciences, NYU, 1986. Ph.D. Thesis.

[17] Alan Jay Smith. Disk cache–miss ratio analysis and design considerations. *ACM Trans. on Computer Systems*, 3(3):161–203, Aug., 1985.

[18] Hoichi Cheong. Towards efficient software-based cache coherence strategies. Technical report, University of Illinois at Urbana-Champaign, 1990. Ph.D. Thesis in progress.

[19] Hoichi Cheong and Alex Veidenbaum. A version control approach to cache coherence. *Proc. ICS 89*, (CSRD No. 832):322–330, June 1989.

# Index